The Last Judgment: Hell, by Coppo di Marcovaldo
(Baptistry, Florence)

GIANTS OF WORLD LITERATURE

Dante

His Life, His Times, His Works

Created by the editors of
Arnoldo Mondadori Editore
Translated from the Italian
by Giuseppina T. Salvadori
and Bernice L. Lewis
Anthology by
Professor Thomas G. Bergin
Yale University

AMERICAN HERITAGE PRESS

NEW YORK

TABLE OF CONTENTS

Miniature portrait of Dante (Riccardian Library, Florence)

The Poet, in his own Words

For a person to speak of himself is unseemly. To praise or blame oneself is to be avoided as if it were bearing false witness, for there is no man who may be a true and proper judge of himself, since self-love will mislead him. [All the same] I say that in certain circumstances it is [sometimes] permissible to talk of oneself. And among these circumstances two stand out. One is when one cannot prevent disgrace or great danger without talking about oneself. The other is when, by speaking of oneself, other men may find the discourse most useful. I am moved by fear of disgrace, and I am moved by the desire to instruct others.

But we, to whom the world is our native country, just as the sea is to the fish, though we drank of Arno before our teeth appeared, and though we love Florence so dearly that for the love we bore her we are wrongfully suffering exile—we rest the shoulders of our judgment on reason rather than on feeling.

The ignorance of the common man keeps him from making discerning judgments, and just as he believes that the sun is a foot in diameter, so he is deceived by the same false belief when it comes to customs. But we, who are privileged to know the best that is in us must not follow the footprints of the crowd, but must correct their errors. In fact, those who live by intellect and reason and who are endowed with a certain divine liberty are not constrained by any custom, and there is nothing marvelous about this, because these men are not guided by the laws, but rather the laws by them.

Since it was the pleasure of the citizens of that most beautiful and famous daughter of Rome, Florence namely, to cast me out of her sweet bosom—where I was born and grew up to the height of my powers and where with all my heart I wished to peacefully rest my tired soul and finish the time which was left to me— I have wandered, almost begging, through almost every region where this tongue is spoken, showing against my will the stroke of fortune which is often and unjustly charged to the victim. Truly I have been a ship without a sail and without a rudder, driven to many ports and river mouths and shores by the dry wind of miserable poverty; and I have appeared [differently] in the eyes of many who, perhaps hearing reports of me, had imagined me to be another kind of man.

It is certainly true: I am one of the last lambs in the pastures of Christ. It is true: I take advantage of no pastoral authority because I am not rich. But this means that I am who I am not thanks to riches but by the grace of God and the love of His kingdom.

Besides, I have as my teacher the Philosopher who, in fixing the eternal principles of the moral law, has taught that the truth must be preferred to all friends.

. . . among so many who usurp the pastoral office, among so many sheep if not scattered at least forgotten and abandoned in their pastures, mine is the only compassionate voice, the voice of a private citizen, which now proclaims that the Church is almost on the edge of the abyss.

To all those who will read this paper Dante Alighieri of Florence, the last of the true philosophers, sends greetings in the name of Him who is the source of truth and light.

From: *Convivio* I, 2; *De Vulgari Eloquentia* I, 6; *Epistle* XIII to Cangrande della Scala; *Convivio* I, 3; *Epistle* XI to the Italian Cardinals; *Questio*, prologue.

Medieval Florence

Who were the taxpayers? How many hospital beds were available?
What was the city like in Dante's day? What was included in the city budget?

THE PEOPLE. In 1300 there were 90,000 people (excluding the clergy) living in urban Florence, and another 80,000 in the rural areas and the province itself. In the city 25,000 men were eligible for military service (that is, aged fifteen to seventy). There were also 1,500 noblemen and 250 knights. Annual births totaled 5,500 to 6,000, with males outnumbering females five to three. Each year 8,000 to 10,000 children learned to read. Of these, 1,000 to 1,200 were also taught arithmetic, and 550 to 600 studied logic and grammar.

CHURCHES AND CLERGY. There were 126 churches, abbeys, and convent chapels in the city and its environs; 57 parish churches, five abbeys with two priors and 80 monks, 24 convents with 500 nuns, 10 fraternal orders, 30 hospital chapels. There were 250 to 300 lay preachers.

COUNTRY VILLAS. A great many Florentines, both nobles and commoners, owned good houses in the country, on which they spent lavishly. Within a six mile radius of the city, there were great and luxurious villas whose like could not be seen in Florence itself.

MEDICAL SERVICES. The city's 30 hospitals, primarily charitable institutions for sheltering the poor and the infirm, had more than 1,000 beds. They were staffed by about 60 doctors and surgeons, and had about 100 pharmacies.

ARTS AND CRAFTS. Trade flourished; there were a great many merchants and artisans, but the total number is not known. We do know, however, that there were a great many shoemakers', clogmakers', and slippermakers' shops, and that there were 146 bakeries. Each year 350,000 gold florins were minted in the city. There were about 80 banks. There were also 80 magistrates and 600 notaries. More than 200 wool shops produced from 70,000 to 80,000 pieces of cloth annually for a turnover of approximately 1,200,000 gold florins. The cloth trade gave work to more than 30,000 people. Formerly, there had been even many more cloth shops—as many as 300, producing more than 100,000 pieces a year.

FOOD. Each year the city's slaughter houses processed approximately 4,000 cows and calves, 60,000 sheep, 20,000

Guelph palace; S. Maria sopra a Porta church.

Porta alla Croce, built around 1284.

Church of Santa Croce: XIV century cloister.

goats, 30,000 pigs. Wine consumption was 55,000 to 65,000 vats, or half a million barrels. Wheat requirements were 140 bushels a day.

PUBLIC OFFICE. The commune of Florence entrusted its numerous public offices mainly to foreigners. Here is a list of the principal magistrates and public officials: the mayor, the public defender, the chief of justice, the captain of the guard, the tax assessor, the official in charge of regulations concerning women's ornaments, the administrator of the trade regulations, the official in charge of the wool guild, the ecclesiastical officials, the grand inquisitor.

PUBLIC EXPENSES. The average annual expenditure of the commune amounted to about 40,000 gold florins and included the salaries of all public officials (the mayor was paid 5,000 florins, the captain of the guard 2,000, the official in control of women's ornaments 330), the upkeep of the priors and their families (who ate and drank up 1,200 florins a year), the maintenance of ambassadors, spies, and messengers, the salaries of guards, municipal couriers, town criers, and bell ringers, subsidies for charity, funds for organizing public ceremonies and pageants. Then there were the very heavy appropriations for arms and the army; these varied considerably with the war in progress at the moment.

TAXES. The commune acquired its funds through taxes and tolls, which brought in about 300,000 gold florins a year. Beside duties on produce entering the city (including salt), there were taxes on millstones, on loans, on mortgages, rents, contracts, on markets in and out of the city, on live and slaughtered animals, on garbage, on fines, on fruit and vegetable stands, and so forth. A tax on the property of convicts and exiles brought in 7,000 florins.

(The above information is contained in chapters 91-94, Volume XI of the *Chronicle*, by Giovanni Villani.)

The Baptistry, a Florentine landmark.

Palace of the Bargello (1255): courtyard.

Palace of the wool guild (fourteenth century)

Dante's Life

Just as the DIVINE COMEDY *reflects the human experience, Dante's life as an artist, citizen, and exile sheds light on the* COMEDY.

Youth

Dante Alighieri was born in May, 1265, in the district between Orsanmichele and the Badia in Ghibelline-dominated Florence. His family, which had pretensions to nobility, was in fact neither particularly illustrious nor particularly important. As proof of this, after the defeat at Montaperti, the Guelph Alighieris were not forced into exile with the leaders of the great families of the vanquished faction. Dante's father was a small landowner, and Dante never mentioned him. About the only information we have, offered by that scandalmonger Forese Donati, is the obscure hint that the elder Dante was a usurer. Dante's mother Bella died a few years after the poet's birth; his father remarried a woman called Lapa, by whom he had three more sons.

A brief allusion in the *Vita Nuova* suggests that the second family was full of affection for the little Dante and that perfect harmony reigned. His eldest half brother, Francesco, later often helped the poet with generous loans.

Opposite, Dante with Brunetto Latini in a fresco by Giotto. Above, Dante's house stood between the tower of the Castagna (left) and the parish church of San Martino del Vescovo, from which the little fifteenth-century chapel (center) took its name. The wall at the right is part of an unauthenticated reconstruction of a so-called House of Dante.

9

Below, San Miniato al Monte, the most beautiful monastic church in the outskirts of Florence. Bottom and right, the two meetings between Dante and Beatrice: at the age of nine, in a drawing by Simeon Solomon (Tate Gallery, London); and at eighteen, in a painting by Henry Holliday (Walker Art Gallery, Liverpool).

The most significant event in Dante's infancy took place outside his home: in 1274 the nine-year-old boy met a girl a few months his junior. She was dressed "in most noble crimson" and adorned in the refined fashion of the day. When he caught sight of her, Dante's senses stirred for the first time and he began to tremble violently. The impression was so profound that from that moment the little Beatrice, daughter of Folco Portinari, became the future poet's muse, his inspiration —"the glorious lady of my mind"—and the first lady of

Italian poetry for all time. Dante regularly attended Florentine schools, but he acquired vast knowledge by studying on his own as well. The secondary schools of his day taught the trivium and the quadrivium, and Dante learned how to read, write, and handle figures; the schools gave him a start at drawing and an introduction to ethics, metaphysics, and astronomy. But the major architect of the young man's cultural education was Brunetto Latini, a solid burgher, an official of the commune of Florence, and a lover of learning. He had

profited by a period of exile to absorb the culture of Europe firsthand, particularly in Paris, where he had earned his living as a notary. On his return to Florence he was sought out by all the young intellectuals because of his vast and impartial knowledge and his wide interests.

First Steps in the Literary World

The young Dante taught himself "the art of saying things in verse." He began to write when he was about eighteen, after meeting Bea-

trice for the second time and feeling the old emotion overwhelm him again. The renewal of his great love turned him decisively toward poetry, and the virtuous austerity of Beatrice inspired him from the first to ennoble this gentlest of women as if she were a heavenly being.

His first lyrics attracted the attention of Guido Cavalcanti, a poet much in vogue at the time and one of the best Italian poets before Dante. Little by little the rich, noble Cavalcanti's interest in the modest young poet turned to friendship.

*Below, Guido Cavalcanti,
poet of the "new style"
and close friend of Dante's.
Bottom, a miniature of a sing-
er and his audience (from
a manuscript in the National
Gallery of Florence).*

Gradually, as the young man's personality matured and his extraordinary talent was refined, the gap between the two men closed.

Arms and Revelry

Dante's first contact with public life was through military service. When still quite young, he fought at Campaldino—one of the countless battles of the eternal wars between the communes of the Italian peninsula. This time it was a war against Arezzo, then predominantly a Ghibelline city. Dante was one of the *feditori,* the cavalry troop chosen to make the assault, and he fought bravely. In the same year, 1289, he took part in another campaign—the conquest of the Castle of Caprona from the Pisans. After his military experience, and before he took up politics, Dante went through a period that can only be described as dissolute—and small wonder, for Dante was a man of strong passions.

Beatrice died in 1290, and Dante relates that to console himself he took up philosophy. At first laboriously, then with increasing interest, he read the works of Boethius and Cicero. During these years he even tried to settle down to family life by marrying Gemma Donati, whom his parents had chosen as his future bride when he was only a boy. But neither family nor philosophy could contain his temperament. In company with his friend Forese Donati and others, Dante discovered the pleasures of gay parties, lavish banquets, and freewheeling exchanges with a whole string of Lisettas, Fiorettas, and Fiammettas. He even went so far as to take part in a public rhyming contest with Forese Donati, a sort of battle of insults in which literary virtuosity often degenerated into vulgarity.

In short, his life became so wild that his friend Cavalcanti felt obliged to reprove him sharply in a sonnet:

And now I care not, sith thy
 life is baseness
To give the sign that thy
 speech pleaseth me,
Nor come I to thee in guise
 visible . . .

However, this stormy period did not last long, because in 1295, five years

On the anniversary
of Beatrice's death,
Dante draws an angel
while growing sadder
at the memory of his lady.
The poet himself
tells the story

in the Vita Nuova,
and it is illustrated here
by the British
pre-Raphaelite painter
Dante Gabriel Rossetti
(Ashmolean Museum,
Oxford).

after the death of Beatrice, Dante went into politics. No one knows what caused such a change of interests. Perhaps there was no one specific reason. Perhaps he was tired of his dissolute life; or perhaps his passion for politics was kindled by a Florentine ordinance of 1295, which extended to the nobility the privilege of holding public office, provided they were members of one of the art or craft guilds.

Dante enrolled in the guild of the doctors and pharmacists, almost certainly by virtue of his philosophical studies.

Florence at the End of the Thirteenth Century

During these years Florence was continually expanding. Its trade flourished, and the town became too restricted for the population, which crowded together in small, gloomy houses dominated by massive towers. The city was already surrounded by three circles of walls, and for a breath of fresh air, to soothe the eye and the spirit, the Florentines had, then as now, to climb the hills around their city.

The new growth of trade and industry had caused a great social upheaval. The nobility was in decline and the middle classes were in power. And they ruled thanks to a sort of bloodless revolution that had taken

14

*The narrow streets and
sentinel towers
of medieval Florence,
as they appear
in a contemporary fresco
(Bigallo Orphanage,
Florence).*

place shortly before, when Giano della Bella made himself the spokesman and standard-bearer for a people oppressed by the nobility. Giano had not only incited the people to free themselves from their yoke, but to subject the nobles themselves, that class which called itself "the Great." As often happens in these cases, once Giano lost his popular support, the nobles revived, and the middle classes, coming to terms with them, consolidated their power. All this took place between 1293 and 1295, while the rivalry between the two chief families, the Cerchi and the Donati, smoldered. The Cerchi were nouveaux riches who had made a vast fortune in business and were making every effort to become part of the aristocracy, although they were not of noble birth. The Donati, on the other hand, were less rich, but enormously proud of their ancient and noble lineage.

All the nobility of blood rallied around the Donati, while the Cerchi were supported by families who had only recently become powerful. In such circumstances

Public life
in the comune of Florence:
above, a group of Whites
are sentenced
to decapitation by
Cante de' Gabrielli da Gubbio,
the chief justice
who later signed
Dante's sentence;
right, Corso Donati
enters the city
with his forces
in November, 1301,
opens the prisons,
and instigates a period
of administrative
turmoil and
confusion (miniatures in
the Vatican Library).

16

Dante is chosen as a member of the embassy sent by Florence to Pope Boniface VIII. It was the last diplomatic mission the poet undertook for his city before his exile.

it was inevitable that the rivalry between the two families assumed a political character. And this happened precisely at the time Dante entered public life. He immediately found himself embroiled in and finally overwhelmed by this intricate conflict.

The division between Guelph and Ghibelline had lost all significance, for at the time Florence was overwhelmingly Guelph. Instead, the city was torn apart by the Cerchi and Donati factions, which soon came to be called the Whites and the Blacks respectively. Pope Boniface VIII added fuel to the flames by supporting Corso Donati, leader of the Blacks, thereby hoping to seize all Tuscany.

Head First into Politics

Dante made his first forays into politics at a time when the political climate could not have been hotter, and the situation more thorny and delicate. And his political career was certainly not a happy one.

From 1295 to 1297 Dante was part of the Special Council of the People; he participated in an election

campaign for the priors and was a member of the Council of the One Hundred. We know nothing more of him until 1300. In that year he served as ambassador to San Gimignano, and then was elected prior from June 15 to August 15. Concerned above all with the welfare of the city, Dante tried to rise above party politics and take a position that favored neither faction. In this spirit he approved the priorate's decision to exile the most violent leaders of both parties after a skirmish between the Blacks and the

Whites on St. John's Eve. His impartiality cost him his friend Guido Cavalcanti, who was exiled along with the others. Indeed, the poet himself may have advised this step. But in Florence it was impossible to stay out of the fray. And Dante was almost forced to side with the Whites in his effort to oppose the subtle maneuvers of the pope, who was constantly trying to insinuate himself into the affairs of Florence by siding with the Blacks.

The following year, his term as prior having expired, Dante and two other Flor-

17

Dante in exile: below,
left, the Abbey of Pomposa,
where the poet spent
the last year of his life;
below, right, the palace
of the Scaligeri family
in Verona, with a

monument to Dante
in the foreground;
bottom, a portrait
of the exile in his maturity
(detail from a painting
by Bertini). Opposite,
the procession of

the Virgin (sixth-century
mosaic in Sant' Apollinare
Nuovo in Ravenna).
It is possible that the
mystical atmosphere of the
Ravenna mosaics inspired
the last cantos of Paradise.

entines were sent on an embassy to Rome. Boniface VIII allowed the other two men to leave, but detained Dante, in whom he recognized a formidable adversary. Meanwhile, the situation at home worsened. Thanks to the decisive intervention of Charles of Valois, the Blacks gained the upper hand in Florence, chased out the Whites, destroyed their houses, and condemned by default those who had already left.

In January, 1302, Dante was fined 5,000 florins, sentenced to two years in prison, and prohibited from holding any public office. Because he did not come to Florence to clear his name, word reached him in Siena in March that a new sentence condemned him to be burned alive.

"You Had Better Leave Florence"

The poet's first reaction was a violent desire for revenge.

He wanted to join the other exiles, seek help, organize an armed band, and re-enter Florence by force. But the exiled Whites were an irresolute lot, trapped by their own petty interests. As for allies, it was not easy to find trustworthy ones. The Whites were too compromised with the pope; to help them would be to take sides openly against the papacy. Nevertheless, there were a few skirmishes, which went under the name of the Wars of Mugello. All

were unsuccessful, and they left behind a train of venomous recriminations and mutual accusations. Dante, disgusted with his own companions, dropped them, and relying on his own resources, decided to go it alone. Leaving Tuscany, he went to Verona to join Bartolomeo della Scala, who shared Dante's Ghibelline views. Here, in the "first hostel," that is, in his first place of refuge, Dante found generous hospitality and made friends with the

young Can Francesco, Bartolomeo's brother, who was later to become Can Grande. The *Divine Comedy* testifies to the poet's stay in Verona. After that there are no trustworthy documents that would allow us to reconstruct Dante's wanderings from city to city. He followed more and less favorable opportunities, fulfilling diplomatic assignments, when he could find them, on behalf of lords who received him grudgingly and those who really

opened their doors to him. He lived more or less like a courtier, spending his talent in the service of noblemen and sharing their hospitality with diplomats, soldiers, adventurers, buffoons, and men of every kind. In 1306 he was with the Malaspina family and went on their behalf to meet the bishop of Luni. Some say he made a quick trip to Paris, but that is only conjecture.

The year 1310 was the year of Dante's great hope. Henry VII of Luxemburg came to Italy; he was a powerful and generous emperor who might have pacified the city-states and united them under a single leadership. Dante was inspired by this marvelous dream, and from the Casentino, where he was perhaps the guest of the count of Battifolle, he encouraged Henry in his glorious undertaking. But once again the city he loved and hated deceived him, exasperated him. The most rascally of the Florentines, jealous of the liberty of their commune, instigated a movement against the emperor that spread rapidly all over Italy. When Henry finally decided to act, his undertaking failed miserably. More embittered than ever, Dante perhaps returned to Can Grande in Verona, perhaps remained in the Casentino, or perhaps sought refuge in Tuscany with Uguccione della Faggiuola. By now he felt like "a boat without a helmsman." He drifted from town to town,

Left, as ambassador from Guido Novello da Polenta, lord of Ravenna, Dante before the Venetian senate. Below, Dante's death, as depicted by the German Romantic painter Anselm Feuerbach. Bottom, the Church of San Francesco in Ravenna, where Dante's remains were first entombed and where they were discovered more than three centuries after they had been stolen and hidden.

guided only by the events of the day. He spent the last years of his life in Ravenna, where it seems his wife and children joined him. We know little of this period too. Possibly he held a teaching post in Ravenna.

At any rate, it is known that Dante fell sick in 1321 while returning from Venice, where he had been sent as ambassador by Guido da Polenta, the lord of Ravenna. It was the end. On the night of September 13 Dante died.

Illustrious Contemporaries

The prominent people of a world in transition pass in review, differing greatly from each other, but all sharply etched.

*Matteo I Visconti
(1250-1322)
gained control in Milan
for his family.*

*The painter Giotto di Bondone
(1266-1337) freed himself
from Gothic and Byzantine
influences to create a
new kind of art, vigorously
plastic, profoundly human.*

*Under King Edward I
(1239-1307), Parliament and
the law in England
began to take shape.*

*Marco Polo (1254-1324)
remained at the
court of Kublai Khan
for seventeen years.
He is at right, with
his father and his uncle.*

*Alfonso X, "the Learned,"
king of Castile (1221-84),
is considered to be the
founder of Spanish literature.*

*His lauaı spirituali have
made Jacopone da Todi
(1230-1306) one of the greatest
of the Italian religious poets.
religiosi italiani.*

The insurrection of the Vespers brought Peter III of Aragon (1239-1285) to the throne of Sicily.

Dino Compagni (1257-1324), like Giovanni Villani, was one of the chroniclers of Dante's time.

Saint Thomas Aquinas (1225-74) adapted the Aristotelian system to Christian thought.

The dream of the Emperor Henry VII (c. 1270-1313) was to unify Italy.

Pope Clement V, in alliance with King Philip the Fair of France, transferred the papacy to Avignon (1305).

In the battle of Meloria (1284) the Genoese Oberto Doria routed the Pisans, with whom Count Ugolino fought.

Albertus Magnus (1193-1280) was not only a philosopher and a theologian, but a distinguished naturalist.

Albert I of Augsburg (1250-1308), Dante's "Albert the German," was king of Germany and duke of Austria and Styria. He was assassinated by one of his nephews.

23

Memorable Dates

City republics are born; great nations begin to grow stronger; and culture develops amid alternating periods of peace and war.

Mongols attack Japan
(miniature from The Book of Marvels)

1256—Mongols invade Persia.
1257—Robert de Sorbon founds the theological college of Paris, the Sorbonne.
1258-65—Barons rebel against Henry III of England.
1259-60—Saint Thomas Aquinas writes the *Summa Contra Gentiles*.
1260—Mamelukes (a military caste dominant in Egypt) stop Mongol expansion.
1261-64—Norway acquires Greenland and Iceland.
1261—Michael Palaeologus reorganizes the Byzantine empire.
1266—Battle of Benevento takes place between Manfred and Charles of Anjou. (As a consequence of Manfred's defeat and death, the control of southern Italy passed to the Angevins.)
1270-74—The seventh crusade takes place.

1273—Rudolph of Hapsburg is elected king of Germany; the power of the Hapsburgs begins with him.
1274-81—In Japan the samurai repel the invasion of the Mongols in a bloody struggle.
1275—Arabs learn the use of saltpeter as gunpowder from the Chinese.
1280—Kublai Khan, having completed the conquest of China, founds the Mongol empire.
1282—The Sicilian Vespers in Palermo; French rule overthrown.
1291—Acre falls into the hands of the Saracens, and so one of their last footholds in the Holy Land is lost to the Christians.
1293—Catholicism is introduced into China.
1295—The so-called Model Parliament is convoked in England under Edward I.
1298—Marco Polo writes the account of his travels.
1302—With the Peace of Caltabellotta, Sicily comes under the control of Aragon.
1302—Battle of Courtrai liberates Flanders from the French. (Flanders falls again to the French in 1305.)
1307—King Philip the Fair has the Knights Templars arrested and persecuted so that he may confiscate their property.
1309—The papacy moves to Avignon.
1324—Marsilius of Padua in his political work *Defensor Pacis* affirms that the state is founded on the sovereignty of the people.
1325—Aztecs found the city of Tenochtitlan as the capital of their kingdom. (It is Mexico City today.)
1327—Ludwig of Bavaria assumes the iron crown in Milan.
1339—Edward III of England lays claim to the throne of France and starts the Hundred Years War.
1346—The English defeat the French at the battle of Crécy.

Mysteries and Legends

Questions, theories, and anecdotes about Dante have all contributed to illuminate the great poet, sometimes indirectly, sometimes vividly.

The Last Cantos of Paradise and Their Secret Hiding Place

Boccaccio writes that after Dante's death and burial, his sons undertook the usual sad task of settling his affairs and putting his manuscripts in order. His sons and friends were most anxious to find the last thirteen cantos of the *Divine Comedy*, which they knew had been written, but had not yet sent to Can Grande della Scala. No matter how long they searched, ransacked, indeed turned the house upside down, they could not find the slightest trace of the precious manuscript. It seemed to have really disappeared. Had it been stolen? Destroyed by Dante himself? Secretly entrusted to someone by the poet? And why?

With the passage of time, Dante's friends resigned themselves to the thought that the last cantos of the poem were lost forever. Then one night, eight months after Dante's death, his son Jacopo had a dream in which his father appeared dressed all in white and bathed in light. The vision said that he had just realized he had not given instructions about the poem before he died and that he had come to rectify this oversight. Dante's ghost then took Jacopo by the hand, led him into the study, pointed to a certain part of the wall, and disappeared.

Disturbed by the dream, Jacopo immediately ran to the house of his friend Giardini, who had been with him when his father died. As soon as Giardini heard the story he got up and accompanied Jacopo back to the study. They removed a mat from the wall where Dante had pointed, and found a small niche. In it were some dusty rolls, already mildewed where they had been exposed to the air. These were the manuscripts of the last thirteen cantos of *Paradise*.

With trembling hands Jacopo and Giardini copied the verses, and it was this transcription that was sent to Can Grande della Scala.

Did Dante Have an Illegitimate Son?

Little more than forty years ago, when it was thought that nothing more would be found out about Dante, an unpublished document from Lucca turned the world of Dante scholars upside down. It was a paper notarized in 1308, witnessed by one Giovanni, son of Dante Alighieri of Florence (*Dantis Alagherii de Florentia*). Was this another of the poet's children, beside Jacopo, Pietro, and Antonia (later Sister Beatrice)? So it seemed; and not only another son but an illegitimate one, because, it was thought, a witness had to be at least eighteen. And if he was eighteen in 1308, he must have been born in 1290, several years before Dante's marriage to Gemma Donati. The marriage is generally thought to have taken place after 1290, which is to say, after the death of Beatrice.

If this theory is not accepted, we must believe that there is a coincidence of names. If another Dante Alighieri lived in Florence during these years, the alarmists said, the whole carefully constructed biography of the poet is in danger of collapsing.

For example, was the Dante *Allegheriis* who was ambassador to San Gimignano in 1300 the poet or another man of the same name? And what about the Dante *Alleghieri* who was sentenced to be burned alive by Cante de' Gabrielli? Was he the poet Dante or another man? And if he was another Dante, why and when was the author of the *Divine Comedy* exiled?

In short, the son who appears in the document risked destroying and nullifying the very life of his own father.

The question has been exhaustibly—and inconclusively —studied and discussed in all its aspects. During the course of research the alternatives changed. It was shown that the alarmists who questioned the poet's identity spoke without foundation. The mysterious Giovanni, son of Dante, could have been the poet's natural son, and with equal probability he could have been the first-born of Dante and Gemma. The minimum age for a witness at the time turns out to have been fourteen, not eighteen.

Moreover, there is no documentary evidence that the marriage of Dante and Gemma took place after 1290; it could well have been celebrated earlier.

This seems all the more likely, because Gemma's dowry certificate is dated 1277. The dowry certificate was usually drawn up at the time of the marriage or a little before. There is nothing to prevent our concluding that according to the common practice of the time, the couple was married when very young, and consummation and cohabitation only took place several years later.

On the other hand, coincidental names were fairly frequent in the fourteenth century. A little after the poet's time there is a record of a Dante Alighieri, father of a Gabriello and a

Dantino Alighieri. And to suppose still another Dante Alighieri is not to destroy the poet Dante's biography, unless we also presume that the other Dante was also a scholar, a politician, and a Guelph partisan of the Whites.

Moreover, we must also remember that in contemporary documents some descriptive qualification was usually added to the name to identify the person more precisely. For example, besides his first name and family name, the poet Dante is also sometimes identified as "son of Bellincione" or as living in the "district of Porta San Pietro." Still, with three children or four, with or without a confusion of names, our poet's life remains the same.

Dante's Troubles and Debts

The old records of the commune of Florence are a rich source of small details and gossip about the Alighieri family. They reveal, for example, that Dante, his two sons, or his half brother, Francesco, were always pressed by creditors and usurers, by debts and legal problems.

It seems that his father, who had died when Dante and Francesco were young, left behind a muddled and difficult

financial situation. The fact is that between 1297 and 1301 the two brothers contracted very large debts—80, 90, and then 277 florins "of good weight in gold." For a six-month loan of 53 florins, Francesco was obliged to turn to a moneylender whose astuteness and total lack of scruples were well known in Florence. This is a sure sign that the financial situation of the Alighieris must have been almost desperate. Francesco later made several loans to Dante, once even for 125 gold florins.

However, Francesco was unable to get back his money from the commune when his brother was condemned and his possessions seized. Thus the question of the 125 florins dragged on into the time of Francesco's sons.

In their turn, Dante's sons sharply reproached their uncle when he sold the whole farm at Camerata for his own account, without taking into consideration that one half belonged to them. Only later, after interminable negotiations, were Jacopo and Pietro able to recover some of the family fortune by claiming their mother's dowry rights on their confiscated patrimony. But then the brothers went to court over the division of the property.

Jacopo was constantly obliged

to juggle financial problems and legal actions on account of women. A widower with children, he had promised to marry Jacopa degli Alfani. She had brought him a dowry of 200 florins; but it seems that Jacopo did not in fact marry her.

We do not know why Jacopo changed his mind. We do know, however, that Jacopa lost patience and finally resorted to law. A referee was designated to arbitrate the dispute, and he decreed that Dante's son must keep his word. There exists a document of a legal action instituted by Jacopa in which the stubborn fiancé is enjoined to keep his promise and marry without further delay, in accordance with the sentence of the referee named by both parties. Furthermore, he is enjoined to publicly acknowledge that he has already received Jacopa's dowry.

Four years later—Jacopo having died in the meantime—Jacopa was still claiming her dowry from his heirs, producing as evidence not a marriage certificate (which would have been the natural thing if the marriage had taken place), but only the deposition made by the referee.

It is logical to suppose that poor Jacopa degli Alfani lost her 200 florins without realiz-

ing her dream of marrying Dante's son.

The Reasons for His Break with the Exiles

It is hard to establish what actually happened between Dante and the "wicked and foolish company." It is not known how long Dante and his companions in exile stayed together, whether he always remained in Arezzo or whether Uguccione della Faggiuola, the Ghibelline chief of the city, had a change of heart, and Dante and a good number of the other exiles went to the more friendly town of Forlí.

In the tangle of hypotheses and suppositions that surrounds every episode in the poet's life, there is good reason to suppose that Dante stayed a certain time in Arezzo and actively participated in the preparations for the first war of Mugello valley. After a series of defeats suffered by the Whites and their allies (the last at Campo Piceno, where Florentine exiles and Pistoians clashed with Florentine citizens and Luccans), Dante understood that serious military preparation backed by subtle diplomatic action would be necessary if there was to be any hope of victory. Thereupon he persuaded even his most impatient companions to conclude a truce. And he proposed that Scarpetta Ordelaffi, lord of Forlí, be named their chief ally and military leader.

The diplomatic mission was successful, and Scarpetta accepted the task without stipulating too many conditions. He kept Dante with him as counselor and secretary while he put his affairs in order for the undertaking. In the execution of his duty, it appears that Dante also went to Verona for the first time and obtained Bartolomeo della Scala's promise of a contingent of cavalry and infantry. The city of Bologna also agreed to help the exiles. In March, 1303, the army, with Scarpetta at the head, prepared to invade the Mugello valley. It was a sizeable force for the time, if it is true, as it seems to be, that there were 6,000 foot soldiers and 800 cavalrymen. The first surprise attacks met with some success. But at Castel Puliciano the exiles found themselves face to face with an army of Blacks, most ably led by Fulcieri da Calboli, and they suffered a quick and open defeat.

Since Dante had first suggested the truce and then organized the new army, even proposing its captain, he appeared inevitably as the man responsible for the disaster. He was blamed on the ground that the truce only allowed the Blacks to find reinforcements; that Scarpetta knew neither how to command nor how to fight; that the whole basis of the campaign had been a catalogue of errors. And as the criticism became more venomous, Dante was even accused of having accepted Florentine bribes. Much less would have been enough to arouse the poet's anger and scorn. Abandoning the whole undertaking, Dante turned his back on the quarrelsome company.

A Violent Love in Maturity

While he was staying in the Casentino, Dante turned forty. His was a sad and harsh maturity. In the midst of his bitterness, he forgot for a time the love poems of the good years in Florence and dedicated himself only to profound study and to compiling weighty works of scholarship, politics, and linguistics. According to Boccaccio's account of him, Dante had even come to look austere: his body was stooped and he walked gravely; his face was lean and his expression severe. He ate and drank moderately, dressed soberly, and enjoyed his own company, absorbed as he was in his own thoughts.

And yet, just then, he found himself suddenly in love. It was an unexpected and overwhelming passion, "a bolt from the blue," by his own definition. In a letter to Moroello Malaspina he confessed: "A woman as radiant as a flash of lightning appeared before me, I don't know how, conforming in every way to my desires by her beauty and behavior. I was completely struck dumb and full of wonder to see her, but my amazement ceased for fear of the thunderclap that would follow. Because, just as thunder immediately follows lightning, so the flame of her beauty was scarcely dying down when I was seized with a violent and imperious love. And as the man does who returns to his country after a long exile, my fierce love killed or banished or enslaved everything that opposed it inside me. It even killed my good resolution to abstain from women and from songs of love; it banished by ceaseless meditation and contemplation of heavenly and earthly things. In short, because my soul no longer rebelled against it, my love put the yoke on my free will so that I had to turn not where I wished to go, but where it wished me to go. Therefore love ruled me and no virtue opposed it. You will find in what way love dominated me by reading on, after this letter." (That is, by reading the canzone: "Love, since I needs must make complaint. . . .") The object of this love remains a mystery. There was talk of a lady in waiting in the court of the counts Guidi;

another theory goes further, asserting dogmatically that it was a servant girl. Dante describes her as "beautiful and evil." That may be true, but to listen to Boccaccio, she was not exactly beautiful. He relates that in the Casentine Alps Dante had longed "for a mountain girl who, truth to tell, was goiterous, however beautiful her face was."

Perhaps the goiter is a wicked invention of the Tuscan storyteller, who was always ready to color his anecdotes. At all events, goiterous or not, the girl must have had a difficult personality, and Dante suffered for a long time.

In the poems Dante dedicated to her, there are notes of sincerity, drama, and passion that the poet had never used before when writing of love.

The idealizations, the angelic women, the gentle hearts, are gone. Instead, there is a passion all too human, turbulent, obsessive, at times desperate, at times almost gross. Because of this anti-Beatrice, who had "a heart of marble," Dante finally lost interest in Florentine political developments and no longer pursued the extreme attempts of the Whites to conquer Florence and throw out the Blacks. And yet, perhaps specifically to witness these events firsthand, he remained in the Casentino. When the exiles were beaten once again and had lost the last hope of returning to their homeland, Dante had no further reason to remain in that part of the country. Indeed, he had every reason to get away as quickly as possible. It was really a desperate flight from the region that had become hateful to him because of his tormented and disturbing love.

Tradition has it that at this point he crossed the Alps and went to Paris.

Dante in Paris

Boccaccio and Villani both state that Dante visited Paris, and although we have no proof of this, the story seems credible enough. In the *Divine Comedy* there are references to places in France and to sites on the road to France that are so precise as to make one think that the poet had indeed seen them.

Denied the hope of returning to Florence, and shaken by an obsessive and disturbing passion for the beautiful lady of Casentino, it is more than likely that Dante decided to study seriously and take his degree. A degree, among other things, would have permitted Dante to teach in the cities he visited in his wanderings. And nothing could have been more natural for the poet than to choose Paris, where the university, still in its infancy, was already becoming the most

important center of European culture. In the straw-littered, squalid classrooms, which faced onto Straw Alley—as Dante himself called it, translating the French *Rue de Fouarre*—all the great medieval thinkers were teaching or had taught: the great Abelard, Albertus Magnus, Bonaventura, Siger de Brabant, Thomas Aquinas.

Dante probably knew French, and he must have known a good deal about Paris—its customs, its people—and about the studies at the university. After all, in Florence he had had as his teacher Brunetto Latini, the notary who lived out his exile in Paris.

At the university, this mature student of philosophy and theology was immediately noticed, not only for his austere looks and his difficult personality but also for his exceptional cleverness. Boccaccio relates that Dante once heard fourteen debates on various subjects. At the end of the discussions, after refuting or resolving the various disputed points, he summarized the fourteen arguments so lucidly that his listeners were astonished. Despite so much skill, he had still not received his degree by the time he returned to Italy. According to some, his failure to do so was caused by a lack of money. It appears that Dante attended his courses regularly and that he had com-

pleted all the requirements for a degree in theology (such as the reading of the Judgments and the oral examination before the doctors), but that at the end he did not have enough money to convene the solemn assembly, which would have granted him the academic title.

Boccaccio states that Dante refused the Paris degree because he wished to take the degree only in Italy; but a chauvinistic gesture of this kind is not in keeping with the cultural climate of the time.

According to still another version, Dante hastily abandoned his studies in Paris when he learned that Henry of Luxemburg, Holy Roman Emperor-elect, was to come down into Italy to assume the iron crown in Milan and the imperial crown in Rome. Crossing the Alps once again, Dante the exile dreamed of a peaceful Italy under the government of the new emperor. Already he saw the gates of Florence flung wide, and the town, as if freed from an evil spell, once again honorable and wise. In the face of such a prospect, of what importance was a degree, even one from the University of Paris?

The Letter
from Brother Ilario

One day a pilgrim approached the monks who stood at the

entrance to the Camaldolese Monastery of Santa Croce del Corvo in the mountains near the mouth of the Magra River. Pale and stern, the traveler looked at the monastery wall. A monk asked him what he was seeking, and he had to repeat the question twice. Finally, the man turned his eyes from the wall and answered that he was seeking peace. There was something strange in the pilgrim's look, and Brother Ilario felt the desire to know him better. He made him come into the monastery, sat down with him in the parlor, and found out that the man was a Florentine exile named Dante Alighieri, who was on his way to Paris. He also discovered that the pilgrim was a poet and had written a poem about the other world.

Pursuing the conversation, the monk immediately gained Dante's confidence, and the poet gave him the manuscript of the Inferno and asked him to deliver it to Uguccione della Faggiola, to whom he intended to dedicate the work. This the monk did promptly. He also wrote a letter to accompany the manuscript in which he described his meeting with Dante, commented on the verses of the poem, and explained why it was written in Italian and not Latin. The letter was discovered between the pages of an ancient Dante codex.

The document has been studied and restudied by Dante scholars, but it still remains a patent fraud. In the first place, in this period, from 1308 to 1309, the Inferno could not possibly have been finished, if indeed it had even been begun. Secondly, Dante would never have entrusted a work that he knew to be valuable to an ordinary monk. On the other hand, it is not clear why, if Dante had wanted to forward the manuscript to Uguccione, he had not seen to it before he undertook this trip. And if indeed he wished to dedicate the poem to the Ghibelline condottiere, why leave the job to the monk without at least writing a note or a dedication in his own hand? As for Brother Ilario's explanatory notes, did he write them at Dante's invitation? And how could a proud and difficult poet have trusted not only the loyalty but also the cultural qualifications of this unknown friar? Would it not have been more logical for Dante himself to write the commentary for his own poem? Moreover, the commentary is clearly the work of a learned man who has studied, compared, and meditated. How could a poor monk possibly have improvised it on the spur of the moment?

It is most probable that the false details were invented to give greater credence to the commentary on the Inferno that an unknown author—perhaps a Brother Ilario at the monastery of Santa Croce del Corvo—had put together after who knows how many years of diligent and perceptive work.

Relations between Dante and Can Grande Were Not Always Easy

Despite the great praise given to the Scala family in the Divine Comedy, relations between Dante and Can Grande della Scala were not always serene. Several anecdotes point up the behavior of the two men, who were more often than not quite sharp during their confrontations.

One day Can Grande, along with Dante and the whole court, were listening to the somewhat vulgar quips and jokes of an entertainer, who succeeded in amusing the whole company. Suddenly Can Grande asked the poet why this actor, rough and silly as he was, knew how to amuse and please everyone, while he, Dante, had never amused anyone, and in fact, bored most of those who knew him. Without hesitation, Dante replied: "It wouldn't surprise you if you reflected that friendship is based on equality of customs and similarity of spirit."

On another occasion, again ac - cording to certain minor chronicles, Can Grande played a joke on Dante that seems rather good-natured if somewhat childish, and certainly not deserving the poet's scourging retort. During a banquet Can Grande secretly ordered the servants to put all the bones discarded by the diners under the table in front of the poet's place. When the tables were removed (which was the custom in those days), the guests roared with laughter to see the great heap of leftovers at Dante's feet. But the imperturbable Alighieri said: "I don't see why you are so surprised. The dogs have eaten their bones while I have left mine behind." (Can Grande means "large dog.")

Perhaps the real reason for this acid reply lies in the contrasting character of the two men. Can Grande was jovial, extroverted, and gay; Dante was taciturn, introverted, and embittered. On the human level, a rapport is difficult between a melancholic and irritable exile and a generous, pleasure-loving young noble. Another source of the lack of understanding could have been the fact that Can Grande, while praising and encouraging the poet in his work, was not in a position to appreciate the true value of the Divine Comedy. It seems that the Veronese nobleman always thought of Dante as a diplomat who had written a good political treatise and who amused himself by also writing verses. It is certain that Can Grande was a most hospitable host, but he never helped Dante's career as a man of letters. He did not allow him to teach in the Studio (the school of advanced studies at Verona, which was on its way to becoming a renowned university). Instead, he preferred Artemisio as the professor of logic. Nor did he award Dante the honorary degree, which he was persuaded without much difficulty to confer on Albertino da Mussato for a tragedy he had written about Ezzelino.

Dante the Sorcerer

One evening, while strolling down a lane by the Adige River, Dante noticed that two young girls drew back as he passed and that they seemed a little frightened. His astonishment grew when he heard one whisper to the other: "Did you see him? He's the one who comes and goes to Hell and brings back news of the damned who live there." And the other answered: "Ah, that's why his complexion is so dark. The smoke must have blackened him." True or false, the anecdote testifies to the great success of the Divine Comedy, which was beginning to be known even among the populace. And it is also proof that the story of his trip beyond the grave quite soon earned Dante the reputation of being a magician and a sorcerer, the man who frequents the land of the dead.

The most delightful anecdote illustrating Dante's purportedly supernatural powers is the story about the Milanese priest Cagnolati, also reputed to be a sorcerer, who became deeply involved in a shady case of black magic. The account of the episode takes up two codices in the secret archives of the Vatican.

At that time in Milan, Matteo Visconti had begun little by little to build his power by intrigues, money, and skillful jockeying. Like all other princes, he did not suffer from an excess of scruples, nor was he overly troubled by the means he used to gain his ends. Since the person then giving him the most trouble was Pope John XXII, he thought up a rather strange method for getting rid of the pope. He called in a renegade priest, Bartolomeo Cagnolati, who was reputed to be an expert in black magic, and in occult practices in general. In great secrecy Visconti entrusted the priest with the job of bringing about the pope's death by sorcery.

Cagnolati at first accepted; but

31

then, repentant or terrified by the rank of the person he had to kill, he fled to Avignon and revealed the plot to the papal court. The pope was terribly frightened and immediately ordered a complete investigation of the affair. Among other facts that emerged, it was revealed that Visconti had brought grave pressure to bear in order to convince the priest to do the job: he had threatened to call in Dante Alighieri of Florence, the man who had been to Hell and who would surely hex the pope to death without difficulty. Cagnolati, so as not to appear a lesser man than his Florentine rival, had promptly accepted the task.

Naturally, the poet, who was in Ravenna at the time, knew nothing of the affair, and perhaps he never did learn of it.

The Changing Fortune of Dante's Remains

Condemned to a life of wandering, poor Dante knew no peace even in death. His remains were first buried in the Church of San Francesco in Ravenna. Six years after his death, the papal legate to Lombardy declared Dante's *De Monarchia* a heretical book and ordered it to be publicly burned along with the poet's body. Only a series of fortunate circumstances prevented the order from being carried out.

However, as time passed, enmity was replaced by admiration. In the early fifteenth century Florence asked Ravenna to give back the body of its exceptional son. Ravenna refused at first, but had to give in a century later when the request was renewed, this time by Pope Leo X, a member of the Medici family of Florence.

However, when Dante's tomb was opened, it was found to be empty. The Ravenna authorities did not know how to explain it, and the Florentines had to resign themselves to the incredible truth.

Dante's body had disappeared. How, when, why, and by whose hand?

It was an absolute mystery. And a mystery it remained until 1865, the year in which it was decided to restore the empty tomb, which the Italians had continued to honor nevertheless. During the restoration in the Franciscan cloister, a laborer broke down a wall and found a wooden chest. It contained human bones and a letter dated 1677 and signed by the prior of the convent, attesting that these were Dante's bones, hidden by the monks to prevent them from being taken to Florence.

Where the poor relics had lain between 1519, when the tomb was opened and found empty, and 1677, when they were walled up in this hiding place,

is, and will always remain, a mystery. Probably they were in some dusty archive or under the false bottom of some vestry wardrobe. At any rate, once they were found, the poet's remains were returned to the urn with public ceremonies and great honors.

But the event had a sequel. In 1878 the Classe Library in Ravenna received a little package containing a few small bones, which were said to have been stolen when the wooden chest was recovered in 1865. In 1886 another little box with similar bone fragments arrived at the Ravenna town hall. And a third box arrived in 1900.

Perhaps all the talk about theft and rediscovery had fired the imagination of the people of Ravenna; or perhaps these sad remains were authentic. Whatever the case may be, a rigorous and scientific examination of all the bones was considered necessary to head off an alarming proliferation of the poet's remains. The skeleton would be entirely restored and every false relic eliminated. This took place in 1921, and since then, Dante's remains have rested in peace at last. In Santa Croce in Florence, there is a great funerary monument to Dante, but the tomb is empty. Not even six centuries after his death was the exile allowed to return to his native city.

A Survey of Dante's Writings

Dante's minor works alone would assure him a place in literary history, but in the DIVINE COMEDY, *the same concepts are transformed into sublime poetry.*

LA VITA NUOVA

LA VITA NUOVA (THE NEW LIFE)

This supremely delicate love story is Dante's first work. It relates the poet's great love for Beatrice in a mixture of prose and poetry, or more precisely, in a series of poems with commentaries or introductions in prose. Following the rules of the *stil. nuovo* ("new style"), which was the school of poetry in fashion at the time, the poet's love is an ecstasy, a contemplation of an idealized woman. It is also a genuine, romantic love, full of anxiety and glances, desire and dreams. This is the love that later infused the *Divine Comedy;* but it is the central theme of the *Vita Nuova.*

Dante and Beatrice were children when they met for the first time; they were only nine years old. When they met again, nine years later, the young man of eighteen once more experienced the agitation of their first meeting—and from this moment love rules his soul. Dante tries to hide his secret love from prying eyes by pretending to be in love with another woman, the "lady of the screen." But the trick gets out of hand, rumors begin to circulate, and Beatrice snubs him.

The young man suffers profoundly.

When Beatrice's father dies, Dante is in such despair, thinking of her sorrow, that soon afterward he falls sick. In a dream—almost a nightmare—he sees Beatrice dead, covered with a white veil. It is a prophetic dream, for on the ninth day of the ninth month of the year 1290 Beatrice does die. Dante, prostrated by grief, is comforted by a compassionate lady; but this consolation is so welcome to him that at a certain point he says: "I came to such a pass at the sight of this lady that my eyes began to take too much pleasure in seeing her; wherefore time and again I was troubled in my heart and held myself to be exceedingly base."

A very real conflict arises in the poet's soul, for he is torn between his feeling for the compassionate lady and the wish to remain faithful to the memory of Beatrice. The thought of Beatrice triumphs at last, and Dante has a miraculous vision—"in which I saw things as made me resolve to say no more of this Blessed Lady until the time when I could speak of her more worthily."

In the *Vita Nuova* the story is told with great delicacy, and the events are, as it were, suspended in the atmosphere of a dream. It is as if the only reality are the poet's feelings, his wonder, his anxieties, his sighs. What he remembers nullifies the sense of place, dims outlines, and veils and transforms people, words, and objects. Therefore the dream can have the sharpness and precision of reality, whereas the real event can seem as vague as a fantasy. We are in the undisputed realm of poetry; in its best moments the *Vita Nuova* anticipates the *Divine Comedy*. Not only the verses but also the prose sometimes achieve a pure lyricism. When the poem and the prose relate the same episode, it almost seems as though a kind of poetic contest is taking place between them, in which sometimes the verse is victorious and sometimes the prose—a malleable and artistic prose that can be bent to every purpose.

Naturally, the lady in the *Vita Nuova* is an angel, whom God sends to earth out of pity for men and as a comfort to them. However, in the story Beatrice also has very human attributes and reactions.

Precisely because of the oscillation in her character between the real and the ideal, the knotty question has arisen as to whether she existed or not in life.

The majority of the critics now appears convinced that the Beatrice of the *Vita Nuova* is the Beatrice who was the daughter of Folco Portinari.

Dante wrote the *Vita Nuova* around 1292. He selected the poems from his early work, arranged them in a progressive order, and wrote the prose passages that provide the thread of the narrative.

Lo amoroso Conuiuio di Dante: con la additione: Nouamente stampato.

IL CONVIVIO

IL CONVIVIO (THE BANQUET)

Composed between 1304 and 1307, the *Convivio* is one of the first works Dante wrote in exile, at the beginning of his wanderings. It is a serious and painstaking work by which the poet hoped to demonstrate the extent and depth of his knowledge, to achieve great fame, and so to obtain from his fellow Florentines the revocation of his sentence. As we know, none of this happened. Dante wanted to prepare a banquet of knowledge, inviting all those who truly hungered for it. To be able to teach them, he had to address them in their everyday language, which the professional intellectuals quite wrongly spurned. That is why the *Convivio* is written in Italian—or better, in the vernacular—rather than in Latin. It is truly a work of cultural enlightenment written for "princes, barons, noblemen, and many other titled people, not only male but female." Dante conceived of it as a series of fifteen treatises; but he only wrote four, of which the first is an introduction. The arguments are set forth in the poetic compositions that precede each treatise—no longer, or at least not solely, poems of love, but ballads heavy with learning. The ballads constitute the "meat" of the feast, while the prose sections are the "bread." In its external form the *Convivio* seems to resemble the *Vita Nuova*; but in reality it is entirely different. Whereas the youthful work is the story of a purely interior beatitude, in the *Convivio* logic and reason prevail, sustained by a precise and effective prose style. The prose is not immune from a certain medieval heaviness; but it already has a clarity of terms and a musical quality that make it the first true and solid Italian prose.

The scholarly content of the *Convivio* is drawn from Aristotle, and therefore will not particularly interest the modern reader. The valid aspect for us is the discussion on the concept of nobility. "Nobility is the perfection of the natural quality in each thing." That is to say, nobility is not hereditary and does not depend on an ancient lineage or on wealth, but on the spirit. Besides intellectual and moral qualities, it includes natural impulses, goodness, and generous feelings. Nobility, elevated by sanctifying grace, then becomes the seed of the happy life, which unfolds first naturally, then rationally, to turn the soul created by God back to God. As hinted above, this is the first time Italian was used in a purely scholarly text. French had already been used for simi-

lar works, but never Italian. And Dante has harsh words for those who look down their nose at their own native language while quick to praise the vernacular of others.

LE RIME

IL CANZONIERE (THE POEMS)

Under this heading is collected all Dante's poetry not included in the *Vita Nuova* and the *Convivio*. The collection was certainly not edited by the poet, who divided his mature years between the worries of exile and work on the *Divine Comedy*. It was, instead, the patient work of Dante scholars, who extracted the

poems from ancient manuscripts, where they were mixed with the poetry of others. The critics exposed the false attributions, put the poems in order according to theme and time; in fact they composed Dante's *Poems*.

In it there are poems of his youth, love poems of his maturity, and poems written for various specific occasions. Besides many small jewels, each with its unique quality, there is a series of poetic compositions that Dante exchanged with Guido Cavalcanti. These are noteworthy for the many things they tell us about the *dolce stil nuovo* ("sweet new style") and its typical characteristics. On the other hand, the poetic contest with Forese Donati—when the two dissolute friends exchanged insults and vulgarities—is interesting only as a document on the customs of the day.

Another group of poems, which some call "stony," or harsh, differs from all the rest and has been the source of much conjecture and many theories. These poems tell of a lady as hard as stone; they are bitter, and the words and images are

35

dry. Nothing is left of the angelic transfiguration of the "new style." Instead, love is violent, earthy, and full of anguish. For this reason some critics feel that these verses were inspired by a violent passion of the poet's mature years. Others, however, see them as allegorical poems; still others consider them to be new artistic experiments.

Naturally, not all of Dante's poems are equally good. But as a whole, the *Poems* is a most important body of work. It alone would have assured Dante a pre-eminent place among the poets of the thirteenth century. Besides their intrinsic value, the poems are a precious record of the poet's artistic evolution. They show his varied approaches and often labored experiments with language and style.

A self-taught poet, Dante began as all novices do, by imitating the well-known forms. Already in his very earliest compositions, in spite of the medieval conceits, the ornaments, and the alliterations, one can discern the poet's taste for a simple and direct form of expression. Amid trite expressions of courtly love, a note of life-giving sincerity rings through. Little by little he refined his art until finally we have lyrics of the purest love, the anguish and grief of the poems on his lady's death, the introspection of an inner conflict, the serious and thoughtful wisdom of the poems of exile.

DE VULGARI ELOQUENTIA

DE VULGARI ELOQUENTIA (ON THE VULGAR TONGUE)

This may be defined as a philological tract. Written in Latin because it was addressed to the learned, the work is divided into two books. The subject is the history of language, drawn in broad outlines from the time of Adam to the Tower of Babel and the confusion of tongues.

The book first treats the various dialects; then the "illustrious vernacular" of Italy. In Europe, broadly speaking, Dante distinguishes three fundamental vernaculars: one used in the south, one in the east, and one in the west. (Vernacular is the language commonly spoken by a people—the language that a child learns without rules, as Dante himself says —in contrast to Latin, the language of the educated.) The three vernaculars are the languages of *oil, oc,* and *si*—so named after the word each uses to express "yes." All three languages share a common origin and similar words.

The Italian vernacular has many dialects; some are rough, like those of Rome, the Marches, Spoleto, Milan, Bergamo, and Sardinia; others are smooth, like that of the Romagna; still others are harsh, like those of Brescia, Verona, Padua, and Venice; and that of the Tuscans is downright obscene. However, a noble vernacular does exist in Italy. One cannot identify it with a particular dialect, for it is spoken in all the cities. This distinguished vernacular is used by the most authoritative writers of every region and in conversation about noble and refined subjects. (This vernacular would be worthy of use at court, if Italy were a kingdom.)

In the second book Dante continues to praise the Italian vernacular. There he distinguishes the various metric forms, verses, styles, and the choice of words, some of which are "hairy," some "courteous and urbane." But at this point the work breaks off abruptly, although it should have gone on to at least four books.

What has come down to us is enough to show Dante in a particular light, that is, as a philologist of vision. His attempt to classify and regroup the dialects anticipates the modern science of philology. At the same time the glorification of the Italian vernacular above all regional divisions plainly presupposes an awareness of a unified Italy at a time when the concept of a single nation was almost non-existent.

Besides, Dante's awareness of a language independent of dialects foreshadows modern aesthetics, which considers the literary language a model that coincides with none of the spoken dialects.

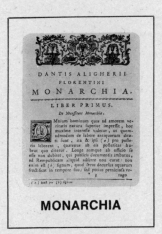

MONARCHIA

DE MONARCHIA (CONCERNING MONARCHY)

De Monarchia is a philosophical and political tract, written in Latin, in which Dante traces in detail his conception of the world—the same conception that we find later in the Divine Comedy.

It is difficult to say exactly when Dante wrote the book, because we lack both reliable information and references in the text to people or events of the time.

It could have been written after the Convivio, because what exists in the Convivio in embryo is fully developed in De Monarchia. It is generally thought to have been written during the time of Henry VII's invasion, years of hope—and disappointment—for a united empire.

Dante had an unshakable faith in the empire—a Holy Roman Empire that would unify all countries and nations under its dominion. The emperor, or monarch, would rule all kings, ministers, and leaders of the people, and acting with justice, he would ensure that all those under him would act the same way. He would allow all humanity to live morally free and in peace. In fact, only the enlightened government of a single man could guarantee the lasting peace that is brought about by intelligence and good will and that permits man the chance for rational progress. In Dante's view, universal monarchy was an indispensable good.

On the eternal question of the relationship between Church and State—a question then phrased in terms of the supremacy of the pope or the emperor— Dante energetically defended the opinion that they should be independent. He points out that men are both citizens and Christians; that they live in this life and prepare to live in the next. It is therefore only just that two authorities should guide them— one temporal, the other spiritual—each independent of the other but both proceeding directly from God. However, since eternal bliss is more important than bliss on earth, the monarch must pay respectful homage to the vicar of God. But that is all, for the pope must absolutely not interfere in political matters. In fact. there is no validity in the temporal power of the pope, historically, juridically, or theologically. In Dante's time such pronouncements were extremely daring.

Obviously, the idea of an enlightened universal monarchy was even then utopian, but Dante upheld it,

pointing to the universality of the Roman empire, a reality that survived in a different way in the Holy Roman Empire. All the same, Dante did not conceive of the universal monarchy as a tyranny that would destroy the characteristics of an individual nation and strangle its liberty.

Dante's political theory is not completely coherent or brilliantly original, as Machiavelli's was. His utopia is not a philosophical unity, as Plato's and Campanella's were. But it does have its own particular structure. It is the echo of the tormented fourteenth century, in which the contradictory and chaotic modern world was born, with its conflicts between the old empire and the independent states, between the divine and the human, between the individual and the mass.

The poet's ideas are clearer when he treats the political relationship between the pope and the emperor. One feels his deep conviction, his absolute certainty of being right; these inspired him to fight Boniface VIII so tenaciously, and for them he paid the price of exile.

Seen in the light of the au-

thor's own life, the De Monarchia is not only a political tract but the spiritual testament of an exile. Whatever the value of the ideals outlined in this book, Dante lived up to them to the end.

EPISTOLAE (THE LETTERS)

Dante's surviving Letters, which number thirteen, were written in Latin to various well-known contemporaries. Heavy with rhetoric and erudition, they are among the least original of Dante's writings in their adherence to the rigid rules of medieval culture. But they are a rich source of information about the life and thought of the poet. Ironically, while important letters concerning Dante's sentence and exile have been lost, three flattering letters to Henry VII's wife have survived. They were written by Dante on behalf of the countess of Battifolle. But even these are useful as examples of the assignments Dante undertook for his hosts during his exile.

Three letters about Henry's descent into Italy confirm the ideas in the De Monarchia and praise the emperor as the defender of peace and justice. They are made more vivid by the glimpse we get of the exile's anxious hope for a political revolution, which would allow him to return to his native city. By contrast, his long letter to Can Grande della Scala contains the first comment on the *Divine Comedy*, a pedantic explanation, to tell the truth, stated according to Aristotelian principles. It states that the poem should be interpreted both literally and allegorically; it explains the meaning of the title; and it gives the argument of the three divisions of the book. Finally, it gives the literal interpretation of the first three tercets of *Paradise*.

On the occasion of the death of Clement V—the pope who transferred the papacy to Avignon—Dante wrote an almost prophetic letter to the Italian cardinals. He rebukes them in fiery terms for having led the Church astray by their greed for money and power. Rome has been deprived of both its beacons, the pope and the emperor, and the blame lies above all with the Italian cardinals. He urges them finally to repent and to repair the damage

they have done by electing a pope who will transfer the papacy back to Rome.

But perhaps the most impassioned of all the letters that remain is the one Dante wrote to a Florentine friend when he found out that he would be allowed to return to Florence if he agreed to dress as a penitent, with a cord around his neck, and go barefoot to the baptistry for a public ceremony during which he would have to pay a fine. Never would he submit to such humiliation. If that was the only way he could enter Florence, well, he would never return. Did not the sun and the stars shine in other places? Would he not find bread elsewhere? In everything Dante was a man of his time—stubborn, proud, and implacable. The fight between him and Florence was a hard one, and neither side gave any quarter.

QUESTIO DE AQUA ET TERRA (AN INVESTIGATION ABOUT WATER AND EARTH) AND ECLOGAE (THE ECLOGUES)

The *Questio de Aqua et Terra* is written in Latin and treats a typically medieval problem: whether at any

point on the surface of the earth water is higher than land. Dante holds that this is impossible.

The little work is simply the text of a lecture that Dante gave in Verona in the presence of all the clergy and scholars on January 20, 1320. Can Grande della Scala had invited him to speak.

The *Eclogues* are an exchange of poetic essays between Dante and one of his learned friends. The interlocutor is Giovanni del Virgilio, a Latin scholar from Bologna, who urged Dante to try for the title of "poet laureate" by writing a work in Latin. Dante replied that he expected to get the laurel wreath for his *Divine Comedy*, and he sent Giovanni ten cantos of the poem. When Giovanni read them he was delighted, proclaiming Dante "Virgil resurrected," and invited Dante to come to Bologna. Dante thanked Giovanni for the offer, but declined because too many other affairs drew him to Ravenna. At this point there is an obscure reference to a certain Polifemo who would prevent Dante from going to Bologna. It has not been possible to make a reasonable historical identification of this presumed enemy of the poet.

The *Eclogues* are pastoral odes of classical inspiration, and Dante has used the purest Latin style in writing them. The substance of the dialogue is veiled by the pastoral fiction. Thus Dante becomes Tityrus the shepherd, Giovanni is Mopsus, another shepherd, and the cantos of the poem are little jugs of ewe's milk.

LA DIVINA COMMEDIA

LA DIVINA COMMEDIA (THE DIVINE COMEDY)

The *Divine Comedy* is a poem made up of an intro-

ductory canto and three principal divisions—*Inferno* (*Hell*), *Purgatorio* (*Purgatory*), and *Paradiso* (*Paradise*). Each of the divisions is composed of thirty-three cantos of about one hundred and forty lines each.

The lines are hendecasyllabic (eleven syllables long), and they are grouped in threes to make interlocking tercets (a form known as *terza rima* in Italian). When the poem was written is a matter of considerable discussion. Most probably Dante began it around 1307 and continued to work on it for the rest of his life.

Dante himself gives the complete title of the poem in a letter to Can Grande della Scala: *Incipit Comedia Dantis Alagherii, florentini natione, non moribus (Here Begins the Comedy by Dante Alighieri, a Florentine by Birth, But Not by Habits)*. The poet called the work a comedy because, like true comedies, it ends happily. Perhaps the title was also a form of modesty. Dante much admired the *Aeneid*, Virgil's tragic epic, and he would not have wanted to suggest that his poem was intended as competition for the Latin master's. The adjective "divine"

was added later, perhaps by Boccaccio. It appears in print in a Venetian edition of 1555. The poem as a whole is the story of a sinner turning toward God.

Above all, the poet meant the *Comedy* to be a work of doctrine and edification, a compendium of the knowledge of his time about science, philosophy, and theology. For this reason the poem is filled with allegorical and moral meaning. For example, Virgil, the Roman poet who sang of the ideals of peace and justice during the time of the Roman Emperor Augustus, guides the poet through Hell and Purgatory. He symbolizes reason and moral wisdom, while at the same time he is the voice of Dante's conscience. Beatrice, the poet's beloved who guides him through Paradise, represents Christian wisdom illuminated by grace, the supreme wisdom of the saints, which alone can lead to God. The whole poem is a perfectly constructed allegory, and in making it so, Dante only followed the rules of his time. There are many medieval works that relate journeys beyond the grave for the instruction of the sinner. But in Dante's poem this is a subtle artifice that allows him to include the entire history of his time. Dante's imaginary journey takes place in 1300, and so he can easily refer to everything that took place before that year. Moreover, by acknowledging the ability of the dead to foretell the future, he allows them to prophesy the public and private events that he wants to reveal.

THE LAYOUT OF THE UNDERWORLD

Under the earth's crust in the northern hemisphere, directly under Jerusalem, there is a large funnel-shaped abyss that leads to the center of the earth. The abyss was created by the fall of Lucifer, the rebellious angel who ended up imprisoned at the bottom of the abyss. The earth he displaced during his fall formed an island in the southern hemisphere, a conical mountain with the Earthly Paradise at the summit, diametrically opposite Jerusalem and at the extreme boundary between the material world and the spiritual one.
Hell is situated in the abyss,

which descends in nine concentric circles. The damned are scattered throughout these circles according to the gravity of their sins. The seriousness of a sin is judged by the degree it violates what man has in him of the divine.
Purgatory is on the conical mountain in the southern hemisphere. The souls are distributed on ledges carved into the mountainside. There are seven terraces, corresponding to the seven capital sins. These, plus anti-Purgatory and the Earthly Paradise, bring the divisions of Purgatory to the prophetic number nine. The numbers nine and three are basic to the architecture of the *Divine Comedy*.
The two kingdoms are joined by a narrow underground passage, which leads from the bottom of the abyss of Hell to the island of Purgatory in the opposite hemisphere.
Paradise, naturally, is in the heavens, where, according to the Ptolemaic system nine spheres revolve ever more rapidly and in ever wider orbits around the stationary earth. Above the spheres is the dazzling Empyrean, where God is enthroned in his splendor, sur-

rounded by the spirits of the triumphant blessed.

HELL

In the middle of his journey through life, Dante, lost in a dark wood, tries in vain to climb a brilliantly lighted hill. Three wild beasts, symbolizing human lusts, bar his path. Virgil appears before the poet and proposes another road to the contemplation of God (that is, the summit of the luminous hill). But it is a rough and frightening road, which twists through the kingdoms beyond the tomb. Dante is uncertain and afraid. Only when Virgil tells him that the privilege of taking this road has been granted him by the prayers of a blessed lady, Beatrice, who is anxious for his salvation, only then does Dante take heart and set off for the threshold of the great beyond. (Virgil will guide him through the places of sin and purification; Beatrice will lead him through the kingdom of the blessed.) Having crossed the fateful threshold, Dante finds in the vestibule of Hell both the souls of the futile, who lived "without infamy and without praise," and the angels who could not decide whose side to take during Lucifer's revolt. They are now condemned to run at breakneck speed behind a banner, and they are continually stung by wasps and hornets. This is the first example of the law of retaliation: all the punishments in Hell and Purgatory relate directly to the crimes committed, either resembling or contrasting with those crimes.

The river Acheron runs between the vestibule and the first circle of Hell. Here the new arrivals pause to await Charon, the demon with "eyes like hot coals" who ferries them to the other bank, where they will be judged by Minos, the monstrous magistrate who indicates the number of the circle of Hell the sinner will inhabit by wrapping his tail around himself the corresponding number of turns. Limbo is the first circle beyond the Acheron. It is inhabited by the souls of unbaptized children and of honorable men who lived before the birth of Christ. There is no punishment in Limbo, only an atmosphere of oppressive melancholy. In this circle Dante meets the great men of antiquity —Homer, Horace, Ovid, Lucan, and many others. Hell proper only begins at the second circle, where the lustful are buffeted by a constant gale. Among them Francesca da Rimini, still clinging to her Paolo, tells the poet her tragic tale.

In the third circle the gluttonous are scourged by a foul rain and watched over by the ferocious Cerberus, a terrible, three-headed dog. Ciacco, a Florentine, talks to Dante of the quarrels between the opposing factions in their city. In the next circles the hoarders and the spendthrifts stagger by, pushing huge rocks; then come the wrathful, the slothful, the envious, and the proud, all of them immersed in the boiling mud of the Stygian swamp.

To cross the swamp, Dante and Virgil avail themselves of the boat belonging to the demon Phlegyas, who lets them off before the gate of the city of Dis. The red-hot walls of the city enclose the deeper and more terrible region of Hell, where the crimes are more serious and the punishments more severe. The punishments often seem to have been suggested by outbursts of indignation, and sometimes by a cruel fantasy.

The devils have decided to bar the entrance of Dis to those who "alive, travel through the kingdom of the dead." They lock all the doors, while on the battlements appear the three Furies, among them Medusa, who tries to turn Dante to stone with her magic. In the nick of time a celestial messenger arrives, and with a wand throws open the gates to the city and sharply rebukes the devils.

The journey continues, and Dante sees the heretics in their flaming tombs, among them Farinata. Then he passes those who committed violence against their neighbors; they are immersed in a river of blood and stricken with arrows by the Centaurs if they dare to raise their heads. Next come those who were violent against themselves, that is, the suicides (among them is Pietro della Vigna), all transformed into gnarled trees; then the profligates, pursued and torn at by ferocious dogs.

The violent against God and

the violent against nature are exposed to an endless rain of fire. However, while the latter (that is, the homosexuals, like Brunetto Latini) can move about, somewhat alleviating their torture, the violent against God must lie still under the lash of the fiery rain. The usurers too are exposed to the rain, but they are seated, and constantly move their hands to protect themselves.

So the two poets reach the end of the seventh circle, where a deep, rugged, and craggy ravine opens before them. To cross it, Dante and Virgil must mount the back of Geryon, a winged monster with a barbed tail, who flies with them slowly to the bottom of the abyss. The eighth circle is divided into ten trenches, connected by bridges. With rising horror, in an atmosphere of increasing hallucination, they enter the place called Malebolge, "all of stone the color of iron." The long parade of sinners continues. In the lower part of Hell the spectacle is ever more horrifying.

There are the panderers, beaten by horned devils; the flatterers, floundering in dung; those guilty of simony, stuck head first into tight holes, the soles of their feet burning; and the sorcerers, with their heads twisted around on their necks so that they can only look behind them.

In the fifth trench the swindlers struggle through boiling pitch, while clouds of devils armed with pitchforks force them to remain completely submerged. The hypocrites, weighed down with heavy leaden capes, drag themselves around the sixth trench. The seventh swarms with snakes of every size, color, and deadliness; these rush for the thieves, twine themselves around their limbs, biting and crushing them. As soon as a thief is bitten, he begins to burn, and in an instant is incinerated, only to immediately rise again from the ashes like the Arabian phoenix. Other damned souls when they are bitten are themselves transformed into serpents, while the snakes that bit them become men. The whole trench boils with strange beings in the midst of metamorphosis: flicking tails become legs, arms disappear into bodies, tongues become forked.

Passing this monstrous spectacle, the poets come upon a flickering of small flames, in which are the false counselors, like Ulysses and Diomedes. Ulysses tells of his last adventure on the boundless ocean and solemnly pronounces on the destiny of man—"made not to live like beasts, but to follow virtue and knowledge."

After talking with Ulysses and Guido da Montefeltro, Dante and his faithful guide continue their journey. They meet the promoters of discord and schism, who are constantly cut to pieces by the razor-sharp swords of the demons. Among the horrible scars and mutilations, towers Bertrand de Born, the Provençal troubadour who divided father and son by his evil counsel and who goes about carrying his own severed head by the hair.

The falsifiers are jammed together in the last trench, a prey to hideous diseases: the alchemists furiously scratch their scabs; the counterfeiters are swollen by dropsy; the liars burn with fever.

Leaving Malebolge, the poet believes he sees a shadowy

landscape with towers, but then he realizes that the towers are actually three chained giants who slowly emerge through the dimness. The giants are Ephialtes, Antaeus, and Nimrod, the man who dared to challenge God by building the Tower of Babel and who now babbles meaningless words. It is Antaeus' task to lower Virgil and Dante down the last precipice. He lifts them up, stoops, and sets them down into the lowest circle of Hell.

Here there are no fire, no demons, no shrieks of the damned. The bottom of Hell is frozen; it is one enormous block of ice. Locked in it, their heads alone showing, are the traitors. Tears of ice seal their eyelids. In this unreal immobility Ugolino della Gherardesca gnaws furiously on the skull of his enemy.

The curtain falls on the horrible tragedy of the damned with the sight of Lucifer, the fallen angel turned monster, whose three mouths are chewing on the three greatest human traitors—Judas, who betrayed Christ, and Brutus and Cassius, who betrayed Julius Caesar and

thereby the empire. Holding fast to the hairs on Lucifer's legs, Dante and Virgil descend still farther, until, at a certain point, they turn their heads southward and begin to climb. They have arrived at the center of the earth, and a narrow passage now will take them "to see the stars again" on the other side of the globe.

The trip through Hell has lasted three days.

PURGATORY

Instinctively, Dante heaves a sigh of relief on emerging from the "dead air" to find the sky above him once more "sweet color, the translucent tint and tone of orient sapphire." Thanks be to God that all is different in Purgatory—the landscape, the air, the light that floods it from above.

Hate, rebellion, and crime are gone. The inhabitants of Hell were intimately bound to the life they had led on earth, and to the sins they were reliving (and would relive for eternity). The penitents in Purgatory, detached from earthly matters, anxiously turn toward a future union with God. The tragedies they endured on earth

are remote, transformed, and no longer make their hearts beat faster.

The very punishments to which the penitents are subjected no longer have the three-dimensional horror of those in Hell. Physical suffering almost vanishes in the face of the more ardent spiritual suffering, but that too is mitigated by resignation and hope. Scarcely arrived on the shores of the island, and while he is still looking around him and gazing at the stars of the southern hemisphere and the splendid southern cross, Dante suddenly sees next to him an old man with a long white beard. It is Cato, the staunch defender of liberty who committed suicide in Utica rather than see the fall of the Roman republic. Now he is the guardian of Purgatory, because the mountain of expiation is indeed the kingdom of liberty—liberty from sin and liberty of the will. Virgil speaks to him with great respect and gets permission for himself and his disciple to climb the mountain. However, before beginning the journey, Virgil collects dew from the grass and washes Dante's face with it, to remove every trace of the filth of Hell.

All of a sudden, a light appears at sea and approaches rapidly. It is an angel standing in the stern of a ship, which is "slender and light"; he propels the craft by beating his great wings. In the boat are seated more than a hundred souls, coming to the kingdom of expiation. Among them is Casella, who during his life set Dante's *canzoni* to music and who now, having disembarked and recognized his friend, sings the famous: "Love that discourses to me in my mind." The spirits crowd around to listen to the "sweet song"; but Cato rebukes them for the delay, and they run toward the mountain slope.

The two poets also hurry toward the mountain, and while Virgil looks for a path Dante can follow, a group of spirits joins them. On learning why a living person is there, one of the souls reveals that he is Manfred, who, although excommunicated, was saved by a last minute act of repentance.

The ascent is steep, and Dante, using his hands,

The angel of God, sitting on the threshold . . .

pulls himself up as best he can. They arrive at the first terrace, which is a kind of vestibule where those who have been slow to repent wait for a chance to enter Purgatory. Dante meets Belacqua, a notorious lazybones in his time. He also meets Buonconte da Montefeltro, a veteran of Campaldino, and finally, after many others, he comes across the gentle and unlucky Pia dei Tolomei.

Virgil too has a singular encounter. He embraces Sordello, a Mantuan like himself. The embrace brings to Dante's lips the famous invective against "servile Italy." Dante proceeds into the little valley of the princes, where the souls of the kings and noblemen are reunited, and there falls

asleep. When he wakes the next morning he finds himself, mysteriously, before the true gates of Purgatory. An angel traces the letter *P* on Dante's forehead seven times, to represent the seven capital sins. Each *P* will be erased by a different angel as Dante passes from ledge to ledge, where he observes sinners as they do penance for the seven capital sins. As he ascends, he meditates on the various examples of virtue or vice being punished.

On the first terrace the proud walk bent under heavy weights and regard sculptures that depict examples of humility. The envious, on the second terrace, sit wrapped in sackcloth, their eyes sewn together with iron wire, while strange voices call out examples of envy punished. Anger is purged on the third terrace, where the spirits are enveloped in dense smoke. On the fourth terrace the slothful run; on the fifth the covetous lie face down on the ground.

On the fifth ledge Dante and Virgil meet the spirit of the Latin poet Statius, who has finished his penance and is on his way toward

*She immersed me
to the neck in the river . . .*

the summit of the mountain. Together the three poets pass the sixth terrace, where the gluttonous, among them Dante's friend Forese Donati, are reduced to skeletal thinness. During the ascent Statius tells of his conversion to Christianity, and Virgil speaks of his companions in Limbo. The conversation becomes progressively more learned, turning to the theory of the formation of the body, of the animal, or conscious soul, of the rational soul, or intellect, and finally to the survival of the soul after death.

In this way the three poets arrive at the seventh terrace, where the lustful burn with fire. Dante too must pass through the flames to purge himself, and the good

Virgil has to evoke the memory of Beatrice to spur his reluctant disciple to enter the fire. Having passed the test, Dante falls into a profound sleep and dreams of a young and beautiful woman who gathers flowers for garlands. It is Leah, symbol of the active life. After still another climb, the poets arrive in the marvelous Earthly Paradise. The moment has come for Virgil to depart. Now, while awaiting the arrival of Beatrice, Dante no longer needs the support of his counselor.

The poet moves alone through the "divine forest, dense and alive," continually turning back toward his master, who watches him affectionately from a distance. Dante presently arrives at a clear brook. On the far bank he sees Matilda, a woman of celestial beauty who walks while "singing and gathering flower after flower." (Perhaps Matilda is the symbol of primitive innocence.) Dante sees a mystical procession advancing: seven flaming candelabra, twenty-four elders crowned with lilies, four strange animals, and the allegorical chariot

of the Church, which undergoes a series of monstrous transformations. Around the chariot dance the three theological virtues and the four cardinal virtues.

And finally Beatrice appears, "wreathed, o'er a white veil, with an olive stem . . . under a cloak of green, apparelled in the hue of living flame." The poet is overcome with emotion. He again feels the old flame kindled within him, and he turns around, wishing to make Virgil a participant in this passionate event. But the good master has disappeared, silently.

Beatrice, who symbolizes the light of God and truth, reproves Dante for his sins and induces him to confess them to her. The confession purifies the poet, who is then plunged by Matilda into the two rivers of the Earthly Paradise. This evokes the memory of his good actions and makes him forget his sins. He is finally ready to ascend into Paradise.

PARADISE

Paradise is the section of the book that deals with blessedness and with the harmony of the will of the blessed with God's will. It is full of theological discussions and learned explanations, which Dante receives from his lady and from many other blessed souls. But above all Paradise is the realm of light, a light that shines, irradiates, blazes, and throbs everywhere—on the faces of the blessed, in the eyes of Beatrice, on the revolving spheres of the heavens. It is a light that becomes ever more blinding as the poet climbs closer to the vision of God.

From the Earthly Paradise, Dante and Beatrice rise swiftly toward the sphere of fire. Passing it, they come to the first heaven, that of the moon, which is inhabited by the spirits of those who failed their religious vows because of the violence of someone else. Here Dante meets Piccarda Donati. In Paradise the blessed all reside in the Empyrean, where they contemplate God. Their distance from God depends on their merit; but they are all content with their state. In order to make Dante understand the architecture of heaven, and in order to demonstrate to him the various degrees of blessed-

ness, the souls group themselves in the seven planetary heavens. According to the rules of medieval astrology, each soul occupies the heaven that influenced him during his lifetime. A single moral virtue has sway in each heaven: fortitude in the heaven of the moon; justice in Mercury; temperance in Venus; prudence in the sun; faith in Mars; hope in Jupiter; charity in Saturn. In the sphere of Mercury are the spirits of those who used their energy to do good. Here Dante meets Justinian, who summarizes and celebrates the history of the Roman empire from Aeneas to Charlemagne. Then Beatrice dispells some of Dante's doubts by telling him of the death of Christ, the redemption of man from original sin, the incorruptibility of everything created directly by God. During the discussion they arrive in the sphere of Venus, where, among the other spirits of those who loved strongly, they meet Charles Martel, son of Charles II of Anjou. (While passing through Florence in 1294, the young Angevin had met Dante and had shown him great friendship,

... but you will recognize that I am Piccarda ...

which was cut short by Charles' untimely death.) Other loving spirits appear to the poet: Cunizza da Romano and Folco da Marsiglia, who curses the shameful avarice of the clergy.

In the fourth sphere, that of the sun, are the learned and the theologists. Dante meets Saint Thomas Aquinas and Saint Bonaventura, who in turn praise those two great champions of the faith, Saint Francis and Saint Dominic.

The fifth is the sphere of Mars, where the souls of those who died fighting for the Christian faith form a cross of light. On the right arm of the cross, Dante sees his great-great grandfather, Cacciaguida, who fell during the second crusade. Cacciaguida speaks of Flor-

Speak, as thou art a Christian, confess: What is faith?

ence in the old days, when the Florentines, enclosed by the first ring of walls, "lived in peace, sober and modest," and he predicts Dante's exile while encouraging him to bear the injustice by trusting in God. Above all, he urges Dante not to be afraid of the truth, but to speak truthfully to all men without worrying about the consequences. Dante and Beatrice continue the ascent. In the sphere of Saturn, the seventh, the spirits of the contemplative are arranged on a miraculous ladder that stretches up to the Empyrean. Saint Peter Damian speaks of the mystery of predestination; Saint Benedict talks of himself and laments the decay of his Order.

The eighth sphere is that of the fixed stars. In the midst of the thousands of brilliant lights, each one a blessed soul, Dante sees the triumph of Christ in the form of a blazing sun. Christ ascends to the Empyrean, and in a burst of splendor, the blessed celebrate the triumph of Mary. Before Dante enters the ninth sphere, Saint Peter, Saint James, and Saint John question him about faith, hope, and charity. He passes the examination concerning the theological virtues without difficulty, and then hears Saint Peter deliver the poem's fiercest invective against the corruption of the papacy. Then Adam joins the three apostles; he reveals to the poet the nature of original sin, tells him how many years have passed since the creation of man, how many years he remained in the Earthly Paradise, and what language he spoke.

After a hymn of thanks to God, the blessed rise to the Empyrean. From the ninth sphere, the *primum mobile,* Dante gazes at nine resplendent angelic choirs, whose virtues and duties Beatrice explains to him. Then she relates the cause, the place, and the time of the creation of the angels, and their powers, their number, and the tragic difference between the faithful and the rebellious angels.

When the angels have vanished, there appears before Dante's eyes the radiant, blinding spectacle of the Celestial Rose, formed by the triumphant spirits and angels grouped around God. It is the paradise of contemplation. Beatrice leaves Dante and takes her seat among the third circle of the elect. Saint Bernard, the most ardent of the mystics, is now beside Dante. He will be the poet's guide from now on, because Dante can proceed no farther by reason, but only through ecstatic rapture. Invoked by Saint Bernard in a marvelous prayer, the Virgin intercedes with God, and Dante receives the ultimate grace: the poet has a vision of the divinity. In an ineffable instant the poet has a glimpse into a realm beyond the limits of human capacity, a lightning flash that the memory cannot retain. And with this vision of the inexpressible, the poem ends.

Art in Dante's Time

Art awakened to new values; compositions became monumental; color was used for dramatic effect; human expressions revealed the spirit of the subjects.

The Virgin, in a detail from the Last Judgement, by the Roman painter Pietro Cavallini (1250-1325) (Santa Cecilia in Trastevere, Rome).

Head of Christ, detail from the Crucifix of Santa Croce, by Giovanni Cimabue (c. 1240-c. 1303) (Church of Santa Croce, Florence, badly damaged in 1966 flood).

49

Detail from the altarpiece of the Blessed Humility, by Pietro Lorenzetti (1280–c. 1348), which unites richness of color with intense expressiveness (Uffizi, Florence).

The interior of the great Church of Santa Croce in Florence,
begun in 1295 by the sculptor and architect Arnolfo di Cambio (1240-1310).

The Madonna of the Ognissanti, by
Giotto di Bondone (c. 1267-1337),
the great master of the new style of
Italian painting (Uffizi, Florence).

Two most significant sculptures: above,
Santa Riparata, by Arnolfo (Duomo Museum,
Florence); right, the pulpit, by Nicola
Pisano (1220-1284) (Baptistry, Pisa).

Pope Innocent III Dreams that Saint Francis Upholds the Lateran, one of a series
of renowned frescoes about that saint's life by Giotto in Assisi.; Also preserved
at Assisi is the chalice of Pope Nicholas IV, executed in 1290 by Guccio di Mannaia.

*Saint Francis is Honored
by a Simple Man,
in another detail
from the Assisi frescoes by Giotto.*

*Art left the church to take its place
in municipal life. Arnolfo di Cambio
built the massive and
harmonious Palazzo Vecchio in Florence.*

Anthology

LA VITA NUOVA (THE NEW LIFE)

A few years after Beatrice's death Dante recalls his first sight of her.

CHAPTER II

Nine times already since my birth the heaven of light[1] had circled back to almost the same point when the now glorious lady of my mind first appeared to my eyes. She was called Beatrice[2] by many people who did not know what her name was. She had been in this life long enough to allow the starry heavens[3] to move a twelfth of a degree to the East in her time; that is, she appeared to me almost in the beginning of her ninth year, and I first saw her near the end of my ninth year. She appeared dressed in the most patrician of colors, a subdued and decorous crimson, bound round and adorned in a style suitable to her years. At that moment, I say truly that the vital spirit, the one that dwells in the most secret chamber of the heart, began to tremble so violently that even the least pulses of my body were strangely affected; and trembling, it spoke these words: "Here is a god stronger than I, who shall come to rule over me." At that point the animal spirit, the one abiding in the high chamber to which all the senses bring their perceptions, was stricken with amazement, and speaking directly to the spirits of sight, said these words: "Now your bliss has appeared." At that moment the natural spirit, the one which lives in that part where our food is worked on, began to weep, and weeping, said these words: "Alas, wretch that I am, from now on I shall be interfered with often." Let me say that from that time on Love governed my soul, which became so readily devoted to him and over which he reigned with such assurance and lordship given him through the power of my imagination that it became necessary for me to tend to his every pleasure. Often he commanded me to seek out this youngest of angels; and therefore I went in search of her many times in my youth and found her so full of natural dignity and admirable bearing that certainly the words of the poet Homer suited her well: "She did not seem to be the daughter of any ordinary man, but rather of a god." And though her image, which remained constantly with me, was Love's assurance of holding me, it was of such a pure quality that never did it permit me to be ruled by Love without the trusted counsel of reason (regarding those things wherein such advice would profitably be heeded.) Since to dwell too long on the passions and actions of my early years may appear frivolous, I shall leave them, and omitting many things which could be copied from my book of memory whence these derived, I turn to those words which are written in my mind under more important headings.

His friends ask Dante for his definition of love, and he replies with a sonnet.

CHAPTER XX

Love and the gracious heart are but one
    thing,
As Guinizelli[4] tells us in his rhyme;
As much can one without the other be
As without reason can the reasoning mind.
Nature creates them when in loving mood:
Love to be king, the heart to be his home,
A dwelling place where Love inactive lies
Sometimes a longer, now a shorter time.
A worthy lady's beauty next is viewed
With pleasure by the eyes, and in the heart
Desire for the pleasing thing is born,
And for awhile this beauty lingers there
Until Love's spirit is aroused from sleep.
A man of worth in ladies does the same.

Dante has a vision of the death of his lady.

CHAPTER XXIII

A few days after this, it happened that a severe illness overtook part of my body and caused me to suffer intense pain constantly for nine days, which in turn made me so weak that it became necessary for me to lie in bed like a paralyzed person. On the ninth day, experiencing almost unbearable pain, I suddenly had a thought concerning my lady. After thinking about her a while, I returned to thoughts of my frail life, and realizing how short life is, even if one is healthy, I began to sob inwardly at such wretchedness. Then sighing loudly, I said to myself: "Some day the most gracious Beatrice will surely have to die." I went so out of my head that I closed my eyes and became convulsed as one in a delirium and began to have these imaginings: How at the outset of my imagination's wandering certain faces of ladies with dishevelled hair appeared to me and they were saying: "You too shall die." And then after these ladies there appeared to me certain faces, strange and horrible to behold, saying to me: "You are dead." As my imagination wandered in this fashion, I came to such a point that I no longer knew where I was. I seemed to see ladies miraculously sad, weeping as they made their way down a street, their hair dishevelled; I seemed to see the sun darken in a way that gave the stars a color that would have made me swear that they were weeping; it seemed to me that the birds flying through the air fell to earth dead, and that there were great earthquakes. Astonished and very frightened, I imagined in this dream that a certain friend came to me and said: "You do not know then that our miraculous lady has departed from this life?" At that I began to sob most piteously, not only in my dream, but with my eyes that were wet with real tears. I imagined I was looking up at the sky, and I seemed to see a multitude of angels returning upwards, and in front of them was a little pure-white cloud. It seemed to me that these angels were singing in glory, and the words of their song seemed to be: *Hosanna in the highest*, the rest I could not hear. Then it seemed that my heart, in which so much love dwelt, said to me: "True it is that our lady lies dead." And so it seemed to me that I went to see the body in which that most noble and blessed soul had dwelt, and so strong was the hallucination that it actually showed me this lady dead. And it seemed that ladies were covering her head with a white veil, and it seemed that her face was so filled with joyous acceptance that it said to me: "I am contemplating the fountainhead of peace." Through seeing her in this dream I became filled with so much humility that I called upon Death and said: "Sweet Death, come to me and do not be unkind, for you have just been in a place that should have made you gracious. Come to me now, for I earnestly desire you; you can see that I do, for already I wear your color." And when I had seen that the rites usually performed on the body of the dead had been administered, it seemed that I returned to my room and from there looked toward heaven; and so vivid was my dream that, weeping, I began to cry aloud: "O most beautiful soul, how blessed is he who beholds you!" As I was saying these words in a spasm of tears and calling upon death to come to me, a young and gracious lady, who had been at my bedside, believing that my sobbing and my words had been due only to the pain of my illness, began in great fright to weep. Then other ladies who were about the room became aware of my weeping through seeing this one weeping, and after making this one, who was a close relative[5] of mine, leave me, they, believing that I was dreaming, drew close to waken me, saying: "Wake up," and "Don't be afraid." As they spoke in this fashion, my realistic dream was broken at the moment when I was about to say, "Oh, Beatrice, blessed art thou." And I had already said, "Oh, Beatrice," when I opened my eyes with a start and saw that I was deceived. Although I had uttered this name, my voice had been so broken by my sobs and tears that I think these ladies were not able to understand. Even though I was very much ashamed, I nevertheless turned toward them, thanks to some warning from Love. And when they saw me, they began saying, "He looks as if he were dead," and to each other, "Let us try to comfort him"; wherefore they said many words to comfort me and asked me what had frightened me so. Having been comforted somewhat and having recognized the falseness of my imagining, I answered them: "I shall tell you what happened to me." Then I began from the beginning and continued to the very end, telling them what I had seen but keeping silent the name of the most gracious one. After I was cured of my illness, I decided to write about what had happened to me, since it seemed it would be a fascinating thing to hear. Therefore, I composed this *canzone: A very young and sympathetic lady,* it is constructed in the manner made clear in the divisions following it.

A very young and sympathetic lady,
  Extremely graced with human gentleness,
  Who stood by me and heard me call on
    death,
  Seeing the piteous weeping of my eyes
  And hearing wild, confusing words I
    spoke,
  Became so filled with fear she wept
    aloud.
  Then other ladies, made aware of me
  Through that one weeping there beside
    my bed,
  Forced her to go away
  And then drew near to try to waken me.
  One said to me: "Wake up,"
  Another said: "Why are you so
    distressed?"
  With this I left my world of dreams and
    woke,
  Calling aloud the name of my dear one,
But in a voice so weak and filled with pain
  And broken so by tears and anguished
    sobs,
  That only in my heart I heard her name.
  Although there was a look of deep-felt
    shame
  That made itself stand out upon my face,

Love made me look these ladies in the
  eye.
The pallor of my face amazed them so
They could not help but start to speak of
  death.
"Oh, let us comfort him,"
Implored one lady sweetly of another.
And many times they said:
"What have you seen that stole away
  your strength?"
Consoled and comforted somewhat, I
  said:
"Ladies, now you shall know what I have
  seen."
While I was brooding on my languid life,
  And sensed how fleeting is our little day,
  Love wept within my heart which is his
    home;
  Wherefore my startled soul went numb
    with fear,
  And sighing deep within myself, I said:
  —My lady some day surely has to die.—
  Then taken by this fright and
    wonderment,
  I closed my heavy wept-out tired eyes,
  And so despaired and weak
  Were all my spirits, that each went
    drifting off;
  And then drifting and dreaming
  With consciousness and truth left far
    behind,
  I saw the looks of ladies wild with wrath
  Who kept repeating to me—You shall
    die.—
Then, drifting in my false imaginings
  And standing in a place unknown to me,
  I seemed to be aware of dreadful things:
  Of ladies all dishevelled as they walked,
  Some weeping, others murmuring
    laments
  That with grief's flame-tipped arrows
    pierced my heart.
  It seemed to me that then I saw the sun
  Grow slowly darker and a star appear,
  And sun and star did weep;
  The birds that fly above fell dead to
    earth;

The earth began to quake.
And then a man appeared, pale-faced
   and hoarse
And said to me: —Have you not heard
   the news?
Your lady, once so lovely, now lies
   dead.—
I raised my tear-bathed eyes to look above
And saw, looking like manna's
   showering,
The angels that ascended homeward
   bound;
In front of them they had a little cloud;
They sang "Hosanna" as they rose with
   it,
If they had said more, I would have
   told you.
Then Love: —I shall not hide a thing
   from you;
Come now to see our lady lying dead.—
My wild illusions
Led me to see my lady lying dead,
And as I looked at her
I saw that ladies hid her with a cloth.
Such was the joyful resignation on her
   face,
It was as if she said: —I am in peace.—
So humbly in my grief I then beheld
What true humility had taken shape in
   her
That I said: —Death, I hold you very
   dear;
By now you ought to be a gracious
   thing
And should have changed your scorn for
   sympathy,
Since in my lady you have been at home.
I am so keen to be one of your own
That I resemble you in every way.
Come to me, for my heart is begging
   you.—
When the last rites were done, I left that
   place,
And when I was alone,
And looking toward high heaven,
   I exclaimed:

—Blessed is he who sees you, lovely
   soul!—
You called to me just then and I am
   grateful.

Beatrice has a marvelous effect on all who meet her.

CHAPTER XXVI

Such sweet decorum and such gentle graces
Attend my lady's greeting as she goes
That every tongue is stammering then
   mute,
And eyes dare not to gaze at such a sight.
She goes benignly in humility
Untouched by all the praise along her way
And seems a creature come from heaven to
   earth,
A miracle manifest in reality.
So charming she appears to human sight,
Her sweetness through the eyes reaches the
   heart;
Who has not felt this cannot understand.
And from her lips it seems there moves a
   spirit
So gentle and so loving that it glides
Into the souls of men and whispers,
   "Sigh!"

Dante speaks of his desire to have others share in his grief for Beatrice, of a vision that came to him, and of his intention to write great things for her.

CHAPTERS XL—XLII

... it happened, during that season when many people go to see the blessed image that Jesus Christ left us as a copy of His most beautiful face, which my lady beholds in glory, that some pilgrims were going down a street which is almost in the middle of the city where the most gracious lady was born, lived, and died. These pilgrims, it seemed to me, were going along very pensive; therefore, thinking of them, I said to myself: "These pilgrims seem to be from distant parts, and I do not believe that they have ever heard mention of this lady; they know nothing of her, but rather their thoughts are of other things than these; perhaps they are thinking of their friends far away, whom we do not know." Then I said within myself: "I know that if they were from a neighboring town they would in some way appear distressed while passing through the center of the mournful city." Again I said to myself: "If I could detain them awhile, I would yet make them weep before they left this city, for I would speak words that would make anyone listening to them weep." Then after these people had passed from my sight, I decided to compose a sonnet in which I should reveal what I had said within myself. And so that it should appear more pathetic, I decided to write it as if I had spoken to them, and I composed this sonnet, which begins: Ah pilgrims. . . .

Ah pilgrims, moving pensively along,
Thinking perhaps of things that are not
here,
Do you travel from towns as far away
As your appearance would make us
believe?
For you are not weeping as you pass
through
The middle of the city in its grief;
You seem to be like those who understand
Nothing about its grievous weight of woe.
And if you stop because you wish to know,
My sighing heart truly whispers to me
That afterwards you will depart in tears:
The city's source of blessings it has lost,
And words that one can say concerning her
Have power to make whoever hears them
weep.

Some time afterwards two worthy ladies sent word to me requesting that I send them some of this poetry of mine; wherefore, taking into consideration their worthiness, I decided to send some poems and to write something new which I should send along with them so that I might fulfill their request more suitably. And then I wrote this sonnet which tells of my condition, and I sent it to them accompanied by the preceding sonnet and by another one. . . .

Beyond the sphere that makes the longest
round,[6]
Passes the sigh which issues from my
heart;
A quickened understanding that sad Love
Imparts to it keeps drawing it on high.
When it has come to the desired place
It sees a lady held in reverence,
And who shines so, that through her
radiance
The pilgrim spirit gazes upon her.
It sees her so, that when it tells me this
I cannot understand its subtle tale
Spoken to the sad heart that makes it
speak.
I know it talks of that most gracious one,
Because it often mentions Beatrice;
This much, dear ladies, I well understand.

After this sonnet there appeared to me a miraculous vision in which I saw things that made me resolve to say no more about this blessed one until I should be capable of writing about her in a more worthy fashion. And to achieve this I am striving as hard as I can, and this she truly knows. So that, if it be the wish of Him in whom all things flourish that my life continue for a few years, I hope to write of her that which has never been written of any other lady. And then may it please that One who is the Sire of Graciousness that my soul ascend to behold the glory of its lady, that is of that blessed Beatrice, who in glory gazes upon the countenance of the One *who is through all ages blessed.*

IL CONVIVIO (THE BANQUET)

Dante speaks of his love for his native tongue.

BOOK I, CHAPTERS 12 AND 13

If flames could be seen plainly issuing from the windows of a house, and one man should ask whether there was a fire in that house, and another should answer 'yes' I would find it hard to say which of the two was more ridiculous. Of like nature would be the question and reply if any one were to ask me if I had love for my tongue, and I were to answer 'yes'. However I have yet to show that not only love but most perfect love for it dwells within me, and I have to denounce its enemies somewhat more. In the course of my demonstration to those who will understand me aright, I shall tell how I became a friend of this language, and how this friendship was confirmed.

I say then (as Cicero writes in his essay *On Friendship*, following the teachings of the Philosopher[1] in the eight and ninth chapters of his *Ethics*) that nearness and excellence are the natural causes that generate love; benefaction, study, and comradeship are the thing that foster it. All of these causes have worked together to beget and nourish the love I bear my native tongue, as I shall briefly show. Now a thing is nearer a man in proportion as of all things of its kind it is most closely associated with him. So a son is nearer his father; medicine, of all the arts, is nearest the doctor; music to the musician, because they are, respectively, more closely associated with the man than the other arts. And of all lands the nearest to a man is the one where he has his home, because it is most closely associated with him. Likewise a man's native speech is closest to him, for it is closely united to him. It has a special, unique place in his mind above all others; not only is it united to him essentially, in itself, but also incidentally: that is to say, it is connected with those closest to him: his relatives, his fellow citizens, his own folk. So a man's vernacular we may call not simply near to him, but most near. So as we said above, if nearness be the seed of friendship, nearness must clearly be among the causes of the love I bear my native tongue, nearest to me above all. Indeed, it was the aforesaid cause, namely that whatever has first sole possession of the mind is closest to it, that gave rise to the custom of primogeniture, for the first born sons are closer to their fathers

and hence more loved.

Further, the excellence of my native language makes me its friend. For you must know that in any given thing we are to love the excellence proper to that thing; as well-beardedness in a man and smooth skin in a woman, sharpness of scent in a setter and speed in a boarhound. And the more appropriate the excellence the more it should be loved, so, although all virtues in man are to be loved, that one which is most human is to be loved most: that is to say justice, which is found only in the rational or intellectual part of man, which is to say the will. Justice is so much to be loved that, as the Philosopher says in the fifth chapter of his *Ethics*: its very enemies, such as robbers and plunderers love it, and we see too that its opposite, injustice, is also hated, in its various forms such as treachery, ingratitude, theft, rapine, cheating, and the like.

. . . So we have shown that the most proper excellence of anything is that for which it is most praised and loved: we must now see what that excellence is in each case. And in matters of speech, the most loved and commended excellence is that of rightly setting forth the conception. And since our native speech has this excellence (as we have shown in a chapter above) it is clear that it must be one of the reasons for which I love it.

Having set forth how my native tongue possesses the two things that made me friendly to it—that is, nearness to me and excellence—I will tell now how the friendship has been confirmed and nourished by benefaction, concord of purpose, and the good will born of long comradeship.

First of all, I, in myself, have received from it the greatest of benefits. For among all benefits the greatest is that one that is most precious to him who receives it, nor is anything so precious as that for the sake of which all others are desired, and all other things are desired for the perfection of the desirer. Hence, since a man has two perfections—the first is that which gives him being, the second that which gives him well being, it follows that if my native tongue has been the cause of both, then I have received from it the very greatest benefit. And it may be briefly shown that it has been the cause of my existence—if my very presence here did not make that obvious.

May there not be many efficient causes for one thing, even though one of them be of higher degree than the others? For the fire and the hammer are efficient causes of the knife, even though the blacksmith be the principal one. Now it was this native tongue of mine that brought together my begetters, for it was the tongue they spoke, just as the fire prepares the iron for the smith who is making the knife; so it is clear that my native speech had a part in my begetting, and so was a certain cause of my being. Furthermore it led me into the way of knowledge which is our specific perfection; in it Latin was explained to me and so through it I began Latin, which was my path to further progress. So it is plain and I readily acknowledge it, that my native speech has been my benefactor in the highest degree. Likewise it has shared my purpose, as I shall prove. Everything naturally studies its own preservation, so if in itself my native tongue could pursue any purpose it would aim for this preservation and this would be by seeking greater stability, which could not attain save by binding itself in numbers and rhymes. And this has been my study too, as is clear enough to need no witness. So the same study has been common to both of us and by this concord our friendship has been confirmed and nourished.

More, we have also the goodwill of comradeship; from the beginning of my life I have lived in goodwill and communion with it, I have used it in speculating, explaining and questioning. So if, as is indeed plain to be seen, friendship grows with comradeship, it is clear that it has grown mightily within me, for I have passed all my time in the company of this native speech of mine. It is therefore apparent that all of the causes that can generate and nourish friendship have combined for this one; the conclusion is that I should have and do have for it not only love but perfect love. . . .

On the immortality of the soul.

BOOK II, CHAPTER 8

I say that of all stupidities, the one that holds there is no life after this one is the most foolish, vilest and most dangerous. For if we turn over all the writings both of the philosophers and other wise writers we shall see that they all agree on this: that there is an immortal part in us. And this above all is apparent in Aristotle's intent in the treatise *On the Soul*, it is the clear and chief intent of every Stoic, it is Cicero's argument, especially in his booklet *On Old Age;* it is the argument of all poets who have spoken according to the faith of the Gentiles; it is the meaning of all law whether of Jews, Saracens, Tartars or any other people who live under any kind of reason. And if all were deceived there would ensue an impossibility dreadful even to set down. For everyone is certain that human nature is the most perfect of all natures here below; this no man denies and Aristotle affirms as much when he say (in chapter XII of *On the Animals*) that man is the most perfect of all animals. So since many living creatures are entirely mortal, as the brute animals, and while they live are without the hope of another life, if our hope were vain our defect would be greater than that of any other animal, for many there have been who have sacrificed this life for the other, and so it would follow that the most perfect animal, man, would be the most imperfect—which is impossible—and that that part of him which is his greatest perfection, his reason, would be the cause of his greatest defect, which would appear quite absurd. It would follow too that nature against itself had put this hope in the human mind (for it has been said that many have hastened to the death of the body in order to live in the other life) and this too is impossible.

Further, we can observe continuous experience of our immortality in the divinations of our dreams, which could not be if there were not some immortal part within us. For the revealer, whether corporeal or incorporeal must be immortal, if we think well and subtly on the matter (I say corporeal or incorporeal because of the various opinions I find on the subject) and whatever is moved or informed by an immediate informer must have some ratio to the informer and no ratio exists between the mortal and the immortal. Further assurance of mortality is given us by the most truthful teaching of Christ, which is the way, the truth and the light: the way because through it without impediment we go to the felicity of that immortality, the truth, because it permits no error, the light because it illuminates the shadows of the world's ignorance. And I say that this teaching assures us above all other reasons because it was given to us by Him who sees and measures our immortality, which we are not able to see perfectly, by reason with some shadow of darkness, occasioned by the combination of the mortal with the immortal. This should be the most potent argument that both parts exist in us; so I believe, so I affirm and so I am certain to pass after this life to another better life, where lives that glorious lady[2] of whom my soul was enamored when I contended in such a way as will be discussed in the following chapter.

On the common opinion that nobility is a matter of inheritance.

BOOK IV, CHAPTER 7

I say that this opinion of the vulgar has become so widespread that without investigation of any reason everyone is called noble who is son or grandson of any worthy man, even though he himself be of no account. And let it be noted that to allow such a false opinion to gain footing is a most dangerous oversight, for just as grass spreads in an uncultivated field and grows up and so covers the ears of wheat that they cannot be seen by one looking from a distance, and finally the fruit is lost, so false opinion in the mind, if it be not chastised and corrected, so grows and multiplies that the ear of reason, that is to say, the right opinion, is hidden and, as it were, buried and lost. Oh, it

is a great thing I have undertaken, seeking now to weed out from such an overgrown field as is the common opinion, left so long without this care. I intend in fact not to clean out all of it but only those parts where the ears of reason are not entirely overgrown; that is I intend to set right those in whom because of their fortunate nature, some glimmering of reason still survives, as for the others, they are to be heeded no more than beasts. To me it seems that to bring a man back to reason when it has been utterly extinguished is no less a miracle than to bring back to life one who has been four days in the tomb. . . .

A bad man descended from noble ancestors is not only base (that is not-noble) but most base. And I shall illustrate by an analogy of a route for which directions have been given, after which I shall ask and answer a question. There is a plain, with fields and paths; it has hedges, ditches, boulders, logs and almost every kind of obstruction except on its narrow pathways; snow has fallen and covered everything so that all of the plain wears the same aspect and no trace of a path may be seen. A man comes from one side of the plain wishing to go to a house on the other side; having no other guide but his ingenuity, which is to say his perception and sharpness of his mind, he goes by the direct path to the place he seeks, leaving his footprints behind him. After him comes another man, wishing to go to the same house and needing only to follow the footprints; this man, though he has guidance by his own fault manages to lose the path that the first man, though without guidance, had found for him; he wanders among the thorns and the ruins and does not reach the place he should reach. Which of these should be called worthy? I answer: the first man. And what should the second be called? I answer: most base. Why is he not called "not worthy", that is, base? I answer: Because "not worthy", that is, base, should be applied to one who, having no guidance, does not travel rightly; but because the second man had guidance, his error and fault cannot be surpassed and so he is to be called not base but

64

basest. And so one who is ennobled in race by his father or some ancestor and does not maintain his inheritance is not only base but basest and deserves more scorn and vituperation than any other baseborn churl.

DE VULGARI ELOQUENTIA
(ON THE VERNACULAR)

Dante defines the vernacular and affirms its dignity.

BOOK I, CHAPTER 1

Since we do not find that anyone before us has treated of the science of the vernacular language, while in fact we see that this language is highly necessary for all, inasmuch as not only men, but even women and children, strive, in so far as nature allows them, to acquire it; and since it is our wish to enlighten to some little extent the discernment of those who walk through the streets like blind men, generally fancying that those things which are [really] in front of them are behind them, we will endeavour, the Word aiding us from heaven, to be of service to the vernacular speech; not only drawing the water of our own wit for such a drink, but mixing with it the best of what we have taken or compiled from others, so that we may thence be able to give draughts of the sweetest hydromel.

But because the business of every science is not to prove but to explain its subject, in order that men may know what that is with which the science is concerned, we say (to come quickly to the point) that what we call the vernacular speech is that to which children are accustomed by those who are about them when they first begin to distinguish words; or to put it more shortly, we say that the vernacular speech is that which we acquire without any rule, by imitating our nurses. There further springs from this another secondary speech, which the Romans called grammar.[1] And this secondary speech the Greeks also have, as well as others,

but not all. Few, however, acquire the use of this speech, because we can only be guided and instructed in it by the expenditure of much time, and by assiduous study. Of these two kinds of speech also, the vernacular is the nobler, as well because it was the first employed by the human race, as because the whole world makes use of it, though it has been divided into forms differing in pronunciation and vocabulary. It is also the nobler as being natural to us, whereas the other is rather of an artificial kind; and it is of this our nobler speech that we intend to treat.

Why speech is necessary to man and to man alone.

BOOK I, CHAPTERS 2 AND 3

. . . Speech was not necessary for the angels or for the lower animals, but would have been given to them in vain, which nature, as we know, shrinks from doing. For if we clearly consider what our intention is when we speak, we shall find that it is nothing else but to unfold to others the thoughts of our own mind. Since, then, the angels have, for the purpose of manifesting their glorious thoughts, a most ready and indeed ineffable sufficiency of intellect, by which one of them is known in all respects to another, either of himself, or at least by means of that most brilliant mirror[2] in which all of them are represented in the fullness of their beauty, and into which they all most eagerly gaze, they do not seem to have required the outward indications of speech. . . .

The lower animals also, being guided by natural instinct alone, did not need to be provided with the power of speech, for all those of the same species have the same actions and passions; and so they are enabled by their own actions and passions to know those of others. But among those of different species not only was speech unnecessary, but it would have been altogether harmful, since there would have been no friendly intercourse between them. . . .

Since, then, man is not moved by natural instinct but by reason, and reason itself differs in individuals in respect of discernment, judgment, and choice, so that each one of us appears almost to rejoice in his own species, we are of opinion that no one has knowledge of another by means of his own actions or passions, as a brute beast; nor does it happen that one man can enter into another by spiritual insight, like an angel, since the human spirit is held back by the grossness and opacity of its mortal body. It was therefore necessary that the human race should have some sign, at once rational and sensible, for the inter-communication of its thoughts, because the sign, having to receive something from the reason of one and to convey it to the reason of another, had to be rational; and since nothing can be conveyed from one reason to another except through a medium of sense, it had to be sensible; for, were it only rational, it could not pass [from the reason of one to that of another]; and were it only sensible it would neither have been able to take from the reason of one nor to deposit in that of another.

Now this sign is that noble subject itself of which we are speaking; for in so far as it is sound, it is sensible, but in so far as it appears to carry some meaning according to the pleasure [of the speaker] it is rational.

On the first speaker and the first word spoken.

BOOK I, CHAPTER 4

Speech was given to man alone, as is plain from what has been said above. And now I think we ought also to investigate to whom of mankind speech was first given, and what was the first thing he said, and to whom, where, and when he said it; and also in what language this first speech came forth. Now, according to what we read in the beginning of Genesis, where the most sacred Scripture is treating of the origin of the world, we find that a woman spoke before all others, I mean that most presumptuous Eve, when in answer to the inquiry of the devil she

said, 'We eat of the fruit of the trees which are in Paradise, but of the fruit of the tree which in is the midst of Paradise God has commanded us not to eat, nor to touch it, lest peradventure we die.'[3] But though we find it written that the woman spoke first, it is, however, reasonable for us to suppose that the man spoke first; and it is unseemly to think that so excellent an act of the human race proceeded even earlier from woman than from man. We therefore reasonably believe that speech was given to Adam first by him who had just formed him.

Now I have no doubt that it is obvious to a man of sound mind that the first thing the voice of the first speaker uttered was the equivalent of God, namely *El*, whether in the way of a question or in the way of an answer. It seems absurd and repugnant to reason that anything should have been named by man before God, since man had been made by him and for him. For as, since the transgression of the human race, every one begins his first attempt at speech with a cry of woe, it is reasonable that he who existed before that transgression should begin with joy: and since there is no joy without God, but all joy is in God, and God himself is wholly joy, it follows that the first speaker said first and before anything else 'God.'

The first speech of mankind.

BOOK I, CHAPTER 6

Since human affairs are carried on in very many different languages, so that many men are not understood by many with words any better than without words, it is meet for us to make investigation concerning that language which that man who had no mother, who was never suckled, who never saw either childhood or youth, is believed to have spoken. In this as in much else Pietramala is a most populous city, and the native place of the majority of the children of Adam. For whoever is so offensively unreasonable as to suppose that the place of his birth is the most delightful under the sun, also rates his own vernacular (that is, his mother-tongue) above all others, and consequently believes that it actually was that of Adam. But we, to whom the world is our native country, just as the sea is to the fish, though we drank of Arno before our teeth appeared, and though we love Florence so dearly that for the love we bore her we are wrongfully suffering exile—we rest the shoulders of our judgment on reason rather than on feeling. And although as regards our own pleasure or sensuous comfort there exists no more agreeable place in the world than Florence, still, when we turn over the volumes both of poets and other writers in which the world is generally and particularly described, and take account within ourselves of the various situations of the places of the world and their arrangement with respect to the two poles and to the equator, our deliberate and firm opinion is that there are many countries and cities both nobler and more delightful than Tuscany and Florence of which we are a native and a citizen, and also that a great many nations and races use a speech both more agreeable and more serviceable than the Italians do. Returning therefore to our subject, we say that a certain form of speech was created by God together with the first soul. And I say 'a form,' both in respect of words and their construction and of the utterance of this construction; and this form every tongue of speaking men would use, if it had not been dissipated by the fault of man's presumption, as shall be shown further on.

In this form of speech Adam spoke; in this form of speech all his descendants spoke until the building of the Tower of Babel, which is by interpretation the tower of confusion; and this form of speech was inherited by the sons of Heber, who after him were called Hebrews. With them alone did it remain after the confusion, in order that our Redeemer (who was, as to his humanity, to spring from them) might use, not the language of confusion, but of grace. Therefore Hebrew was the language which the lips of the first speaker formed.

DE MONARCHIA
(CONCERNING MONARCHY)

Dante points out the need of a central world government.

BOOK I, CHAPTER 4

. . . the task proper to mankind considered as a whole is to fulfill the total capacity of the possible intellect[1] all the time, primarily by speculation and secondarily, as a function and extension of speculation, by action. Now since what applies to the part applies also to the whole, and since the individual man becomes perfect in wisdom and prudence through sitting in quietude, so it is in the quietude or tranquillity of peace that mankind finds the best conditions for fulfilling its proper task (almost a divine task, as we learn from the statement: 'Thou hast made him a little lower than the angels.') Hence it is clear that universal peace is the most excellent means of securing our happiness. This is why the message from on high to the shepherds announced neither wealth, nor pleasure, nor honour, nor long life, nor health, nor strength, nor beauty, but peace. The heavenly host, indeed, proclaims: 'Glory to God on high, and on earth peace to men of good will.' 'Peace be with you' was also the salutation given by the Saviour of men, because it was fitting that the supreme Saviour should utter the supreme salutation—a custom which, as everyone knows, his disciples and Paul sought to preserve in their own greetings.

Supreme authority is essential for arbitration between states and nations.

BOOK I, CHAPTER 10

Wherever there is a possibility of dispute there has to be a judgment to settle it; otherwise there would be imperfection without a remedy to heal it, which is impossible, since God and nature never fail in essentials.

It is clear that a dispute may arise between two princes, neither of whom is subject to the other, and that this may be their fault or their subjects'; therefore a judgment between them is indispensable. However, since neither can take cognizance over the other (neither being subject to the other—and equals do not rule over equals), there needs to be a third person enjoying wider jurisdiction who by right rules over both of them. This person must be either the monarch (in which case our argument is complete) or not the monarch, in which case he himself will have an equal outside his own jurisdiction, and it will again be necessary to have recourse to a third person. Either this process will go on to infinity (which is impossible) or eventually it will lead us back to a first and supreme judge whose judgment will either directly or indirectly solve all disputes: he will be the Monarch, or Emperor.

Therefore monarchy is necessary to the world. And the Philosopher appreciated this truth when he wrote: 'Things resent being badly ordered; but to have different rulers is bad; therefore, one Prince.'

EPISTOLAE (THE LETTERS)

Dante's letter to Can Grande della Scala, lord of Verona, dedicating PARADISE *to him, tells how the poet means his poem to be read.*

LETTER X; PARAGRAPHS 7 AND 8

For the elucidation, therefore, of what we have to say, it must be understood that the meaning of this work is not of one kind only; rather the work may be described as 'polysemous,' that is, having several meanings; for the first meaning is that which is conveyed by the letter, and the next is that which is conveyed by what the letter signifies; the former of which is called literal, while the latter is called allegorical, or mystical. And for the better illustration of this method of exposition we may apply it to the following verses: 'When Israel went out of Egypt, the house of Jacob from a people of strange language; Judah was his sanctuary, and Israel his dominion.' For if we consider the letter alone, the thing signified to us is the going out of the children of Israel from Egypt in the time of Moses; if the allegory, our redemption through Christ is signified; if the moral sense, the conversion of the soul from the sorrow and misery of sin to a state of grace is signified; if the anagogical, the passing of the sanctified soul from the bondage of the corruption of this world to the liberty of everlasting glory is signified. And although these mystical meanings are called by various names, they may one and all in a general sense be termed allegorical, inasmuch as they are different (*diversi*) from the literal or historical; for the word 'allegory' is so called from the Greek *alleon*, which in Latin is *alienum* (strange) or *diversum* (different).

This being understood, it is clear that the subject, with regard to which the alternative meanings are brought into play, must be twofold. And therefore the subject of this work must be considered in the first place from the point of view of the literal meaning, and next from that of the allegorical interpretation. The subject, then, of the whole work, taken in the literal sense only, is the state of souls after death, pure and simple. For on and about that the argument of the whole work turns. If, however, the work be regarded from the allegorical point of view, the subject is man according as by his merits or demerits in the exercise of his free will he is deserving of reward or punishment by justice.

LA DIVINA COMMEDIA
(THE DIVINE COMEDY)

INFERNO (HELL)

The poem, and the poet's pilgrimage, begin on Maundy Thursday of the year 1300. He tells us of the fears that beset him, the beasts that threaten him, the comforting

68

appearance of Virgil, who outlines the journey ahead.

HELL, CANTO I

Midway upon the journey of our life[1]
    I woke to find me astray in a dark wood,
    confused by ways with the straight way at
       strife.
Ah, to find words, if such there be, that could
    describe this forest wild and dense and dour,
    by which, in thought, my terror is renew'd!
So bitter it is that death is scarcely more;
    but of the good I found there I will treat
    by saying what else there I'd discerned before.
I cannot well recall how I entered it,
    so drowsy at that moment did I feel
    when first from the true way I turned my feet.
But after I had reached the base of a hill
    where to an end that valley came which had
    so pierecd my heart with fear and pierced it
       still,
I looked up, and I saw its shoulders clad
    already with the planet's beams[2] whose light
    leadeth men straight, through all paths good
       or bad.
Then did the fear a little lose its might,
    which in my heart's lake had persisted there
    through the long hours of such a piteous
       night.
And as a man, whom, gasping still for air,
    the main lets 'scape and safe on shore arrive,
    turns to the perilous wave, his eyes a-stare,
so did my spirit, still a fugitive,
    turn back to view the pass from whose fell
      power
    no person ever yet escaped alive.
My tired limbs somewhat rested, I once more
    pursued my way across the lone hillside,
    so that the firm foot was always the lower.
And lo, just where the steep began, there hied
    a leopard,[3] light and nimble in the extreme,
    covered with hair by spots diversified;
nor did it shun me, rather did it seem
    so much to block my road of set design,
    that, to retreat, my feet were oft in trim.
The hour was that when dawn begins to shine:
    the Sun was mounting with the stars whose
      ways

marched with his own, when first[4] by Love
      divine
were set in motion those fair presences;
    thus the sweet season and the time of day
    alike conspired within my heart to raise
good hope of that wild beast with skin so gay;
    yet not such as to leave me undismay'd
    when there appeared a lion[5] in the way;
which appeared coming against me, with his
      head
    held high and with a raging hunger, so
    that even the air appeared thereof afraid;
and a she-wolf,[6] that looked as lean as though
    still burdened with all ravenings—yea, her
      might
    ere this had made much people live in woe;
which, for the fear that issued from the sight
    of her, o'erwhelmed me with a lassitude
    so heavy, that I lost hope of the height.
And even as he who joys in gaining, should
    the time arrive which makes him lose, will
      suit
    whate'er he thinks of to his saddened mood;
such was I rendered by the unresting brute,
    which, coming against me, pushed me pace by
      pace
    back to the region where the Sun is mute.
While I was falling back to that low place,
    before my eyes presented himself one
    who seemed enfeebled through long
      silentness.
To him, in that great waste where else was none,
    '*Miserere mei*,'[7] I cried, 'whatso thou be,
    whether a shade or real man!' Whereon
'Not man—man once I *was*,' he answered me:
    'my parents, natives of the Lombard State,
    were Mantuans by birth, both he and she.
Sub Julio[8] was I born, albeit 'twas late,
    and lived at Rome when the good Augustus
      reign'd,
    what time false gods that lied were
      worshipped yet.
Poet was I, and sang of virtue's friend,
    that just Anchìsiades[9] who came from Troy,
    when flames had brought proud Ilium to an
      end.
But thou, to misery so fearful why

turn back? Why climb'st thou not the blissful
    mount,
which is the cause and principle of all joy?'
'And art thou, then, that Virgil, thou that fount
    whence pours a stream of speech so broad and
    bright?'
    thus I replied to him with bashful front.
'O of all other poets the glory and light,
    may the long study and great love that made
    me search thy volume stead me in this plight.
Thou art my master and my author: led
    by thee alone, from thee I learned to take
    the fair style which with honour crowns my
    head.
Behold the beast which turned me backward:
    make
    me safe from her, renownéd sage, for she
    causes each vein and pulse in me to quake.'
'Another course must needs be held by thee'
    he answered, when he marked my sobbing
    breath,
    'wilt thou from out this savage place win free:
because this beast, which now occasioneth
    thy cries, lets no one pass along her way,
    but so impedes him as to cause his death;
and is so evil, so malign, no prey
    can ever glut her greedy appetite,
    which feeding does but aggravate, not stay.
Many are the animals she's paired with: quite
    as many more there will be, till the Hound[10]
    comes, who with painful death shall quell her
    might.
Nor lands nor pelf he'll feed on—nought beyond
    wisdom and love and valour; and between
Feltro and Feltro his birthplace shall be
    found.[11]
Safety for that poor Italy he'll win
    which Turnus, Nisus and Euryalus bled
    and died for, and Camilla the virgin.[12]
'Tis he will hunt the wolf from stead to stead,
    till back in hell he puts her by duress,
    e'en there whence first by envy she was sped.
Therefore I judge this fittest for thy case—
    to follow me, and I will be thy guide
    and draw thee hence through an eternal
    place,[13]
where thou shalt hear them crying whose hope

hath died,
    shalt see the olden spirits in pain who attest
    by shrieks the second death wherein they
    abide;
and thou shalt see those who contented rest
    within the fire,[14] as hoping in the end,
    come when it may, to arrive among the Blest.
To whom[15] thereafter wouldst thou fain ascend,
    there'll be a soul more meet for this than I;
    she,[16] when I leave thee, will thy steps
    befriend:
for that imperial Ruler, there on high,
    since I was alien to his ordering,
    will have none to his court through me draw
    nigh.
In all parts he is emperor, there he's king;
    there is his city and his lofty seat:
    oh blest whom thither he elects to bring!'
And I made answer: 'Poet, I entreat
    thee by that God thou knewest not, that so
    I may escape this evil and worse than it,
to lead me thither where thou saidst but now
    I may behold Saint Peter's gate and find
    those thou describest as so full of woe.'
Then he moved on, and I kept close behind.

The poets approach the gates of Hell.

HELL, CANTO III, LINES 1-30

'Through me ye pass into the city of woe,
    through me ye pass eternal pain to prove,
    through me ye pass among the lost below.
Justice did my sublime creator move:
    I was created by the Power divine,
    the sovereign Wisdom and the primal Love.[1]
Save things eternal, ere this being of mine
    nought was, and I eternally endure.
    Ye that come in, henceforth all hope resign.'
These words in letters of a hue obscure
    I saw inscribed above a gate and said:
    'Master, their meaning makes me feel unsure.'
And he to me, like one experiencéd:
    'Here needs must all misgiving straight be
    check'd;
    all craven scruples needs must here be dead.
We've reached the place I told thee to expect,
    where thou shalt see the folk to sorrow

bann'd
through having lost the good of the intellect.'
Having said this, he laid on mine his hand
with cheerful mien and put me, thus
consoled,
among the things of that secluded land.
There sighs, sobs and loud lamentations rolled
resounding 'neath the starless firmament,
so that at first my tears ran uncontrolled.
Uncouth tongues, horrible utterances were
blent
with words of woe, accents of anger, sound
of hands that joined with voices loud and
faint
to make thereof a tumult, swirling round
without cease, in that air forever dyed,
as sand does, when the whirlwind is
unbound.

*Dante and Virgil, leaving the first circle,
Limbo, descend to the second, that of the
lustful.*

HELL, CANTO V

So from the circle that comes first I went
down to the second, which engirds less space,
but more pain, such as goads to loud lament.
There presides Minos,[1] grisly sight to face,
snarling; inspects the faults as they come in,
dooms and, by how he girds him, allots their
place.
I say, each ill-born spirit, once within
his presence, leaveth nothing unconfess'd;
and he, that grand appraiser of all sin,
sees with what place in Hell it tallies best;
as many grades as down he'd have it go,
so often with his tail he belts his waist.
Passing before him in an endless row,
they go in turn each to the judgment; then
they speak, they hear, and straight are hurled
below.
'O thou that com'st to the hostelry of pain,'
to me, when he beheld me, Minos cried,
letting his great charge unperformed remain,
'ere entering, look in whom thy hopes confide;
beware lest the entry's breadth should prove
a liar!'

'Why keep on clamouring?' answered him
my guide.
'His going is fated and brooks no denier:
'tis so willed there, where there is power to do
that which is willed, and more forbear to
enquire.'
Now begin moans that, as they louder grow,
force themselves on my ear: now I am come
thither where many wailings strike me thro'.
I came to a place, of light completely dumb,
which bellows like the sea when a storm
rages,
if cross-winds battle therewith for
masterdom.
The blast of hell, which nothing e'er assuages,
seizes and, as it sweeps the spirits along,
a whirling, buffeting war upon them wages.
When they arrive at the brink o' the landslip,
strong
is the outcry there, wailing and lamentation;
there they revile God's power with
blasphemous tongue.
Condemned to be tormented in this fashion
are, I was told, the carnal sinners, they
who submit reason to the sway of passion.
And as their wings, come winter, bear away
the starlings in a dense flock, far outspread,
so does that blast the evil spirits for aye:
now here, now there, now up, now down, they
are sped;
and by no hope, I say not of repose,
but of less pain, are ever comforted.
And as of cranes a long succession goes
strung out upon the air, chanting their dirge,
so saw I approach us, crying aloud their
woes,
shades borne upon the aforesaid gusty surge:
hence 'Master, who may yonder people be,'
I asked him, 'whom the black air so doth
scourge?'
'The foremost of those,' then he said to me,
'concerning whom thou askest to have word,
held over many tongues the empery.
Lascivious vice so broke her that she dared
to make, by law, lust licit in her days,
to annul the scandal which she had incurr'd.
She is Semiramis[2] who, legend says,

71

succeeded Ninus and his wife had been:
hers was the land which now the Soldan
  sways.
Then the self-slayer comes, that love-lorn
  queen[8]
who to Sichaeus' ashes broke her faith;
and next, lascivious Cleopatra, seen
with Helen, look! for whom, while she drew
  breath,
such ills were done and suffered: see the
  great
Achilles, who in war with love met death.
See Paris, Tristan,' and a thousand yet,
and still more, were the shades he pointed to,
and named, whom love from life did separate.
After I'd heard my teacher thus run through
so many knights and dames of yore, my
  mind,
was well nigh wildered, overcome by rue.
I began: 'Poet, much do I feel inclined
to address yon two, together going by,
who seem to float so lightly on the wind.'
And he to me: 'Watch till they come more
  nigh;
and then by that same love which they obey,
do thou entreat them, and they will comply.'
So when the wind had drifted them our way,
I lifted up my voice: 'O souls toil-worn,
come, speak with us, saith not Another nay.'
As doves, when longing summons them, return
on raised and steady wings to their sweet
  nest,
cleaving the air, by their volition borne;
so they, from out the troop where Dido's placed,
at once through the malign air tow'rds us
  sped,
such power had my compassionate request.
'O kind and gracious being, unafraid
to venture through the perse air visiting
us who in dying stained the world blood-red,
had we for friend the universe's King.
we would petition him to give thee peace
who pitiest so our perverse suffering.
All that thou fain wouldst hear and speak of,
  this
we will both hear, and speak with you
  thereo'er,

while the wind, lulled as now, for us doth
  cease.
My native city[4] lies upon the shore
where to the sea, in search of peace, flows
  down
the Po, with each its tributary power.
Love, that soon makes the noble heart its own,
seized *him* for the fair body, from me
  removed;
and still I'm sore-bested by the way 'twas
  done.[5]
Love, that from loving lets off none beloved,
seized *me* for the beauty of him so strongly,
  that
it still hath, as thou seëst, my master proved.
Love led us to one death: predestinate
to Cain[6] is he by whom our blood was shed.'
These words were borne to us from them;
  whereat,
when I had heard these souls, thus sore-bested,
I bowed my face, and held it down so long,
that 'On what musest thou?' the poet said.
'Ah me, sweet thoughts how many, and what
  strong
desire brought these unto the woeful pass!'
When first I spoke, these words from me
  were wrung.
Then, turning back to them, now I it was
who spoke: 'Francesca,' I said, 'thine agonies
move me to weep, such pity and grief they
  cause.
But tell me, in the season of sweet sighs
what sign made Love that led you to confess
your vague desires? How opened he your
  eyes?'
And she to me: 'Nought brings one more
  distress,
as well thy teacher knows, than to recall
in time of misery former happiness.
But if to know the primal root of all
our love thou hast so great a longing, I
will do as one that weeps, yet tells withal.
Reading we were one day, entranced thereby,
of Lancelot, how by love he was fast held:
we were alone and deemed no danger nigh.
That reading oft and oft our eyes impell'd
to meet, and changed our faces' hue: but o'er

us one point, and one point alone, prevail'd.
When read we of the smile, so thirsted for,
being kissed by such a lover, he that may
now from myself be parted nevermore,
all trembling, kissed my mouth: destined to
play
our Gallehault[7] was the book and he, as well,
who wrote it: further read we not that day.'
while the one spirit said this, throughout the
tale
so piteous were the tears the other shed,
I swooned, as though in death: and down I
fell
as a man's body drops, when dropping dead.

*In the fourth circle, which holds the souls
of the avaricious and prodigal, Virgil explains to Dante the natue of Fortune and
her operations.*

HELL, CANTO VII, LINES 67-96

'This Fortune, sir, on which thy words but
touch,
what *is* she?' I said: 'that also tell me now—
she who has worldly goods so in her clutch.'
And he to me: 'O foolish creatures, how
great is the ignorance which makes you trip!
My view of her is this, imbibe it thou.
Wisdom supreme, which caused the heav'ns to
leap
into existence and gave *them* their guide[1]
so, that they share, in equal partnership,
each raying on each, the light to each supplied,
likewise ordained a general leader who,
as steward, o'er *earthly* splendours might
preside
and shift from folk to folk, in season due,
the vain goods, and from blood to blood, in
ways
past all that human wits oppose thereto.
Thus, one folk rules, another languishes,
pursuant to her judgment which, as 'twere
a snake in grass, is hidden from man's gaze.
Your wisdom has no means of countering her;
she foresees, judges, and pursues her reign,
no less god, than the gods who reign
elsewhere.

Her permutations have no respite: main
necessity compels her to be swift,
so fast they come who must their turn
obtain.
Yea, this is she whom men so freely lift
upon the cross and whom they blame amiss,
and curse when they should rather praise
her gift.
But she is blesséd and hears nought of this:
with the other primal creatures, blithe as
they,
she turns her sphere, rejoicing in her bliss.

*Dante's conversation with Virgil is inter-
rupted by a voice coming from one of the
fiery caskets wherein the souls of the heretics burn forever; we are in the sixth circle.*

HELL, CANTO X, LINES 22-93

'O Tuscan, walking through the city of fire
alive, and speaking in such seemly wise,
be pleased to halt awhile and to stand nigher.
Thy way of speech proves thee, beyond
disguise,
a native of that noble fatherland,
which, maybe, I used o'er much to victimize.'
This sound from out a coffer close at hand
came of a sudden: therefore by my guide,
for dread, I somewhat closer took my stand.
'Nay, but turn round: what ails thee, then?'
he cried.
'See there, that's Farinata,[1] risen upright:
all of him, up from the waist, can be
descried.'
I had already fixed on him my sight;
and he, uplifting breast and forehead, made
as were he holding hell in huge despite.
My guide, with bold quick hands upon me laid,
to him, where mid the vaults we saw him
show,
urged me on, saying: 'Be thy words well
weigh'd.'
When I at his tomb's foot was standing now,
he eyed me awhile: then, almost with
disdain,
he asked me: 'Of what lineage are *thou?*'
I, eager to obey, spoke out quite plain:

I hid not, but detailed my kindred all;
at which he slightly raised his eyebrows, then
thus answered: 'They were fiercely inimical
to me, my forbears and my party, so
that twice by scattering them I wrought their
fall.'[2]
'They from all quarters and both times,
although
chased forth, returned,' I answered him,
'which is
an art that *yours* have ill learned hitherto.'
Then clear to sight, in the same tomb as his,
rose from his side a shade, high as the chin:
I think that it had risen upon its knees.
It peered all round, as had its impulse been
to see if someone else was there with me;
but vain the hope and, this once clearly seen,
weeping it said: 'If lofty genius be
thy passport through this prison, of light
forlorn,
where is my son? Why is he not with thee?'
And I to him: 'I come not here self-borne:
he, who waits there, p'r'aps brings me by
this road
to her, to be brought to whom your Guy[3]
thought scorn.'
By now his words, together with the mode
of punishment, had read for me aright
that spirit's name, as my full answer show'd.
'What' cried he, suddenly risen to his full
height,
'saidest thou "thought"? Lives he no longer,
then?
Strikes not upon his eyes the gladsome
light?'
Ere answering I made some delay: and when
aware of this, he straight, without more said,
fell backward, nor appeared outside again.
But he, that other, the great soul who'd bade
me halt, changed not his aspect, nor so much
as sideways bent, nor even turned his head.
'And if'—pursuing our previous talk—'with
such
ill-success they have learned that art,' said
he,
' 'tis *that* torments me more than does this

couch.
But not re-kindled fifty times shall be
the lady's face[4] who rules here, ere how great
that art's dead weight is shalt be felt by thee.
Now tell me—so the sweet world mayst thou yet
re-visit—why that people against mine
in all its laws is so unfuriate?'
'The slaughterous rout[5] that made incarnadine
the Arbia' I replied to him 'is why
such prayers are uttered in our
temple-shrine.'
Shaking his head, he answered with a sigh:
'There I was not alone nor, sooth, had e'er
marched with the others save with warranty.
But it was I alone, in the place[6] where
all voted Florence should be swept away,
yes, I alone, who boldly championed her.'

*Dante learns from Virgil about the ethical
structure of Hell.*

HELL, CANTO XI, LINES 16-111

'My son,' he then continued to reply,
'ringed by these rocks and graded like the
rounds
which thou art leaving, three small circles lie.
Damned spirits fill them all: but, that good
grounds
thou have henceforth to know them at mere
sight,
understand how and why they are in bonds.
All kinds of malice that in heav'n excite
abhorrence aim to hurt: which aim doth or
by force or fraud on others wreak its spite.
But fraud, as man's peculiar vice, before
all else displeases God; hence lowest are set
the fraudulent, and pain afflicts them more.
The violent fill the whole first circle; yet,
since persons on whom force is wrought are
three,
it is in three rings built, each separate.
God, man's self, and his neighbour—each may
be
rough-handled: each, I say, and what is his,
as thou shalt hear me prove convincingly.
By force are death and painful injuries

wrought on one's neighbour: and, on what he
  owes,
destruction, fires and ruinous levies.
Hence homicides and whoso deals foul blows,
  spoilers and plunderers, all in divers bands
  the first ring persecutees with divers woes.
A man may on himself lay violent hands,
  and on his goods; hence in the second ring
  with justice, bootlessly repenting, stands
whoe'er doth strip himself of your world, fling
  his goods away on the hazard of a die,
  and there weep, where for gladness he should
  sing.
Force can be wrought upon the Deity
  by at heart denying and by blaspheming it,
  and viewing its boons in Nature scornfully;
therefore the smallest ring stamps, as is meet,
  Cahórs and Sodom[1] with its seal, and those
  who speak the scorn of God their hearts
  secrete.
The fraud whose gnawing every conscience
  knows
  a man may use tow'rds one who trusts him
  and
  tow'rds one who doth no trust in him repose.
The latter mode destroys, thou'lt understand,
  only the bond of love which nature makes:
  hence in the second circle, thither bann'd,
nest hypocrites, and flatterers, whoso takes
  to witchcraft, forging, theft and simony,
  procurers, barrators and suchlike jakes.
By the other mode both loves are made to die,
  the natural and what supervenes thereon,
  source of the trust which forms a special tie.
Hence in the smallest circle, and the one
  wherein the whole world centres and Dis[2]
  reigns,
  all traitors are eternally undone.'
'Master,' I said, 'thy discourse well explains
  and well indeed distinguishes what rules
  control this gulf and all its denizens.
But tell me: those,[3] stuck in the slimy pools,
  whom the wind drives, and whom the
  raindrops smite,
  and who, when clashing, vent such bitter
  howls,

if worthy of his anger in God's sight,
  why aren't they punished in the city of flame?
  And if not, why are *they* in such a plight?'
'Why go thy wits so far astray?' thus came
  his answer: 'thou art wont to show more
  skill;
  or is thy mind pursuing some other aim?
Hast thou not in thy recollection still
  those words with which thy *Ethics*[4] treats the
  three
  main dispositions adverse to heav'n's will—
incontinence, malice, bestiality
  run mad? and how incontinence earns less
  blame, as offending God in less degree?
If thou mark well this dictum, and their case
  recall, and what they are, whose sins provoke
  chastisement up above, outside this place,
thou'lt well see why they're set from this vile
  folk
  apart, and why upon them with less wrath
  the divine vengeance plies its
  hammer-stroke.'
'O sun that show'st to all dim eyes the path,
  thou so content'st me, when thou solvest
  aught,
  that doubt hath charms not less than
  knowledge hath.
Once more,' said I, 'go somewhat back in
  thought
  to where thou saidst that usury offends
  the divine goodness, and untie that knot.'
'Philosophy,' he said, 'for whoso bends
  his mind to her, notes, nor in one sole part,
  how Nature, in the course she takes, descends
from the intellect of God and from its art;
  and, if thou notest well thy *Physics*,[5] there
  thou'lt find, not many pages from the start,
that your art[6] does its best to follow her,
  e'en as the pupil does his master, so
  that your art is God's grandchild, as it were.
From these two, if thou recollectest how
  Genesis[7] opens, it behoveth men
  to get the means by which they live and
  grow;
but usurers another way have ta'en:
  and, since they set their hope elsewhere,

despise
Nature, both in herself and in her train.

Dante, riding on the back of the Centaur Nessus, has crossed the river of boiling blood, in which those guilty of violence against their neighbor are submerged; he now finds himself in the grotesque forest of the suicides.

HELL, CANTO XIII, LINES 1-78

Not yet had Nessus as he waded back
    reached shore, when we for our part pushed
      on through
    a wood unmarked by any beaten track.
Not green the leaves, but of a dusky hue;
    not smooth the boughs, but gnarled and
      interwound;
    not fruit-trees there, but poisonous brambles
      grew.
Not rougher brakes or thicker could be found,
    to lurk in, by those wild beasts that fight shy,
    'twixt Cécina and Corneto,[1] of tilled ground.
Hither, to roost, the loathsome Harpies fly,[2]
    who chased the Trojans from the Strophades
    with dismal presage of mischief drawing
      nigh.
Broad-wing'd, a human face and neck have
    these,
    great feathered belly, and claws for toe and
      heel;
    they utter mournful cries on the strange trees.
Then the good master thus began: 'I will
    thou shouldst, ere entering farther,
      understand
    thou'rt now in the second ring, and shalt be,
      till
thou comest to the waste of horrible sand.
    Look well, then, and thus things that would
    my tale
    discredit, thou shalt here see close at hand.'
I heard now all around me one long wail,
    and saw no person whence it could proceed:
    wherefore I stopped, deeming my wits to fail.
I think that *he* thought that *I* thought that mid
    the tree-trunks all those voices made their
    way

from people who, whence *we* then stood, were
    hid.
And so my master said: 'Break off a spray
    from aught that's planted here, and thou'lt
    soon know
    how far the thoughts thou hast are gone
    astray.'
Then, putting out my hand, from a great sloe
    I plucked a tiny twig, and therewithal
    its trunk cried out: 'Why dost thou rend me
    so?'
I saw 't grow dark with blood, then heard it call
    out once again: 'Why maim'st thou me?
    Awakes
    my cruel lot no pity in thee at all?
Each of us, once of human shape, here takes
    a stock's: thy hand ought surely to have
    shown
    more mercy, had our souls been those of
    snakes.'
As from a green brand which, one end alone
    on fire, at the other oozes from the wood
    and hisses by reason of the wind thence
    blown,
so from the broken splinter words and blood
    came forth together: whence I, like one
    un-nerved,
    thereupon let the tip fall where I stood.
'If what my verse alone till now has served[3]
    to show him he'd been able to believe
    beforehand, poor hurt soul,' my sage
    observed,
'thee had he ne'er stretched forth his hand to
    reave;
    but 'twas the thing's being past belief that
    made
    me prompt his deed, for which I too now
    grieve.
But tell him who thou wast, that so, instead
    of some amends, he may revive thy fame
    on earth, to return whereto he is licenséd.'
'So sweet thy words are, that, enticed by them,
    I cannot be mute,' the trunk said: 'and do ye,
    if talk beguiles me a little, forgive the same.
'Twas I that held the one and the other key
    of Frederick's heart,[4] which I grew so adept
    at locking and unlocking silently,

that from its secrets nigh all men I kept:
  so faithful was I to my glorious charge,
  that I for it lost strength, nay, scarcely slept.
The drab against whose strumpet eyes no targe
  is proof in Caesar's household[5]—she that is
  the vice of courts and death to men at large—
set against me all minds aflame, and these,
  inflamed, in turn inflamed Augustus,[6] so
  that gracious honours turned to obloquies.
My mind that, with contemptuous relish, now
  by dying thought to escape contempt, to my
  own righteous self dealt an unrighteous blow.
But by the strange roots of this tree do I
  swear that I never with my lord broke faith,
  whom all so justly held in honour high.
If either of you to the world re-journeyeth,
  let him restore my memory, 'neath the stroke
  still prostrate whereby envy sought is death.'

*The souls of the violent against nature are
condemned to eternal, restless roaming over
the burning sands of the seventh circle.
Dante tells of his moving encounter with
one of these sinners.*

HELL, CANTO XV, LINES 1-99

Now one of the hard margins bears us on,
  steam from the brook so shadowing overhead,
  that of the fire water and banks get none.
As Flemings 'twixt Wissánt and Bruges,[1] in
    dread
  of the spring tide when it is blown their way,
  build dikes, that the sea's inrush may be
    stay'd;
and as along the Brenta, so that they
  may guard their towns and castles, Paduans
    rear
dams, ere Carinthia feels the warmth of May;
not otherwise were the embankments here,
  save that he'd built them not so high and
    wide,
  who'er he was, that master-engineer.
Already from the woodland we had hied
  so far that, had I turned to look, it could
  no longer, where I was, have been descried,
when we met souls approaching in a crowd
  beside the embankment who, as each passed
    by,

eyed us, as one man, comes the evening,
    would
another, when the new moon's in the sky;
  puckering at us their eyelids in such wise
  as does the old tailor at his needle's eye.
Submitted thus to such a family's
  inspection, I was known of one, who caught
  my skirt, and cried: 'Can I believe my eyes!'
I, when to me he stretched his arm out, brought
  my gaze to rest so squarely on his baked
  appearance, that his scorched face stayed me
    not
from recognizing him with my intellect;
  and '*You* here, Ser Bruetto!'[2] stooping down
  my face to his, I said: and my heart ached.
And he: 'May't not displease thee, my dear son,
  if Brunetto Latini turn with thee
  a short way back, and let the file pass on.'
'With all my heart I beg you to; and be
  it your wish,' I said, 'that I sit with you, I will,
  if he there, whom I'm going with, agree.'
'O son,' he said, 'who of this herd stands still
  one instant, lies ten decades then supine
  and powerless to brush off the fiery ill.
Move forward, then: I at these skirts of thine
  will follow, then rejoin my company,
  who, as they go, for aye lament and pine.'
I dared not step down from the path to be
  on the same level with him, but kept my head
  bent low, like one who walks respectfully.
And he began: 'What chance or fate has led
  thee ere thy last day down into this pit?
  And who is this, whose guidance lends thee
    aid?'
'Up there,' I answered him, 'in the life lit
  by sunshine, in a valley I went astray,
  ere half my sum of days was yet complete.
From it I turned at dawn but yesterday:
  as to it I re-turned did he appear
  and leads me home now by this narrow way.'
And he to me: 'An thou pursue thy star,
  thou canst not fail to reach the glorious port,
  if I judged well in the glad life up there;
and had my days not been o'ersoon cut short,
  seeing heav'n thus kind to thee I would have
    lent
  thy work my aid and been thy strong support.

But that ungrateful commons, on evil bent,
  who down from Fiésole³ came long ago,
  and still of rock and mountain keep some
    taint,
shall for thy good deeds, make themselves thy
    foe:
  and with good reason, for sweet figs are seen
  to fruit but ill where harsh crab-apples grow.
Long deemed by the world purblind, they've
    ever been
  a greedy envious folk, whose pride doth pass
  all limits: from their ways see thou keep
    clean.
Thy fortune holds for thee such honour as
  that either side will long to make a meal
  of thee: but far from goat shall be the grass.
Let the brute-beasts of Fiésole have still
  themselves for fodder and not touch the tree
  (if any yet springs up in their dung-hill)
sprung from the holy seed left anciently
  by those few Romans who remained there
    when
  'twas made the nest of such malignity.'
'Had I been able' I replied 'to attain
  to my desire in full, you had not yet
  been banished from the natural state of men;
for on my mind is stamped your affectionate
  and kind paternal look—heart-breaking
    now—
  when in the world you taught me early and
    late
the art by which man grows eternal: how
  deep is my gratitude, so long as e'er
  I live, 'tis meet my tongue should clearly
    show.
What you narrate of how my steps shall fare
  I write, and keep with other texts to gloze
  by a wise lady, if I attain to her.
Yet thus much I would fain to you disclose:
  so conscience chide me not, I'm unafraid
  of Fortune—well prepared for all her blows.
Unto my ears have arles like this been paid
  before now; so let Fortune whirl her sphere
  e'en as she pleases, and the churl his spade.'
On that, my master rightward to his rear
  turned his cheek round, then, eyeing me for a
    spell,

said: "Well they listen, who profit by what
  they hear.'

*In the "pouch" of the grafters, the fifth of
the Evil-pouches that make up the eighth
circle, high-spirited demons play games with
the sinners. The pouches are connected by
bridges; our poets are crossing the bridge
from the fourth pouch as the action begins.*

HELL, CANTO XXI

From bridge to bridge thus came we, talking
    then
  of things my Comedy deems off the mark
  to sing now, and had reached the summit,
    when
we stopped to see in the next fissured arc
  of Evilpouches the next wailings, all
  quite futile; and I saw it strangely dark.
As boils in the Venetians' arsenal,
  when winter comes, the viscous pitch to aid
  them caulk their ships that need an overhaul,
for none can sail, and one constructs instead
  his new boat, and one plugs, with like
    concern,
  the ribs of that which many a voyage hath
    made;
one hammers at the prow, one at the stern;
  some patch the mainsail, some the jib; to
    twine
  cordage and to make oars do others turn—
so, not by fire, rather by art divine,
  was boiling down below there a thick tar,
  which smeared the bank along the entire
    incline.
I saw this, but saw naught within it, bar
  the bubbles the boiling raised, and the whole
    mass
  heave and, compress'd, subsiding near and
    far.
I still was gazing intently down, whenas
  my leader said: 'Look out, look out ' and me
  drew close to him from the place in which
    I was.
Then I turned round, like one in haste to see
  what he must flee from, whom the sudden
    shock

of fear yet so completely unmans that he
  stays not his going to take one moment's stock
  of what he sees; and I beheld a black
devil come running behind us up the rock.
Ah, how fierce he looked! how set to attack
  he seemed to me in his gest and cruel eye,
  with wings spread wide and feet that
    skimmed the track!
For freight his shoulder, which was sharp and
    high,
  bore the two haunches of a sinner: 'twas
  the sinews of the feet he gripped him by.
He shouted from our bridge: 'Ho, Evilclaws,
  here's one of St. Zita's elders![1] Thrust him
    under:
I'm off to his city again for more, because
it's amply stocked with many a such-like
    bounder:
  except Bonturo,[2] all are jobbers there,
  where "no"'s exchanged for "yea" to grab
    more plunder.'
He hurled him down and turned back o'er the
    bare
  hard crag, and never did unleashed mastiff
    strain
  its utmost so, to track a thief to his lair.
The wretch plunged and, besmeared, bobbed
    up again;
  but the fiends, under the bridge, began to
    jeer:
'Here for the Holy Face[3] one seeks in vain:
It's not like swimming in the Serchio[4] here!
  so unless thou want'st our grapples at the
    catching,
  let nought of thee above the pitch show
    clear.'
With countless prongs pricking him then and
    scratching
  they cried: 'Dance here, submerged, so that
    remote
  from sight thou, if thou canst, may'st do thy
    snatching."
Not otherwise cooks bid their scullions note
  where meat seethes in the pot and thrust it
    deep
  down with their flesh-hooks, that it may not
    float.

My kind lord said to me: 'That thou mayst slip
  their notice, find some splinter which
    somewhat
  will screen thee, squat down, and behind it
    keep.
Nor, what rebuff so'er to me be wrought,
  fear thou, for these are things to me well
    known:
  I've faced this traffic before and mind it not.'
Then past the bridgehead on he went alone,
  and need there was, when on the sixth blank
    he
  had set foot, that a bold front should be
    shown.
For with the fierce tempestuous savagery
  of dogs that rush out at some poor man, who
  suddenly, where he stops, prefers his plea.
out from beneath the little bridge they flew
  and turned against him all their gaffs; but
    straight
  cried he: 'No mischief, now, from any of you!
Before those hooks of yours in me be set,
  one of you first step forth to hear me: an so
  ye then will, then on gaffing me debate.'
They all exclaimed: 'Let Malacoda[5] go!';
  so one moved—the rest halting—and came
    near
  him growling out: 'What good will it do him,
    though?'
'Thinkest thou, Malacoda, that thou here'
  my lord said 'seest me come thus far uncow'd
  by all your hindrances, unless it were
by Will divine and Fate that bodes me good?
  Let me pass on, for 'tis in Heaven will'd
  that I show to another this wild road.'
Then how crestfallen he, of late so fill'd
  with pride! He let the hook drop at his feet
  and to the rest said: 'Strike not, we must
    yield.'
My leader then to me: 'Thou that dost sit
  squat on the bridge there where the rock is
    crack'd,
  come down now: thou mayst safely venture
    it.'
Therefore I moved and came to him—swift to
    act;
  for all the fiends advanced, and the fear rose

within me that they might not keep the pact.
And once I saw the footmen in like throes
 of fear, when issuing under treaty from
 Caprona,[6] at seeing themselves so girt with
  foes.
With my whole frame, as close I could come,
 I drew up to my guide, while well in view
 keeping their looks, which were not
  humoursome.
They lowered their prongs and 'Wouldst thou
  like me to,
 I'll tickle him on the rump' was saying one,
 the rest replying: 'Ay, nick it for him, do!'
But he, that demon who had just begun
 to parley with my leader, turned sharp round
 and said: 'Be quiet, be quiet, Scarmiglión.'
And then to us: 'By this crag will be found
 no means of progress, for the sixth arch lies
 in the pit's depth, all shattered to the ground.
But if it still seems pleasing in your eyes
 to go on, take this bank, and soon there'll
  show
 another crag, o'er which a pathway hies.
Yesterday, five hours later than 'tis now,
 twelve hundred sixty and six years[7] had gone
  by
 exactly since this bridge's overthrow.
I'm sending that way scouts of mine, to spy
 on any venturing out to take the air:
 go with them, they'll not treat you spitefully.'
'Alichin, Cálcabrin, step forward there!'
 he went on: 'and Cagnazzo, thou as well:
 let Barbariccia lead the ten, d'ye hear?
Next Libicocco and Draghignazzo, fell
 Ciriatt' o' the tusks and Graffiacane: then
 mad Rubicante and, lastly, Farfarél.
Scout round the boiling bird-lime; give these
  twain
 safe conduct to the next rock-rib that on,
 unbroken, goes o'er each successive den.'
'Ah me, sir, what a sight!' said I: 'alone,
 without an escort, pray, if thou know'st how,
 let's travel; for on my part I want none.
If thou'rt as wary as thou art wont, dost thou
 not see the way they gnash their teeth, the
  way
 they threaten us mischief with their lowering

brow!'
And he: 'I would not have thee feel dismay:
 let them go gnashing on, if so they like;
 'tis at the boiled ones that they bristle and
  bay.'
To the left hand they wheeled along the dike;
 but first, as signal tow'rd their captain, each
 had bitten tongue with teeth; and he to
  strike
a bugle's note, had utilized his breech.

*In the seventh pouch, which contains the
souls of thieves, Dante, in awed fascination,
witnesses strange metamorphoses of snake
and sinner.*

HELL, CANTO XXV, LINES 46-151

If credence, Reader, thou art slow to lend
 to things I'm going to say, no wonder; for
 myself, who saw them, well might deem
  them feign'd.
While I was eyeing them with all my power,
 lo, a six-footed serpent darted out
 in front of one and clung to him all o'er.
With its midfeet it clasped his paunch, and got
 with those in front firm hold of the arms
  likewise;
 then fanging both cheeks, sank therein its
  snout.
Its hindfeet it extended to his thighs
 and thrust its tail between these and behind—
 over the loins—stretched upward made it rise.
Never did ivy round a tree so wind
 and root itself, as that dread beast between
 and o'er the other's limbs its own entwined.
Then like hot wax they stuck, each melting in
 to the other's shape, and mixed their hue:
  which made
 neither to seem now that which it had been,
as upward over paper creeps ahead
 of where it burns a colour that is brown,
 not black yet, though the white begins to
  fade.
The other two, who'd watched this being done,
 both cried: 'O me, how thou art changed,
  Agnél![1]
 See how thou now art neither two nor one.'

The two heads, one now and inseparable,
   showed us two countenances in one face,
   so fused that which was which we could not
     tell.
The arms, no more four strips, became a brace;
   into limbs, such as ne'er were seen, the chest
   and belly turned, the thighs and legs no less.
All former features were by now effaced:
   two and yet none the monstrous image
     show'd,
   and, thus transformed, away it slowly paced.
As the green lizard, 'neath the mighty goad
   of the dog-days, seems lightning if, to gain
   another hedge, it streaks across the road;
so seemed, as tow'rd the guts of the other twain
   it darted, a small serpent, all aflame,
   livid and black as any pepper-grain.
And it transfixed that part in one of them
   whence to begin with we receive our food;
   then dropped, and lay outstretched before the
     same.
The pierced one gazed at it, but spoke not—
     stood,
   rather, quite still and yawned, as though by a
     fit
   of fever or by drowsiness subdued.
The serpent stared at him, and he at it:
   one from the mouth, one whence he felt the
     sting,
   smoked fiercely, and I saw the smoke-jets
     meet.
Silent henceforth be Lucan,[2] would he sing
   of poor Sabellus and Nasidius: let
   him wait and hear the word that now takes
     wing.
Of Cadmus and of Arethusa's fate
   silent be Ovid: him into a snake,
   her let his muse into a spring translate,
for all I care, since never did he make
   two natures, front to front, interchange so
   that both forms could each other's matter
     take.
They mutually responded— this is how:
   the serpent caused its tail to split fork-wise,
   the stung one pressed his feet together below.
So closely, of themselves, the legs and thighs
   clave each to each, that soon, where they had
     joined,
   no mark remained apparent to the eyes.
The split tail took the shape that had defined
   the limbs being elsewhere lost; and e'en as its
   skin softened, so grew hard the other's rind,
I saw his arms draw in at the armpits
   and, in proportion as they thus withdrew,
   the beast's two short feet lengthen out by
     bits.
Next, the hindfeet by intertwining grew
   into man's privy member, and from his
   the wretch of such-like feet had put forth
     two.
While the smoke with unwonted colour is
   investing both, and causing hair to sprout
   over that part and stripping it from this,
the one stood up, t'other fell down, without
   turning, howe'er, the baleful lamps aside,
   under which each assumed the other's snout.
His erect one tow'rds his temples plied,
   and from the smooth cheeks ears then issued,
     made
   out of the excess of stuff which thither hied.
That which did *not* run to the back, but stay'd,
   out of that surplus formed for the face a nose
   and thickened the lips so much as need for it
     bade.
He that was lying prostrate, forward throws
   his snout, and into his head draws back his
     ears,
   as a snail might its horns, if so it chose:
his tongue, once whole and apt for speech,
     appears
   now cleft, and in the other's which was split,
   the fork now closes up, and the smoke clears.
The soul, turned brute, the process once
     complete
   that made it such, fled hissing down the
     valley,
   and the other, sputtering words out, followed
     it;
and, turning to it his new back, did but dally
   to say to the one left: 'I'd have Buoso[3] run,
   as I did, on all fours along this alley.'
Thus did I see the seventh ballast go on
   to and fro changing; and if here my pen
   at all errs, be my excuse the strange things

done.
And though it happened that my eyes were then
  a bit blurred, and my mind dismayed, yet not
  so privily could those souls escape my ken,
but that I well marked Puccio,[4] the hip-shot:
  in him alone, of the triple fellowship
  that came first, had no change at all been
    wrought:
the other[5] was he whom thou, Gavíll', dost
  weep.

*Completely swathed in fire, the souls of the
false counselors move through the eighth
pouch; Dante's attention is drawn to a
double flame that clothes the shades of
Ulysses and Diomed. At Virgil's behest, the
shade of Ulysses describes his last voyage.*

HELL, CANTO XXVI, LINES 85-142

Of the ancient flame the larger of its pair
  of horns began to shake and murmur then,
  e'en as a flame wearied by gusty air.
Next, waving to and fro its tip, as fain
  to emulate a tongue that talks, it cast
  a voice abroad and spake as follows: 'When
I quitted Circe who had held me fast
  for more than twelve months near Gaëta,[1] ere
  Aeneas had so named it, at long last
no fondness for my son, nor filial care
  of my old father, nor the love I owed
  Penelope which should have gladdened her,
could quench the ardour which within me
    glowed
  to gain experience of all lands that be,
  and of man's nature whether bad or good;
but I put forth upon the wide deep sea
  with one ship only, and with that small band
  of comrades who had not deserted me.
I saw both coasts, e'en to Morocco and
  as far as Spain and the Sardinians' isle
  and, of that sea, each other wave-girt land.
I and my comrades had grown old the while,
  and slow, ere we approached the narrows
    where
Hercules[2] set his landmarks up to foil
the aim of whoso would beyond them dare:

I left Seville to starboard, Ceuta I'd
  already seen to larboard disappear.
"O brothers, who have reached the west," I
    cried,
  "thro' a hundred thousand perils, do not let
  our senses' last brief vigil be denied
the chance which now is offered them to get
  experience of the world undenizen'd,
  by following the Sun e'en farther yet.
Think of your breed: nature did not intend
  mankind to live as brutes, but to pursue
  virtue and knowledge to the very end."
So keen-set for the voyage I made my crew
  with this short speech, that I should scarce
    have kept
  them back thereafter, had I wanted to.
And so, our poop turn'd tow'rd the morning,
    shaped
  we our course, with oars made wings for the
    mad flight,
  and gaining still to larboard, on we swept.
Night was now seeing all the stars which light
  the other pole, and ours had sunk so low
  it rose not from the ocean-floor to sight.
Five times re-lit, as many quenched, had now
  the light been 'neath the moon, since first to
    run
  across the vast deep we had turned our prow,
when, by its distance dimm'd, there loomed
    upon
  our view a mountain,[3] so immensely high,
  as of its size, meseemed, I had seen none.
We cheered, but soon it turned to a woeful cry
  for from the new land rose a whirlwind,
    found
  the ship and smote its forepart violently.
Three times it caused her to whirl round and
    round
  with all the waters: at the fourth—for thus
  Another willed—it raised the poop and
    downed
the prow, until the sea closed over us.'

*As Ulysses departs, another flame-clad soul
makes its way toward the poets; it is the
soul of the great Ghibelline leader Guido*

da Montefeltro. *In response to the poet's plea, Guido discloses his identity and tells his story.*

HELL, CANTO XXVII, LINES 61-129

'If to a person who should ever go
  back to the world I thought that my reply
  were made, this flame would flicker nevermoe.
But seeing that from this gulf none e'er, if I
  hear truth, returned alive, I have no fear
  that, answering, I shall smirch my fame
    thereby.
I was a man of arms, turn'd cordelier,[1]
  thinking, so girt, to make amends: and true
  that thought had surely come, to this I swear,
but for the high priest—ill befall him—who
  replunged me in my former sins; I would
  thou hear how this befell, and wherefore too.
While I informed the bones and pulp I owed
  to her who bore me, all my doings smacked
  not of the lion's but of the vulpine brood.
Shrewd wiles and covert ways, of these I lacked
  none, and so deftly practised them, I made
  their sound go forth to Earth's remotest tract.
Come to that stage of life when men are led,
  if they are wise, to haul their tackle in
  and lower their sails, it irked me then, instead
of pleasing me (as once), to live in sin;
  repentant and confessed, I took the vows,
  ah me! and my salvation it would have been.
The prince[2] of modern Pharisees—who chose
  to wage a war hard by the Lateran
  and not with Saracens and not with Jews;
for all his foes were Christians to a man,
  and none had joined in conquering Acre, and
    none
  in trading where the Soldan's fiat ran—
heeded not in himself his supreme throne
  or holy orders or that cord in me,
  which used to emaciate those who girt it on.
As Constantine, to cure his leprosy,
  summoned Sylvester from Soracte's side,[3]
  so call me in as master-leech did he,
to heal him of the fever of his pride:
  he asked me for advice—I deemed him just
  a drunkard blethering, and no word replied.

Then spake he again: "Let not thy heart
    mistrust;
  I, from now on, absolve thee: and teach me
    thou
  how to lay Palestrina in the dust.
Heaven I have the power, as thou dost know,
  to lock and unlock: since two are the keys,
  whose worth my predecessor[4] rated low."
Then, pushed by weighty arguments like these
  to a point where speech seemed, more than
    silence, fit,
  "Father, since thus to cleanse me thou dost
    please
from that sin I'm about now to commit,
  large promise with scant keeping—this,"
    I said,
  "will make thee triumph in thy lofty seat."
Francis[5] came afterwards, when I was dead,
  for me; but a black cherub cried: "Forbear
  to take him: let no trick on me be play'd.
Down among my familiars must he fare,
  because the advice he gave was fraudulent,
  from which time forth I've had him by the
    hair.
For none can be absolved save he repent,
  nor both repent and will the sin's
    commission:
  the contradiction won't thereto consent."
Ah, wretched me, how conscious of perdition
  was I, when seizing me he said: "May be
  thou didst not think that I was a logician!"
He bore me off to Minos: eight times he
  wound his tail round his hard back, in fierce
    ire
  gnawed it awhile, and then pronounced on
    me:
"This is a sinner for the thievish fire";
  so, where thou seest, I'm lost, forever borne
  along, lamenting, clad in this attire.'

In the lowest circle of Hell, the eternal home of traitors, Dante finds two sinners locked in the ice of Cocytus, one engaged in ferociously gnawing the skull of the other. The aggressive shade explains the cause of his savagery.

HELL, CANTO XXXIII, LINES 1-75

Lifting his mouth up from the savage feast,
  that sinner wiped it on the hair of the head
  which in its hinder part he had laid waste.
And then 'Thou wilt that I renew' he said
  'a desperate grief, which but to think of, ere
  I speak thereof, weighs on my heart like lead.
But if my words are to be seeds to bear
  fruit of ill fame unto this traitor whom
  I'm gnawing, I will with tears the truth
    declare.
I know not who thou art, nor how thou art come
  down here: but from thy speech it seems to
    me
  it must be Florence that thou hailest from.
Know, then—I was count Ugolín,[1] and he
  is the archbishop Roger[2]: now I'll tell
  thee why I'm such a neighbour as thou dost
    see.
That I, who deemed his word reliable,
  was captured and then killed—the effect of
    his
  ill schemes, why mention? for thou know'st it
    well.
But that which thou canst *not* have heard, that
    is,
  how cruel my death was, thou shalt hear, and
    then
  know if from him I've suffered injuries.
A narrow slit within the mew which men
  now call the "tower of famine" after me,
  and which as prison needs must serve again,
had let me already through its opening see
  many moons, when a nightmare for me drew
  abruptly aside the veil of things to be.
I saw this man as lord and master who
  was chasing wolf and wolf-cubs tow'rds the
    mount[3]
  which shuts off Lucca from the Pisans' view.
With braches eager, lean and trained to hunt,
  Gualandi and Sismondi he had sent
  before him, with Lanfranchi, on in front.[4]
I saw the father and the sons, forspent,
  being quickly overtaken as they fled,
  and then their flanks by the sharp tushes rent.
When I awoke before the dawn, with dread

I heard my children moaning in their sleep
  (for they were with me) and demanding
    bread.
Right cruel thou art, if thou from tears canst
    keep,
  thinking on what my heart forbode: if thou
  weep'st not, at what, then, dost thou ever
    weep?
They'd woken, and the hour was nearing now
  when our next meal was due, and his dream
    stirr'd
  a doubt in each one, which he feared to show;
and at the foot of that grim tower I heard
  the door being nailed up; whence I gazed
    upon
  the faces of my sons but spake no word.
I wept not, so within I'd turned to stone:
  but *they* wept; and my darling Anselm cried:
  "What ails thee, father? Why look'st thou so
    wan?"
E'en at this tears I shed not, nor replied
  all that day, nor the following night, until
  the next sun rose upon the world outside.
When a faint ray of light began to steal
  into the woeful prison, and on four
  faces my own looks now were visible,
I bit both hands, my anguish was so sore;
  and they, who deemed I did it to relieve
  my hunger; straightway rising from the floor,
said: "Father, wouldst thou feed on us, we'd
    grieve
  much less: this sorry flesh in which we're clad
  thou gav'st us: now strip off what thou didst
    give."
I calmed me then, not to make them more sad:
  both that day and the next we all sat dumb:
  why opened not the hard earth? Would it
    had!
Gaddo, when to the fourth day we were come,
  flung himself full length at my feet with the
    cry:
  "My father, food—why dost not give me
    some?",
and there died; then, as *thou* seest *me*, did I
  between the fifth and sixth day even so
  see the three, one by one, fall down and die.
I crawled among them, groping, being now

blind, and two days kept calling them though
    dead:
· then fasting was more powerful than woe.'

At earth's very center, frozen forever in the
ice ring called Giudecca, stands Lucifer.
Dante describes the spectacle.

HELL, CANTO XXXIV, LINES 28-126

The imperial monarch of the realm of woe
    stood forth at midbreast from the ice; and me,
in size, a giant doth not more outgo
than *his* arms do the giants: thus thou'lt see
    now, how enormous needs must be that whole
    which with a part so fashioned would agree.
If he was once fair, as he now is foul,
    and scorned the Being by whom he had been
      made,
    well may from him come all that damns the
      soul.
And oh, my astonishment, when on his head
    I saw no fewer than three faces![1] one
    in front, and that was of vermilion-red;
to this face the two others were joined on
    just midway above 'twixt where begins and
      ends
    each shoulder, and all three joined at the
      crown.
The right was coloured of the tint which blends
    yellow with white; the left, of that we find
    in such as come from whence the Nile
      descends.
Beneath each two great wings came out,
    design'd
    to fit such a colossal bird: I ne'er
    set eyes on sails at sea of the like kind.
They had no feathers, but in fashion were
    like to a bat's: and these he flapped about,
    so that from him went forth three currents of
      air,
which caused Cocytus to congeal throughout.
    With six eyes wept he, and o'er three chins
      beneath
    dripped tears, with slaver, gout on bloody
      gout.
In each mouth he was bruising with his teeth
    a sinner, as with a brake, and torturer

he was thuswise of three of them therewith.
For him in front the chewing was, in compare,
    nought to the clawing, which oft-times
      scarified
    his back so, that of skin it was stripped bare.
'The soul up there worst punished,' said my
    guide,
    'is Judas called Iscariot, who kicks
    his legs without, and has his head inside.
Of the other two, who hang head-downward, fix
    thine eye on him i' the black snout—Brutus,
      he!
    Look how he writhes, but neither moans nor
      speaks;
and the other's Cassius, limbed so stalwartly.
    But night is re-ascending, and we now
    must go, for we've seen all there is to see.'
I clasped him round the neck, he showing me
    how;
    and, having chosen time and place with care,
    when the wings opened wide enough to allow
his clutching of the shaggy flanks, he there
    and then from shag to shag descended by
    this means 'twixt icy crust and matted hair.
When we had reached the exact point where the
    thigh
    turns in the socket at the haunch's swell,
    my guide, with labour and with agony,
turned head to where his shanks had been; the
    fell
    then gripped he like one mounting upward, so
    that I supposed us climbing back to Hell.
'Hold fast,' the master said, panting as though
    forspent, 'for 'tis by stairs like these that we
    must part from evil and such utter woe.'
Then, issuing where a rock was tunnelled, me
    he first set down beside the edge: anon
    himself to where I sat stepped cautiously.
I raised my eyes and thought to look upon
    Lucifer standing as I'd seen him last,
    and saw him, legs in air, set upside down.
If this perplexed me and I stared aghast,
    judge they, to whose dull wits it does not
      pierce
    what point it was through which I had just
      pass'd.
'Up' said my master 'on thy feet: for there's

a long way yet to go, and rough the road,
  and the sun's back already at mid-tierce.'
It was no palace-chamber where we stood:
  call it a natural dungeon—scarce a ray
  of light, the floor to tread on far from good.
'Ere from the abyss I pluck myself away,
  dear sir,' when risen to my feet I said,
  'to clear he of error spare me a word, I pray:
where is the ice? and he, how on his head
  is he thus fixed? and how in one short hour
  has the Sun on from eve to morning sped?'
And he: 'Thou think'st thou standest, as before,
  yonside the centre, where I grasped the hair
  of the evil worm which through the world
      doth bore.
So long as I descended thou wast there;
  but when I turned myself, thou passedst then
  the point to which weights draw from
      everywhere.
Hence, 'neath the counter-hemisphere, 'tis plain,
  thou now art, and not that whose spans
      o'ervault
  the great dry land and 'neath whose zenith
      was slain
the Man born, as he lived, devoid of fault:
  'tis on the small sphere, forming the other
      face
  of the Judecca, that thy feet now halt.
Here it is morn, when there eve: and the place
  of him whose hair as ladder served us well
  he's still, as erstwhile, fixed in, motionless.
On this side headlong out of heav'n he fell;
  and the land, then on this side prominent,
  for fear of him made of the sea a veil,
and came to our hemisphere; and, maybe, bent
  on fleeing from him, that now on this side
      found
  left here a void and rushing upward went.'

PURGATORIO (PURGATORY)

Dante and Virgil, emerging from the dark channel of the earth through which they have made their laborious ascent, find them-selves on the Island of Purgatory; it is the hour of dawn. The poet begins this second *and happier division of his* Comedy *with a brief invocation.*

PURGATORY, CANTO I

To scud o'er better waters hoisteth sail
  the little vessel of my genius, quit
  henceforward of a sea that is so fell;
and of that second realm my song will treat,
  which is the human spirit's purifier
  and for ascending heavenward makes it meet.
But here with life dead poesy re-inspire,
  O holy Muses, since to you I'm bound;
  and here Calliope[1] rise somewhat higher,
swelling my song with that full-throated sound
  which smote the wretched Pies[2] and made
      them own
  their hope of pardon would be fruitless found.
Sweet colour, the translucent tint and tone
  of orient sapphire, gathering high in heaven
  serene, and pure down to the primal zone,
made using of my eyes a joy re-given,
  once I had issued forth from the dead air
  against whose gloom my eyes and breast had
      striven.
The radiant planet,[3] love's own comforter,
  was setting all a-laugh the eastern sky,
  veiling the Fishes, that scorted her.
I turned to the right and bent my mind thereby
  on the other pole, and saw four stars, the
      same
  as, save the first folk,[4] none did e'er espy.
Joyous seemed heaven of their twinkling flame:
  O widowed northern clime, bereft indeed,
  in that thou mayst no longer gaze at them!
After mine eyes had ceased thereon to feed,
  turning awhile to the other pole, where shone
  the Wain[5] no more, which 'neath it now lay
      hid,
I saw beside me an Ancient, all alone,
  worthy of so much reverence in his mien,
  that more to father is not owed by son.
Long and with white hairs mingled therewithin
  his beard was, to his tresses like, and these
  in two bands falling to his breast were seen.
The rays of the four holy luminaries
  so lighted him, that as a face would look
  having the sun before it, so did his.

'What men are ye, that breasting the blind
   brook
   have fled the eternal prison-house?' Thus fell
   his words, as he his goodly plumage shook.
'What guide, or what to lamp you, could avail,
   as ye came forth from where the deep night is,
   which evermore makes black the pit of hell?
Are the laws broken that control the abyss?
   or some new counsel changed in heaven to
   allow
   you, that are damned, to approach my
   cavities?'
My leader then took hold of me and now
   his words, now hands, now gestures made it
   clear
   he would to reverence bend my legs and
   brow.
He answered: 'Of myself I came not here:
   from heaven came down a lady, who beside
   this man besought me as savior to draw near.
But since it is thy will to have more supplied
   touching our state, how it truly came to pass,
   mine cannot be, that thou shouldst be denied.
Unto his life's last eve this man that has
   ne'er seen it, yet thro' his folly came so nigh,
   that to turn back brief time indeed there was.
So, even as I have said, despatched was I
   to rescue him, nor was there other way
   than this alone which I have travelled by.
Shown him I have, in their complete array,
   the wicked, and now plan that he shall see
   those spirits who purge themselves beneath
   thy sway.
Of how I've brought him, long the tale would
   be;
   power from on high its aid on me bestows
   to guide him to the seeing and hearing thee.
Now please thee grace his coming: for he goes
   in search of Liberty, and that how dear,
   he who renounces life for her well knows.
Thou know'st it, who for her sake didst not fear
   in Utica death's sting nor to discard
   the robe which shall at doomsday shine so
   clear.[6]
For us the eternal edicts are not marred;
   since this man lives, nor me doth Minos bind:
   but mine's the zone where by their chaste

regard
thy Marcia's eyes, O holy breast, thou'dst find
   still praying thee to deem her thine again:
   for *her* love's sake, then, be to us inclined,
Let us go through thy seven kingdoms; then
   thanks will I bear back, touching thee, to her,
   if to be mentioned there below thou deign.'
'Marcia so pleased my eyes, while over there
   I sojourned,' he replied, 'that all she would
   that I should do, I did without demur.
Now that she dwells beyond the evil flood,
   the law laid down, when forth from there I
   came,
   ordains she may no longer sway my mood.
But if that, as thou say'st, a heavenly dame
   moves and directs thee, flattery may be
   spared:
   suffice it that thou ask me in her name.
Go, then, and be it thy task this man to gird
   with a smooth rush and bathe his face,
   thuswise
   renewing what all that soils it hath impaired.
For 'twere unseemly aught should cloud his
   eyes
   the first time that a minister he views
   numbered with those who serve in Paradise.
This islet, where its lowest verges lose
   their vantage o'er the breakers, bears a ring
   of rushes bedded in the muddy ooze.
No other plant that grows a stalk whence spring
   leaves or that hardens, can in that place live,
   because it yields not to the buffeting.
Then do not hitherward your steps retrieve;
   the rising Sun will show you where a way is
   which to the mount will easier access give.'
He vanished; and nought saying did I upraise
   and draw me backward, wholly intent upon
   my leader, and to him direct my gaze.
And he began: 'Follow me close, my son:
   let us turn back, for this way steadily
   down doth the plain to its low limits run.'
The matin hour had now begun to flee
   before the advancing dawn, and far away
   I recognized the shimmering of the sea.
We paced the lonely level, like as they
   who, the road lost, go seeking it anew
   and, till they find it, deem they vainly stray.

As soon as we had come to where the dew
  fought with the Sun, since it but slowly there
  evaporated where a cool air blew,
both of his hands outspread with gentle care
  on the fresh herbage did my master place;
  whence I of his contrivance well aware,
held up to him my tear-bedrabbled face;
  unto my checks did he thus quite restore
  that colour of which Hell had left no trace.
Then came we down upon the desert shore,
  which never yet saw mariner so skilled
  as to return who sailed its waters o'er.
There did he gird me as another willed:
  oh marvel! such, as by his hand 'twas torn
  from earth, in that same place which it had
    filled
the humble plant was instantly re-born.

*A holy bark arrives, laden with souls of the
saved, and among them Dante meets a
friend.*
            PURGATORY, CANTO II, LINES 10-133

We by the margin of the sea yet stay'd,
  like folk who, while their road they ponder
    o'er.
  linger in body, in heart have onward sped.
And lo! as through thick vapours, just before
  the daybreak, Mars burns with a ruddy glow
  down in the west above the ocean-floor,
such appeared—may I once more see it so!—
  a light that o'er the sea came on: nor flies
  aught that for speed can be compared thereto.
From which when I'd an instant turned my eyes
  to question him who led me, I again
  saw it, now brighter and increased in size.
On either side of it I noticed then
  a something white, and underneath it out
  loomed by degrees another no less plain.
My master all this time had uttered nought
  until the first white objects showed as wings:
  then, when he knew the pilot past all doubt,
'Bend, bend thy knees,' he cried: 'God hither
    brings
  his angel: fold thy hands: so fashioned are
  all here appointed to such ministerings.
See how he scorns all man-invented gear,
  so that he wills no oar nor other sail

than his own pinions between shores so far,
See how he lifts them heavenward and how well
  the air do those eternal feathers ply,
  which unlike mortal hair change not nor fail.'
Then as drew nigh to us and still more nigh
  the bird of God, he yet more brightly shone,
  so that mine eyes endured him not close by,
but down I bent them; he to shore came on
  with a ship, which so swiftly and lightly hied,
  that of its bulk the water swallowed none.
Like one whose bliss by his look seemed
    ratified,
  on the poop stood the heavenly mariner;
  and more than a hundred spirits sat inside.
In éxitu Israël de Aegypto[1] were
  the words that all were chanting, with the
    rest
  which in the sequel of that psalm occur.
Then with the sign of the holy cross he bless'd
  them all, whereat they flung themselves
    ashore;
  and off he sped, as he had come, in haste.
The throng that there remained the aspect bore
  of strangers to the place, and their survey
  resembled his who would new things explore.
On every side shone, arrowing forth the day,
  the Sun, who with his well aimed shafts had
    now
  from the mid-sky chased Capricorn[2] away,
when the new-comers raised each one his brow
  towards *us*, saying; 'Show us, if ye know,
  of access to the mount the where and how.'
And Virgil answered: 'Thought it is not so,
  haply ye deem us expert in this isle,
  but we, like you, do on a journey go.
We came just now, ere you did a brief while,
  by another way, which was so steep and rude,
  we'll deem the ascent henceforth child's play,
    not toil.'
The souls, who from my breathing understood
  that I was still alive, grew pale, thereby
  betraying their wonder and its magnitude.
And as to hear his news the folk crowd nigh
  an envoy with an olive-branch and none
  of trampling on his neighbour seemeth shy,
so on my face those happy spirits, one
  and all, kept gazing and became almost

forgetful of going to put their beauty on.
I saw one soul out of the spell-bound host
   advance to embrace me, and thereto so fain,
   that he impelled me to the like accost.
Oh shades, in all but outward aspect, vain!
   Behind him thrice my clasping hands I bent,
   thrice to my own breast brought them back
     again.
My face, I think, revealed my wonderment;
   whereat the spirit smiled and backward drew,
   and I, pursuing it, a step forward went.
Gently it bade me pause: and then I knew
   who it was, and begged it, staying awhile, to
     allow
   us time for talk, ere setting forth anew.
'I in my mortal body loved thee, and now
   thence freed, I love thee as dearly,' answered
     he;
   'therefore I stay; but wherefore journeyest
     thou?'
'Casella mine, that I once more may be
   here where I am, I make this journey,' I said;
   'but how hath so much time been taken from
     thee?'
And he to me: 'None wronged me, if instead
   of granting, he who embarks both when and
     whom
   he wills, to me this passage oft forbade;
for 'tis a just will which his own springs from:
   nathless, for these three months past he has
     ta'en,
   with full consent, all who have wished to
     come.
Whence I, who to the shore had turned me then,
   where Tiber's water with sea-salt is sown,
   by him was gathered in with heart full fain.
Straight to that river-mouth he now has flown;
   for always, there, assemble such of those
   as do not unto Acheron sink down.'
And I: 'If no new law hath made thee lose
   memory or practice of the song of love
   which used to give all my desires repose,
may it please thee somewhere with the strains
     thereof
   to soothe my soul, for which its mortal
     mould
   has made my coming here so toilsome prove!'

'Love that within my mind doth discourse hold'
   he then began so sweetly that I hear
   the sound within me still its sweets unfold.
My master, I, and all the folk who there
   were with him seemed as well content as
     though
   our minds for nothing else had thoughts to
     spare.
Fixed on the strains, we stood entranced, when
     lo!
   the venerable Ancient with us is,
   crying; 'How now, ye laggard spirits, how
     now?
What negligence, what dallying is this?
   Run to the mountain, there to cast aside
   the slough that, clouding God, delays your
     bliss.'
As doves that, gathering corn or tares, abide
   together, all assembled at their feed
   quietly, nor display their wonted pride,
if aught be seen from which their fears proceed,
   incontinently leave their food to lie,
   because some greater care compels their
     heed;
so I that lately-landed company
   saw quit the song and, like one going, yet
   not knowing just whither, tow'rds the hillside
     fly:
nor was our parting less precipitate.

*Among the souls who wander about the
lower slopes of Purgatory, waiting to begin
their penance, Dante encounters Manfred,
son of the Emperor Frederick, slain while under excommunication at Benevento (1266).*

PURGATORY, CANTO III, LINES 88-145

When those in front on my right flank espied
   the sunlight broken on the ground where lay
   my shadow reaching to the steep hillside,[1]
they stopped short, and drew back a little way,
   and all the others following, though left
   in ignorance of the cause, did even as they.
'I, ere it be by question from me reft,
   confess this is a human body ye see,
   by which the Sun's light on the ground is
     cleft.

Marvel not at it; but believers be,
   that not without power from on high he
     stands
   here, and would scale this wall of rock and
     scree.'
The master thus; and that deserving band's
   reply was: 'turn—join and precede us, then:'
   and signal made they with the backs of their
     hands.
'Whoe'er thou art, turn thee about again,
   as thus thou goest,' said one; 'bethink thee
     now
   if yonder I came e'er within thy ken.'
I turned and scanned him closely, noting how
   that comely he was and blond and nobly
     graced,
   but by a sword-stroke cleft was one
     eye-brow.
When I, responding humbly, had confess'd
   never to having seen him, he exclaimed
   'Now look!' and showed me a wound high on
     his breast.
He added, smiling: 'Manfred am I named,
   a grandson of the Empress Constance's;
   so, prithee, go thou, when by earth reclaimed,
to my fair daughter, who bore Sicily's
   and Aragon's chief honour 'neath her side,
   and, whate'er else be rumoured, tell her this.
When pierced by these two stabs whereof I died
   my body lay, weeping did I commit
   myself to Him whose pardon is ne'er denied.
My sins were horrible; but infinite
   Goodness hath arms so wide that they
     embrace
   readily whatsoe'er turns back to it.
And if Cosenza's pastor,[2] who in chase
   of me was sent by Clement, then had found
   time to peruse this aspect of God's face,
my body's bones had still lain in the ground
   at the bridge-head near Benevento trenched,
   under the shelter of the high-heaped mound.
Forth from the Realm[3] now the wind drives
     them, drenched
   with rain, hard by the Verde,[4] where they'd
     been
   transported at his hest with tapers quenched.
But through their malediction none, I ween,

is e'er so lost, that the eternal Love
   cannot return, while hope has speck of green.
True, such as, though at last they contrite
     prove,
   in contumacy of Holy Church have died,
   this bank once reached, must stay outside
     thereof
for thirtyfold the time they willed to bide
   in their presumption, if to abridge this strict
   decree no pious voice on God hath cried.
My welfare, then, do thou hereafter seek 't
   by telling my good Constance[5] of these
     wounds
   and how thou 'st seen me, and of this
     interdict;
   (for here from those o'er there much good
     abounds.)

Bonconte da Montefeltro, a great Ghibelline leader, killed at the battle of Campaldino (1289), answers Dante's question with regard to the disposal of his body (which was never recovered). Bonconte was the son of Guido of INFERNO *XXVII; their matching narratives are at once human revelations and lessons in dogma. But the intervention of the gentle Pia at the end of the canto is more moving than the circumstantial account of the soldier's fate.*

PURGATORY, CANTO V, LINES 94-136

'Oh, at the Casentino's foot,' said he,
   'crosses a stream, Archiano named, whose
     source
   in Apennine lies o'er the Hermit'ry.[1]
Just at the junction, where its name perforce
   is lost, I arrived, stabbed in the throat,
     fordone,
   fleeing on foot and bloodying my course.
There I lost sight, and with my latest groan
   I uttered Mary's name, and there I fell:
   and in that spot remained my flesh alone.
I'll tell the truth: do thou the same re-tell
   'mongst living men; God's angel snatched me,
     and "Why
   dost rob me, O thou from heav'n?" cried he of
     hell.

"Thou carriest off and dost to me deny
   this man's eternal part for one small tear:
   but deal with the other otherwise will I."
Thou knowest full well how in the atmosphere
   moist vapours gather and mount skyward till,
   condensed by cold, they turn to water there.
He joined that ill will, which seeks only ill,
   with the intellect, and stirred the fog and
     blast
   in virtue of power his nature doth instil.
Then he o'erspread the vale, when day was past,
   from Pratomagno to the great range with
     black
   clouds, and the sky above made overcast,
so that to water the charged air changed back:
   rain fell, and through the gullies foamed in
     spate
   all of it that the earth refused to take:
as in the great ghylls it converged and met,
   tow'rds the royal river with such boisterous
   speed did it rush, that nought its course could
     let.
The swol'n Archián at the outlet of its fosse
   found my corpse stiff and pushed it on, thus
     found,
   to the Arno, and on my breast undid the cross
I'd made of myself when vanquished by the
     wound:
   it rolled me along its banks and o'er its bed;
   then with its spoils covered and wrapped me
     round.'
'Ah, when unto the world thou shalt have made
   return, and rested from the way's long strain,'
   the third after the second spirit said,
'me, who am Pia,[2] may'st thou think of then:
   'twas Siena made, Maremma that unmade
     me:
   he knows it who with his own jewel, when
our mutual troth had first been plighted, wed
     me.'

*Virgil, inquiring directions from a soul sitting apart, mentions that he is of Mantuan origin, whereupon the soul springs up and warmly embraces him, happy to greet a compatriot. The shade is that of the poet Sordello, who, although he wrote in Proven-*çal, *was born near Mantua. The spectacle moves Dante to a bitter outburst as he contrasts the cordiality of this meeting with the factionalism rampant in Italy.*

PURGATORY, CANTO VI, LINES 76-151

Ah, enslaved Italia, sorrow's hostelry,
   ship without pilot in a raging gale,
   not lady of provinces, but harlots' sty!
Thus did his zeal that noble soul impel,
   merely at the sweet sound of his city's name,
   to bid his fellow-townsman there all-hail;
and now in thee war ceases not to inflame
   thy living men, and one of the other devours,
   though the same wall, same moat encloses
     them.
Search, wretch, thy sea-coasts all about thy
     shores,
   then look within thy breast, if any part
   in thee enjoy the boon of peaceful hours.
What boots it that for thee Justinian's art[1]
   retrimmed the bit, if no one mounts the
     steed?
   The shame would, but for that, less keenly
     smart.
Ah, folk that should be given to prayer, and
     need
   but to let Caesar fill the saddle again,
   paid ye to God's direction proper heed,
look how this beast, for lack of spurs to train
   and curb its ardour, still more savage grows,
   ever since ye laid hand upon the rein.
O German Albert,[2] who thine eyes dost close
   to her, grown wild and vicious, though by
     right
   'tis thou who shouldst bestride her saddle-
     bows,
may a just judgment from the stars alight
   upon thy blood: be't strange and manifest,
   that thy successor may thereat take fright.
For, like thy father,[3] thou—held back, in quest
   of lands o'er there, by greed that nought
     abates—
   hast let the empire's garden run to waste.
Come and see Montagues and Capulets,
   Monaldi and Filippeschi,[4] O heedless man:
   these dreading ill which those e'en now

91

besets!
Come, cruel! come and see how oppressive can
   thy nobles be, and the ills they've wrought
      make good;
   and thou'lt see Santafiór, how it needs thy
      ban!
Come, see thy Rome, in lonely widowhood
   weeping, and calling day and night: 'Oh,
      why,
   my Caesar, dost thou leave me in solitude?'
Come and see how they love each other, thy
   good folk, and if nought else thy pity move,
   come for thy own repute's sake, shamed
      thereby.
And, be't lawful for me, O highest Jove
   who wast on Earth for us once crucified,
   I'll ask, do thy just eyes elsewhither rove?
Or art thou thus preparing, but dost hide
   in thy unfathomed counsel, some good end
   by our weak vision wholly undescribed?
For all the lands of Italy now bend
   to tyrants, and no churl exists but he's
   a right Marcellus,[5] be he faction's friend.
Thou, my own Florence, well may'st be at ease
   with this digression, withers quite unwrung,
   thanks to thy folk who are so prompt with
      pleas.
Many love justice, but their bows are strung
   with caution, and they shoot the word with
      care;
   but *thy* folk have it on the tip of the tongue.
Many refuse the common load to share:
   but *thy* folk eagerly respond, nor wait
   to be asked, but cry: 'For me 'tis light to bear.'
Count thyself—and with reason—fortunate:
   thou wealthy, thou at peace, and thou so
      wise!
   a truth I leave the facts to demonstrate.
Athens and Lacedaemon, who made rise
   the ancient laws and civic discipline
   scarce showed at all wherein well-living lies,
compared with thee, who of a thread so thin
   dost make provisions, that to mid-November
   lasts not what thou dost in October spin.[6]
How often hast thou, since thou canst
      remember,
   changed customs, coinage, laws and offices,

rejointing limbs only to re-dismember!
This called to mind, seeing clearly thy disease,
   thou'lt see thyself resembling that sick dame,
   who, laid on down, by tossing seeks to ease
her aches, but goes on suffering just the same.

Sordello guides the poets to a little dell
where the souls of princes are preparing for
their evening rest.

PURGATORY, CANTO VII, LINES 70–84
AND CANTO VIII, LINES 1–6

'Twixt steep and level wound a path, which now
   led us along that corrie's flank, to wit
   there where, by more than half, its rim sinks
      low.
Gold and fine silver, rotten wood self-lit,
   violet, white lead, cochineal, sky-blue,
   fresh emerald at the instant it is split,
each by the herbage and the flowers which grew
   within that bosom in colour were outdone,
   e'en as the greater doth the less subdue.
Nor in that place had Nature limned alone,
   but from a thousand perfumes, there allied,
   made one scent, undetermined and unknown.
Thence on the flowers and grass I souls espied,
   'Salve regina'[1] singing, seated where
   owing to the vale they appeared not from
      outside.

Now was the hour that shoreward turns the eye
   of men at sea and makes the bosom swell,
   the day they've bidden beloved friends
      goodbye;
And stabs with love as tolls a distant bell
   the newly started traveller if he hears
   the sound which seems the dying day to knell.

Dante, borne aloft while dreaming, finds
himself before the gate of Purgatory and is
allowed to enter.

PURGATORY, CANTO IX

Already, from the amorous arms releas'd
   of old Tithonus, she[1] who shares his bed
   stood glimmering at her window in the east;
the sky that faced her was with gems inlaid

set in that creature's[2] shape whose blood is
  cold
and tail inflicts a blow that people dread;
and of the steps she climbs with, two, all told,
  had Night made at the spot where we then
    were,
  and the third, now, began its wings to fold;[3]
when I, who bore of Adam's load my share,
  vanquished by sleep, upon the grass reclined,
  all five[4] of us being still seated there.
About the hour which morn comes close
    behind—
  when the small swallow[5] starts her mournful
    lays,
  haply to keep her first laments in mind,
and when the soul, since more from flesh it
    strays,
  and less do thoughts the ranging fancy coop,
  as seer, almost prophetic power displays—
in dream meseemed I saw, as I looked up,
  an eagle poised on high, with plumes of gold,
  with wings wide open, and prepared to stoop;
and there meseemed I was where once of old
  abandoned were his mates by Ganymede[6]
  when rapt to where the gods high council
    hold.
I thought: 'Perchance, 'tis only here he did
  or e'er does strike: prey he might clutch
    elsewhere
  he deems, perchance, unworthy of his heed.'
Then seemed he, having wheeled a little there,
  to swoop down, awful as lightning, me his
    aim,
  and snatch me upward e'en to the fiery
    sphere.[7]
There meseemed he, and I too, was aflame:
  and so the imagined conflagration baked,
  that, broken, sleep perforce to an ending
    came.
Not otherwise, Achilles, having waked,
  did shudder, and wild glances round him dart,
  not knowing where he was or what to expect
(when him by stealth, press'd sleeping to her
    heart,
  from Chiron Scyros-wards his mother bore,
  whence the Greeks later caused him to
    depart),[8]

than shuddered I, as soon as from before
  my face sleep fled; and I turned pale, like one
  who, panic-struck, stands frozen to the core.
Beside me was my Comfort, he alone,
  the Sun already up more than two hours,
  and I now faced and on the sea looked down.
'Fear not, we have reached a point now, which
    ensures
  thy safety,' said my lord, 'and things look
    fair:
  relax not, but exert thine utmost powers.
Thou art now come to Purgatory: see where
  the rampart runs which hems it in all round;
  see—where the rock seems cleft—one enters
    there!
Before this, ere the day had passed beyond
  its dawn, and while thy inner self was laid
  asleep, down there where flowers bedeck the
    ground,
there came a lady thither, and she said:
  "I am Lucy,[9] let me lift this sleeper, so
  that I may ease his journey by my aid."
Sordello, with those noble forms below,
  remained behind: she took thee, and with day
  came upward; in her tracks I mounted too.
She laid thee here: her lovely eyes, 'twas they
  which showed me first that open entrance,
    then
  did she and sleep together pass away.'
As one who, doubting, feels assured again,
  and into confidence transmutes his fear,
  when once the truth has been to him made
    plain,
so changed was I; and, seeing me of good cheer,
  my leader moved on up the rocky steep,
  and I behind, tow'rds where the cliff rose
    sheer.
Reader, well see'st thou how my theme I keep
  exalting: therefore marvel not if I
  support it with more cunning craftsmanship.
We reached a point, as we were drawing nigh,
  from which, where there had first seemed but
    a breach
  like to a cleft a wall is parted by,
I saw a gateway, and below—by which
  to approach it—three steps, coloured
    differently,

and a gate-ward who as yet refrained from
   speech.
As more and more thereto I oped mine ee
   I saw he sat upon the topmost stair,
   such in his visage as I could not dree.
And in his hand a naked sword he bare,
   which back to us-ward so the sunbeams
      threw,
   that all my attempts to face it fruitless were.
'Speak thence: What will ye? Who escorteth
      you?'
   he began: 'Look well, lest it be your fate
   to find the ascent a risk ye'll sorely rue.'
'A lady of heaven, well knowing our estate,'
   my master answered him, 'did but just now
   say to us, "Go ye thither, there's the gate".'
'And may she speed your steps in good' was
      how
   the gatekeeper resumed with courteous mien:
   'Come to our stairs, then; for we so allow.'
There came we, and the first great stair[10] had
      been
   made of white marble, polished with such
      skill,
   that mirrored was my very self therein.
The second, coloured perse or darker still,
   was of rough stone and calcined as by heat,
   cracked through from side to side and head to
      heel.
As for the third, whose mass surmounts them,
      it,
   meseemed, was porphyry, as flaming-red
   as blood one sees a spurting vein emit.
God's angel, both feet planted on this tread,
   was sitting on the threshold: to my view
   this last of solid adamant[11] seemed made.
Over the three steps then my leader drew
   me upward with a good will, saying: 'Entreat
   him humbly now that he the lock undo.'
Devoutly I cast myself at the holy feet:
   in mercy I begged that he would let me in,
   but first upon my bosom thrice I beat.
Seven P's[12] upon my brow, the wounds of sin,
   he traced with the sword's point, and 'see that
      these
   thou wash away,' he said, 'when thou'rt
      within,'

Ashes, or earth when delved, if dry it is,
   would of one colour with his vesture be,
   and from beneath it he drew forth two keys,[13]
the one of gold, the other of silver; he
   first with the white, then with the yellow,
      wrought
   so with the gate that he contented me.
'Whene'er the wards of either key get caught
   within the lock so that it turns awry,'
   he said to us, 'this passage opens not.
Costlier the one: but the other, ere thereby
   the lock be turned, needs wisdom and great
      skill,
   for it is that which doth the knot untie.
From Piers I hold them; nor should I do ill
   he told me, if suppliants at my feet fall prone,
   rather to ope, than keep it bolted still.'
Then of that holy gate he pushed upon
   the valve, saying: 'Enter; but be warned—
      outside
   must he return whose glance is backward
      thrown.'
When on the hinges turned, as it swung wide,
   the pivots of that sacred door, which are
   of metal strong and resonantly gride,
not roared so loud, less strident was by far,
   Tarpeia,[14] when wrested from it was the good
   Metellus, and it then was left stripped bare.
I turned, alert for the first sound, and could
   hear *Te Deum laudamus*,[15] so I deemed,
   in accents blent with notes that sweetly
      flow'd.
That which I heard the like impression seemed
   to give me, as may here oft-times be got
   when, chanted to an organ, what is hymned
is at some moments heard, at others not.

*On the terrace of wrath Mark the Lombard
answers Dante's question: Why is the world
degenerating and why are the old-fashioned
virtues disappearing? Is the cause in our
stars or in our nature?*

PURGATORY, CANTO XVI, LINES 64-104.

A deep sigh, which grief forced into an 'oh',
   broke from him first: then 'Brother,' he
      began,

'the world is blind, and thence, 'tis clear,
  com'st thou.
All causes are referred by living man
  to the heav'ns alone, as did they everything
  move with themselves on some predestined
    plan.
But this, if true, would to destruction bring
  free choice, nor were it justice to requite
  good deeds with joy and ill with suffering.
The heav'ns *do* your first impulses incite;
  I say not all, but, grant it said, e'en then
  to discern good from ill ye are given light
and free will; which, though subject to great
    strain
  in its first battles with the heav'ns, in the end
  will, if well nourished, total victory gain.
Ye are, though free, by a mightier force
    constrain'd,
  by a better nature; and through this holds
    sway
  the mind in you, which the heav'ns lack
    power to bend.
Hence, if the world at present goes astray,
  in you is the cause, in you it should be sought,
  to which I'll put thee now on the right way.
Forth from His hand, who yearns to her in
    thought
  ere she exists, comes, like a little maid
  all tears and smiles, eager to play with aught,
the little simple soul, in life unread,
  save that, by her glad Maker moved, with
    zest
  she turns to that by which her joy is fed.
Of trivial good at first she tries the taste;
  thereby deceived, back to it doth she run,
  if on her love no curbing hand be placed.
Whence need of law for curb, and need of one
  skilled to discern, in kingly state aloof,
  of the true city at least the bastion.
Laws there *are*, but by what hand put to proof?
  No one's: because the leading shepherd, who
  can chew the cud, fails to divide the hoof;
Wherefore the people, seeing their guide pursue
  only that good whereof their greed is fain,
  pasture on that, and other foods eschew.
Your corrupt nature, then, is not your bane;

ill guidance—*that* is why the world hath trod
  the way of sin; see *there* the cause writ plain.

*Half way up the mountain, on the terrace of
sloth, Dante has a dream in which the
temptations of the flesh appear symbolically
before him and are routed by Conscience
and Reason.*

PURGATORY, CANTO XIX, LINES 1–33

About the hour when, vanquished by the Earth
  or whiles by Saturn, the diurnal heat
  ebbs, and the Moon is colder for its dearth—
when geomancers[1] see the sign, to wit
  their 'Greater Luck', rise in the east ere dawn
  by a path which will not long stay dark for it;
I dreamt a woman nigh to me had drawn,
  halting of speech, on feet distorted, eyes
  asquint, with hands maimed, and in colour
    wan.
I gazed at her; and as the Sun supplies
  fresh strength to cold limbs weighed down by
    the night,
  so of her tongue my look unloosed the ties
that bound it, then in brief while set upright
  her crippled frame, and dyed her pallid cheek
  the colour in which lovers most delight.
When thus unfettered was her power to speak,
  she fell to singing so, that had I willed
  to pay no heed my will had proved too weak.
'I'm,' she sang, 'I'm the sweet-voiced Siren
    skilled
  to enchant mariners in mid-ocean, so
  with pleasing magic is my utterance filled.
I turned Ulysses from his course, to go
  after my song: to me once closely bound,
  few quit me, such contentment do they know.'
Nor had her mouth yet closed upon the sound,
  when at my side a saintly dame appear'd
  with all speed her bewitchments to confound.
'O Virgil, Virgil, who is this?' I heard
  her fiercely say: and he, with eyes intent
  upon that guileless one—her only—near'd
then seized the other and her drapery rent
  in front and thereby bared her belly; me
  this wakened with the stench that from it
    went.

95

On the highest cornice of Purgatory Dante and Virgil encounter a file of penitents walking through the purging flames, which shoot forth from the side of the mountain. Dante learns that these are souls cleansing themselves of lust.

PURGATORY, CANTO XXVI

'As thus along the edge in single file
  we went, and the good master 'Profit by
  my warnings and take heed' kept saying the
    while,
the Sun, whose radiance all the western sky
  was turning now to white from palest blue,
  struck me on my right shoulder, so that I
made the flame with my shadow a ruddier hue;
  and as the shades passed by, I could perceive
  the hint, though slight, was marked by not a
    few.
'Twas this that did to them the occasion give
  for talk of me; and one to another turned,
  saying: 'Yon body seems not make-believe.'
Anon, so far as each the way discerned,
  some made tow'rds me, while always giving
    heed
  not to come out where they could not be
    burned.
'O thou who walkest—not that less thy speed,
  but, chance, from reverence—in the others'
    wake,
  reply to me athirst in this glowing gleed:
reply not needed only for my sake,
  since all these thirst therefór, as ne'er did yet
  Indian or Ethiop for cool water-break.
Tell us how comes it that thou here art set
  a wall to sunlight, as if still unmewed
  by death within the meshes of his net.'
Thus one of them addressed me—and I should
  have made me known at once, had not just
    then
  another sight my wonderment renewed.
For midmost of that path of fiery pain
  came on, encountering this, another band
  of souls that made me pause with eyes
    a-strain.
I see there all the shades on either hand
  in haste exchanging kisses, each with each,

content with brief salute, nor making stand.
Thus in their dusky troop do emmets, which
  touch each another's snout, perhaps thereby
  to enquire the way or what their luck may
    teach.
Their friendly greeting ended, instantly
  ere thence a single footstep bears them on,
  each party strives to outdo the other's cry;
'Sodom and Gomorrah'[1] shout the new folk:
  'Gone
  within the heifer is Pasiphaé'[2]
  the rest, 'that to her rut the young bull may
    run.'
Then, like to cranes which flying some might be
  to the Rhiphaeans,[3] some to the sandy waste,
  those from the frost, these from the sun to
    flee;
the one band going, the other coming, haste
  to turn with tears to their first songs again,
  and to the cry which suits them each the best;
and close beside me drew up, now as then,
  those same who had addressed to me their
    prayer,
  intent on listening, as their looks made plain.
I, who had twice seen what their wishes were,
  began: 'O souls, assured of entering
  a state of peace, come that time whensoe'er,
not left behind on earth or in their spring
  or winter are my limbs, but here with me
  these with their blood and with their joints I
    bring.
Long blind, by climbing thus I learn to see:
  I owe it to a heavenly lady's grace
  that of your world my mortal is made free.
But—so may what ye most wish soon take
    place,
  in such wise that the heaven may be your inn
  which full of love and amplest is in space—
tell me, that I may write it yet within
  my pages, who are you and who the throng
  going off behind your backs, and what their
    sin?'
Not otherwise, when first he goes among
  townsfolk, does some wild hillman, roughly
    bred,
  stand wonderstruck and, staring, hold his
    tongue,

than each soul did in the aspect it display'd;
  but once of their amazement they were quit
  (which in a noble heart is soon allay'd),
'O happy thou, who gain'st, to grow more fit
  for dying,' resumed my previous questioner,
  'experience of our coasts, and shippest it!
The folk who come not with us, used to err
  in that for which once Caesar,[4] triumphing,
  heard "Queen" against him shouted: whence
    at their
departure from us they, to feel the sting
  of self-reproof, shout "Sodom", as thou'st
    heard,
  and on the fire their shame as fuel fling.
Our own sin was hermaphrodite: we err'd,
  since beast-like we pursued the lust of sense,
  and this to keeping human law preferr'd;
therefore, to our own shame, when parting
    hence,
  we cite the name of her who bestialized
  herself within the beast-shaped wicker-fence.
Now of our deeds, and guilt, art thou apprised:
  wouldst haply know by name who we here
    are,
  time fails me, nor thereof am I advised.
Me would'st thou know, to that there is no bar;
  I'm Guido Guinicelli,[5] and purge me now,
  since I repented, when from death not far.'
As, while Lycurgus raged with grief, her two
  sons felt, to re-behold their mother's face,[6]
  felt I, to hear—though not transported so—
him name himself who fathered me, nor less
  others as well, my betters, all that e'er
  used rhymes of love with sweet and tender
    grace.
And, hearing not nor speaking, did I fare,
  deep in my thoughts and gazing long at him,
  nor, for the flames, durst I approach more
    near.
Anon, full fed with looking, my extreme
  desire I stressed to serve him every way,
  adding the oath which men most cogent
    deem.
And he to me: 'By what I hear thee say
  is left on me an imprint, stamped so clear,
  that Lethe cannot rase nor turn it grey.
But if the oath thou sworest was sincere,

pray tell me what it is that makes me think,
  judging by word and look, thou hold'st me
    dear?'
I answered: ' 'Tis the words with words you link
  so sweetly, which will still, if nothing breach
  the modern use, endear their very ink.'
'O brother,' he replied, 'yon spirit which
  I point to'—and he showed me one ahead—
  'forged with yet greater skill his mother-
    speech.
Of prose-romancers and love-poets he led
  the field, and quite outdistances the bard
  named "of Limoges",[7] whatever fools have
    said.
Rumour it is, not truth, that they regard;
  fixed in their own opinions, they disown
  reason and art, which speak but are not
    heard.
Thus, in old times, did many with Guittón,[8]
  praising but him, from mouth to mouth, till
    now
  truth, with most minds, has come into its
    own.
But, if so highly privileged art thou
  that thou may'st to the cloister go, wherein
  Christ is the college-abbot, prithee vow
to say me there a paternoster, in
  so far as we of this world need such aid,
  where 'tis no more within our power to sin.'
Then, haply, to leave others room who made
  their way close by, he vanished through the
    fire,
  like fish that, diving, in deep water fade.
To the soul shown me I drew a little nigher,
  and said my wish to know his name was well
  arraying a place for it, and none was higher.
And he[9] without reserve took up his tale:
  'Swich[10] is my plesure in youre curteis[10] ple,[10]
  that I ne can ne will my name concele.
Ich am Arnaut, who wepynge, syngynge se[11]
  in mynde past folie and, bifore me playne,
  with joye se my longe soght felicite.
Now, preie you, by that power whiche not in
    vayn
  up this high montaigne-staire hath lad you
    sure,
  bethynke you in due sesoun of my payne!'

Then hid he in the fire that makes them pure.

*At the end of the long climb Dante has a
dream in which Leah, symbolizing perhaps
the active life of innocence, appears to him.
He wakes to find himself in the Earthly
Paradise, which Virgil encourages him to
explore.*

PURGATORY, CANTO XXVII, LINES 94-142
AND CANTO XXVIII, LINES 1-42

About the hour, I think, when from the East
  by Cytherea's first rays, who seems to flame
  with ever-burning love, the mount was kiss'd,
I dreamt I saw a young and lovely dame
  who, culling blossoms, through a meadow
    went,
  and from her, as she sang, these words there
    came:
'Whoso should ask my name I would acquaint
  that I am Leah;[1] to make me a wreath with
    these
  my lovely busy hands is my intent.
I deck me here at the glass, myself to please:
  but from her mirror at no time will rise
  my sister Rachel: here all day she is.
She is as fain to see with her fair eyes
  as I to deck me with my hands am drawn:
  her seeing, and *me* working, satisfies.'
Now through the splendours that precede the
    dawn,
  whose rise wayfarers the more gladly greet
  as, homing, lodge they a stage farther on,
the dark was fleeing on all sides, and with it
  fled sleep from me; whence to my feet I rose,
  seeing the great masters risen to their feet.
'That sweet fruit, which the care of mortals
    goes
  in search of along branches numberless,
  today shall set at rest thy hunger-throes.'
With words like these did Virgil's voice address
  itself tow'rds me; and never Easter-gift
  was there to match them for delightfulness.
So much I longed, and longed again, to lift
  me heavenward, that thereafter I was ware
  how to each step my pinions grew more swift.
When, quickly scaled, beneath us the whole

stair
  now lay, and on the topmost step we stood,
  on me did Virgil fix his eyes, and there
thus spake: 'My son, the temporal thou hast
    view'd
  and the eternal fire, and reached a place
  where vision of mine no farther may intrude.
I've drawn thee here with judgment and
    address;
  from now on let thy pleasure guide thee:
    forth
  from the steep ways thou art, the strait no
    less.
See there the Sun shine, fronting thee, the earth
  gay with young grass and flowers and
    springing trees,
  to which the soil here, of itself, gives birth.
While the fair eyes are coming, now at ease,
  which, weeping, made me come to thee, 'tis
    thine
  to sit and thine to wander among these.
Expect no longer word from me, nor sign:
  thy will could not be sounder, freër,
    uprighter;
  'twere wrong to do not as its hests enjoin;
thee o'er thyself I therefore crown and mitre.'

Eager forthwith to enter and survey
  the divine forest, quick with foliage, meet
  for tempering to the eye the new-born day,
I lingered not, but making haste to quit
  the edge, I took the plain by slow degrees
  o'er soil that from all sides was smelling
    sweet.
A soft air, having no inconstancies
  within itself, was smiting on my brow
  but no more roughly than a gentle breeze;
wherewith in tremulous accord each bough
  was thither bending where the sacred hill
  casts its first shadow on the world below;
yet not so far deflected, but that still
  the little birds upon the topmost sprays
  could without pausing ply their varied skill;
which with their song were welcoming the day's
  first hours exultantly among the leaves,
  that kept a burden to their roundelays,
such as from branch to branch the ear perceives

gathering among the pines on Chiassi's shore,
when Aeolus freedom to Scirocco gives.
By now my feet, tho' slow, had paced the floor
of that primeval wood so far, that I
to whence I'd entered could look back no
more,
and lo! my farther going was halted by
a stream, which leftward with its ripples
plied
the herbage that upon its bank grew high.
All waters here, e'en the most purified,
would from some mixture fail to seem
immune,
compared with that one, which doth nothing
hide
though dark its movement, very dark, in tune
with the perpetual shade, which ne'er to cast
one ray allows the Sun there, nor the Moon.
I stayed my feet, but with my eyes I passed
beyond the brook, so as to let them dwell
on the may-boughs in daedal verdure
massed;
and, there, to me appeared, as things may well
suddenly appear, that for sheer wonderment
all other thinking from the mind dispel,
a lady,[2] quite alone, who onward went
singing, and choosing blossoms, flower from
flower,
which all along her way their colours blent....

*Dante meets Beatrice, who reproaches him
and invites him to defend himself.*

PURGATORY, CANTO XXX, LINES 22-154
AND CANTO XXXI, LINES 1-91

I've see ere now, as the dawn brighter grew,
the eastern parts all rosy, and elsewhere
the heaven arrayed in a deep, tranquil blue,
and the Sun's face come forth, the misty air
his beams so tempering, that the visual
powers
found them, a long while, not too bright to
bear;
unto me thus, within a cloud of flowers,
which, by angelic hands tossed upward, came
falling back on, and round, the car in
showers,

wreathed, o'er a white veil, with an olive stem
a lady appeared, under a cloak of green
apparelled in the hue of living flame.
Straightway my spirit—which so long had been
free from the crushing stupor that, before,
would make it tremble in her presence—e'en
tho' the eyes revealed but thus much and no
more,
through hidden virtue which from her flowed
out,
of by-gone love now felt the o'ermastering
power.
So soon as that exalted virtue smote
my vision, which already, ere I was done
with boyhood's days, had caught me by the
throat,
I turned me leftward, as a child will run
to its mummy trustfully, when 'tis its aim
to escape some fear or grief it fain would
shun,
intent on saying to Virgil: 'Barely a drachm
of blood that trembles not is left me still:
I recognize the signs of the ancient flame';
but Virgil had forsaken us, my leal
companion: Virgil, sweetest father; he,
Virgil, to whom I gave me for my weal;
nor to my cheeks, dew-cleansed, could all that
she,
man's ancient mother, lost, avail that they
should not with tears once more polluted be.
'Dante, for all that Virgil goes his way,
not yet, weep thou not yet; for needs must
thou
weep when thou feel'st another sword in
play.'
Like to an admiral who on poop or prow
comes to inspect and hearten crews on board
of other ships, that they their best may do;
at the car's left-hand rim—when to the word
I turned which is my own name, and which
here
only because I must do I record—
I saw the lady, seen of me whilere
veiled 'neath the angelic festival, had stay'd
her eyes on me this side the barrier,
albeit the veil descending from her head,
encircled with Minerva's leaf, remain'd

such that her face and form were not
  display'd.
In queenly wise still haughty, yet she deign'd
  to speak on, like to one who does not cease
  from words, but keeps her warmest for the
  end:
'Look at me well! Yes I'm, yes I'm Beatrice!
  How durst thou approach the mountain?
  Didst, then, thou
  not know that here man finds himself in
  bliss?'
I dropped my eyes to the clear fount below,
  but, seeing myself therein, drew them anon
  to the green turf, such shame oppressed my
  brow.
Harsh as is deemed the mother by the son
  I deemed her; for the taste of love when blent
  with sternness takes a tang of tartness on.
She ceased; and the angels sang incontinent
  'In te, Domine, speravi', but their song
  no farther than to pedes meos went.[1]
Like snow, that mid the living beams along
  Italy's spine congeals, as drives and packs
  it tight the bora, when its blast is strong,
then, melting, if but breathes the land that lacks
  a shadow, and trickling through itself,
  appears
as 'twere a candle which the fire attacks:
even so was I devoid of sighs and tears
  ere they began to sing whose notes always
  echo their notes who roll the eternal spheres;
but instantly, when in their dulcet lays
  I heard their pity for me, more than if they
  had asked her: 'Lady, wherefore such
  dispraise?'
the ice that clamped my heart, without more
  stay
  turning to breath and water, from my breast
  through mouth and eyes with anguish forced
  its way.
She, on the same side of the car still placed,
  stood moveless, and thereafter her discourse
  to the compassionate spirits thus address'd:
'Ye, where the day eternal hath its source
  keep watch, so that from you nor sleep nor
  night
  can steal one step of the ages in their course;

hence with more care I pick my words to indict
  him who on yon bank weeps disconsolate,
  that fault with sorrow may be matched
  aright.
Not only through the working of the great
  wheels which direct each seed to a destined
  end
  according to the stars that with it mate,
but through largess of graces which descend
  rained down by God from clouds enskied so
  high,
  that never mortal sight thereto attain'd,
this man in his new life potentially
  was such that each right habit would have
  wrought
  in him a wondrous harvest by and by.
But all the more malign and rank a plot
  of ground becomes with bad seed and
  untill'd,
  the more good earthy vigour it hath got,
Awhile my face was both his strength and
  shield:
  and, showing him my youthful eyes, I led
  him with me, in the right direction held.
So soon as of my second age I made
  to cross the threshold and changed life, he
  then
  abandoned me and after others stray'd.
When I had risen from flesh to spirit, and when
  my beauty and virtue had increased, not more
  but less he loved them, less thereof was fain.
And ways not true he turned his steps to
  explore,
  phantoms of good pursuing that were lies,
  such as no promise of fulfilment bore.
Nor helped it that in dreams and otherwise,
  conveyed through inspirations sought by
  prayer,
  I called him back: such did he little prize.
So low he fell, that insufficient were
  by then all means of saving him, except
  to show him those who of being saved
  despair.
For this I visited the portal kept
  for the dead, and his guide up hither not
  unheedful of my prayer was, when I wept.
God's high degree were to derision brought,

if Lethe should be crossed and viand so
delicious tasted without any scot
of penitence which may cause tears to flow.'

'Ho! thou yon-side the sacred rivulet'—
turning her discourse with its point tow'rds
me,
sharp tho' I'd found it when but edgeways
set—
she thus resumed, continuing instantly:
'Say, say, is 't true? For with so grave a
charge
'tis meet thy own confession should agree.'
So baffled was my power, that to the marge
of utterance rose my voice, but then died
down,
ere from its organs it was set at large.
Whiles she forbore, then cried: 'Why silent?
Own
thy guilt; for by the water in no wise
have thy sad memories yet been overthrown.'
Fear and confusion, miserable allies,
forced from my mouth a 'yes', but breathed
so low,
that to perceive it there was need of eyes.
As an arblast that snaps both string and bow,
when it goes off from being too tightly
drawn,
and the bolt hits the mark with feebler blow,
thus I, by that sore burden weighed upon,
broke down, outpouring sighs and tears,
which drown'd
my voice so, that it barely a passage won.
Whence she: ' 'Mongst those desires that had
their ground
in me, and led thee onto love the Good
which to all aspiration sets a bound,
what crossed thy way that forced thee to
denude
thyself of hope of pressing still ahead?
what pits or what chains sapped thy
fortitude?
And, what advantages, what charms display'd
upon the face of the others, lured thine eye,
that unto *them* thy court was to be paid?'
After the heaving of one bitter sigh
scarcely my voice found utterance, and my

lips
with difficulty framed words to make reply.
Weeping, I said: 'The present world that steeps
things in a false light turned my steps aside,
when once your countenance was in eclipse.'
And she: 'Hadst thou kept silent or denied
what thou confessest, not less fully known,
thy fault were: 'tis by such a judge descried.
But when there breaks forth from the sinner's
own
mouth his self-accusation, in our court
turns counter to the edge the grinding-stone.
Howbeit, that with thine error now comport
thy shame, and that in future, if thou hear
the Sirens, thou behave in manlier sort,
put by the seed of weeping, and give ear:
so shalt thou learn how contrary was in
worth
the course my buried flesh should have made
thee steer.
Nought to which art or nature e'er gave birth
so pleased thee as did the fair limbs wherein
I
was prisoned—limbs resolved now into
earth;
and if that, through my death, the sovereign joy
thus failed thee, how should mortal things so
much
have lured thee that thou wert bewitched
thereby?
Thou shouldst in sooth, when stung by the first
touch
of perishable things, have soared aloft
after myself who was no longer such.
Nor should thy wings have drooped, to wait
with soft
compliance for more blows from some light
girl
or vain thing else, no sooner donned than
doff'd.
The young bird waits, when first his plumes
uncurl,
for two or three; but before those full-fledged
in vain ye spread the net, the missile hurl.'
As children, after hearing some keen-edged
reproof, stand dumb, ashamed, with eyes
downcast,

owning with sorrow to the fault alleged,
even so stood I; and she: 'If cause thou hast
   to grieve through hearing, do but lift thy
     beard
   and greater grief through looking shalt thou
     taste.'
With less resistance, when 'tis blowing hard
   in Europe or the land Iarbas sway'd,
   uproots itself an oak tree, stoutly rear'd,
than I my chin then lifted, as she bade;
   and when by 'beard' she asked for visage,
     there
   well did I note the venom in what she said.
And when my countenance was all laid bare,
   that now those first-created substances[2]
   had ceased from scattering flowers, my sight
     was ware;
and then my eyes, still little at their ease,
   saw Beatrice turned tow'rds the Creature[3]—
     him
   who in two natures one sole person is.
Tho' veiled and on the far side of the stream,
   to excel her former self, yea, even more
   than here she excelled all others, did she
     seem.
Thereat remorse with nettle-sting so sore
   my conscience pricked, that aught else which
     to its love
   most wrenched me, that the most did I abhor.
So deep within me self-conviction drove
   its barb, that I fell conquered: and my last
   state she alone knows who was cause thereof.

PARADISO (PARADISE)

Dante the wayfarer stands with Beatrice in
the Earthly Paradise; Dante the author
arms himself for his great task, the depic-
tion of Heaven itself.

PARADISE, CANTO I

His glory, in whose being all things move,
   pervades Creation and, here more there less
   resplendent, shines in every part thereof.
Within the heaven[1] his brightest beams caress
   was I, and things beheld which none
     returning

to earth hath power or knowledge to express;
   because, when near the object of its yearning,
   our understanding is for truths made strong,
   which memory is too feeble for relearning.
Yet of the realm that saints and angels throng
   so much as I could treasure up in mind
   shall now be made the matter of my song.
Apollo,[2] to my crowning task be kind;
   make me thy chosen vessel, round whose
     brow
   thy darling bay might fitly be entwined.
So far with one Parnassian peak[3] hast thou
   met all my needs: but I require the twain,
   to dare the arena that awaits me now.
Enter my breast in such a mood as when
   thou from the scabbard of his limbs didst tear
   forth Marsyas;[4] breathe in me that matchless
     strain.
O power divine, let me but so far share
   thyself, that I, dim memory though it be,
   the blessèd kingdom may in words declare,
and thou shalt see me come to thy loved tree
   and crown myself with laurel, then indeed
   made fit to wear it by my theme and thee.
For Caesar's triumph or for poet's meed
   so seldom is it gathered,[5] mighty sire,
   (woe worth the sordid ends of human greed)
that the Peneian frondage[6] should inspire
   with gladness the glad Delphic deity,[7]
   whene'er in any man it wakes desire.
From tiny spark a flame may leap full high:
   haply some bard, praying in worthier wise,
   may after me from Cirrha[8] win reply.
Through divers openings dawns on mortal eyes
   the world's bright lamp; but that we see
     display
   four circles with three crosses joined, supplies
his beams with happier course, wherein, with
     ray
   of happier star conjoined, he mouldeth fair
   the mundane wax more after his own way.[9]
This point, or near it, had caused morning
     there,[10]
   here eve: and all of half the heavens were
     white
   on that side, and on this all darkling were,
when I saw Beatrice, with visage bright

turned leftward, gazing full upon the Sun:
  eagle thereon so never fixed his sight.
As from the first the second ray will run
  and upward re-ascend, like traveller fain
  to turn home, when his outward voyage is
    done,
so to her gesture, through the eyesight ta'en
  into my fancy, was my own inclined,
  and I gazed Sunward, past the wont of men.
There much is granted, which our senses find
  denied them here, through virtue of the spot
  fashioned of old expressly for mankind.
So long I gazed—tho' long I bore it not—
  as to perceive him sparkling all around,
  like iron which from the furnace flows
    white-hot;
and suddenly the light of day I found
  increased twofold, as though the Omnipotent
  the heaven with a second Sun had crown'd.
Stood Beatrice with gaze still wholly bent
  upon the eternal wheels; and I on her
  fixed mine, withdrawn now from the
    firmament.
So gazing did I feel in me the stir
  that Glaucus[11] felt, when he consumed of
    yore
  the grass which made him as the sea-gods
    were.
Since words may tell not what it means to
    outsoar
  the human, let the example satisfy
  him for whom grace hath fuller proof in store.
O Love, the lord of heaven, if nought was I
  of self save what in man[12] thou new-createst
  thou know'st, who with thy light didst raise
    me on high.
Whenas the wheel[13] which thou for aye rotatest
  by being desired thereof, had charmed my ear
  with tones which thou, its tuner, modulatest,
I saw such vast fields of the atmosphere
  lit by the Solar flame, that neither flood
  nor deluge ever formed so wide a mere.
The unwonted sound, the light's great
    magnitude
  such craving roused in me to realise
  their cause, as ne'er till then had fired my
    blood.

Then she, who saw me as with my own eyes,
  opened her mouth to calm my troubled mind,
  ere I to frame a question, and thuswise
began: 'Thine own false fancies make thee
    blind;
  hence unperceived are things thou wouldst
    perceive,
  hadst thou but left thy vain conceits behind.
Thou'rt not on Earth still, as thou dost believe;
  but lightning, fleeing its proper home, ne'er
    tore
  as thou art thine now rushing to retrieve.'
Stript of my first doubt by the dulcet lore
  instilled thus briefly by my smiling guide,
  yet in new doubt was I enmeshed the more,
and said: 'Awhile I rested, satisfied,
  from my great wonder; but I marvel yet,
  how up through these light bodies I can
    glide.'
My question with a pitying sigh she met,
  then eyed me with a mother's anxious care
  for child whose brain delirious dreams beset,
and began thuswise: 'All things whatso'er
  have order among themselves, and this
    indeed
  is form, which makes the World God's image
    bear.
Herein do the higher beings the impress read
  of that eternal Worth, which is the end
  whereto the aforesaid rule has been decreed.
In this same order ranked, all natures bend
  their several ways, through divers lots, as
    near
  and farther from the source whence all
    descend;
thus onward unto divers ports they steer
  through the great sea of being, each impell'd
  by instinct, given to make it persevere.
This tow'rd the Moon keeps blazing fire upheld;
  this is in mortal hearts what makes them
    move;
  this doth the Earth into one structure weld:
nor only creatures void of reason prove
  this bow's impelling force, but every soul
  that is endowed with the intellect and love.
The providence, which rules this ordered whole,
  keeps making ever tranquil with its light

the heaven wherein the swiftest sphere doth
   roll;
and thither, as to pre-appointed site,
   that bow-string which doth all its arrows
      shoot
   at happy mark, now speeds us by its might.
'Tis true that, as a form will oft ill-suit
   with the result which art would fain effect,
   the stuff being deaf, hence unresponsive to it,
so from this course the creature may deflect
   itself at whiles; for, though thus urged on
      high,
   its power to swerve aside remains uncheck'd
(even as fire may oft be seen to fly
   down from a cloud), should the first impulse
      bring
   it Earthward, by false pleasure wrenched
      awry.
If I deem right, thou shouldst be wondering
   no more at thine ascent, that at a rill
   for rushing downward from its mountain-
      spring.
Marvel it were in thee, if, with a will
   unhindered, thou hadst hugged a lower
      plane,
   as in quick fire on earth, if it kept still.'
Therewith she turned her face to heaven again.

*In the sphere of the moon Dante learns
from a nun the basic truth of Heaven and
its hierarchy.*

PARADISE, CANTO III, LINES 37-108

'O spirit born for bliss, who in the sun
   of life eternal dost the sweetness try
   which, save by taste, is understood of none,
'twould please me well if thou wouldst satisfy
   my wish to know thy name and your estate.'
   Whence she with laughing eyes made prompt
      reply:
'To rightful wish our love unlocks the gate
   freely as His doth, whose own graciousness
   he wills that all his courtiers imitate.
On earth I was a virgin-votaress;
   and if thou search thy memory 'twill be clear
   to thee despite my greater loveliness
that thou behold'st Piccarda,[1] stationed here

among these other blessèd ones, and blest
   myself too in the slowest-moving sphere.
Our hearts, aflame with joy, which draws its
      zest
   from the Holy Ghost alone, are glad to be
   formed to his order, here where we are
      placed.
And giv'n us is this station, seemingly
   so low, because our vows, since we had paid
   less than we vow'd, were void to some degree.'
Whence I to her: 'Your faces, thus array'd,
   glow with I know not what of heavenly sheen,
   making one's former notions of you fade:
hence was my recollection not so keen;
   but now thy words awake old memories,
   so that more clearly I reshape thy mien.
But tell me, ye who tarry here in bliss,
   would ye not fain ascend to regions higher,
   to see more and make more friends than in
      this?'
All smiled at first to hear me thus inquire;
   then with such radiant gladness she replied,
   methought her burning in love's primal fire:
'Brother, our will is wholly pacified
   by virtue of love, which makes us will alone
   what we possess, and thirst for nought beside.
Wished we to make a loftier seat our own,
   our wish discordant with His will would be,
   who hath assigned this planet for our throne;
the which these orbs admit not, as thou'lt see,
   if here to be in love must needs befall,
   and thou regard love's nature carefully.
Nay, 'tis essential to the being we call
   blest, that it should the will of God fulfil,
   so making one the very wills of all:
therefore, our being thus, from sill to sill
   this whole realm through, alike the realm
      doth please
   and Ruler who in-wills us to his will.
And solely in his will exists our peace;
   it is that ocean whither all things fare
   which it creates and nature bids increase.'
Thus learned I how in heaven everywhere
   is Paradise, albeit the highest good
   sheds not its grace in one sole measure there.
But as may be if, sated with one food
   and greedy for another, we have pled

for this, declining that with gratitude,
such was my gesture, such the words I said,
  to learn from her what web it was
    wherethrough
  she had not drawn the shuttle to the head.
'Shines higher enskied,' quoth she, 'as guerdon
    due
  to perfect life and high desert, a dame²
  whose rule on earth girls, robed and veiled,
    pursue,
that so till death, both day and night the same,
  they may attend that Spouse who will reject
  no vows, if love to his will conformeth them.
Shunning the world, did I in youth elect
  to follow her; and, in her habit wrapt,
  I pledged me to the pathway of her sect.
Thereafter men, for ill than good more apt,
  forth snatched me from the cloister's peaceful
    ways;
  and God knows on what later life I happ'd.

*The poet, entering the fourth sphere, in-
vites his readers to reflect on the wonderful
order of the cosmos.*

PARADISE, CANTO X, LINES 1-99

The ineffable and uncreated Worth¹
  gazing with Love upon his Son's dear face—
  the Love that each eternally breathes forth,
hath all things that revolve in mind and place
  with so much order made, that none can view
  his works and taste not of his graciousness.
Raise, then, thy vision, Reader, as I do,
  unto the lofty wheels,² straight to that part
  where the one motion strikes the other
    through;³
and there with joy begin to admire the art
  of Him whose eye is never turned aside
  from masterpiece framed after his own heart.
See how the circle⁴ where the planets glide
  thence branches off obliquely, with the intent
  that Earth, which calls them, may be satisfied.
And had their pathway not been thus-wise bent,
  vain were much heavenly virtue and well nigh
  all potencies down here would pine and faint;
and were it farther or less far to lie
  out of the straight, in either hemisphere

grave loss of order would be caused thereby.
Now, Reader, in the banquet persevere,
  reflecting on this foretaste of the meat,
  if, unfatigued, you would enjoy good cheer.
I've set the board: henceforth 'tis yours to eat;
  since all the care I lavish on my rhyme
  is claimed now by the theme whereof I treat.
Of nature's servants, he,⁵ the most sublime,
  who stamps with heavenly worth the
    mundane clay
  and gives us light as means to measure time,
conjoined with that part⁶ thou hast heard me
    say,
  circled the spirals wherein earlier
  his orb presents itself from day to day;⁷
and I was with him; yet no more aware
  of my ascension, than a man may know
  the thought within his brain before it's there.
'Tis Beatrice, 'tis she who guideth so
  from good to better by such instant flight,
  that, to record it, time is far too slow.
How needs must that have been itself most
    bright,
  which in the Sun, whose orb I entered, shone
  distinguished, not by colour, but by light!
Art, wit, experience—none, though called upon,
  could aid me paint it for the fancy's eye;
  yet men may trust and yearn to gaze thereon.
Nor wonder if such heights should prove too
    high
  to be imagined; since none ever met
  the Sun's full blaze who was not quelled
    thereby.
Thus shines the exalted Sire's fourth
    household,⁸ set
  in that bright heaven, to whom for endless
    bliss
  he shows how he doth breathe and how beget.
'To him, the angels' Sun, who unto this,
  the visible Sun, hath raised thee by his grace,
  give thanks, give thanks,' commanded
    Beatrice.
Never was mortal so disposed to place
  his mind on God, and none surrendered e'er
  his heart to God with so much willingness,
as I did, when I heard that call to prayer;
  and so on Him was all my longing stayed,

that Beatrice, eclipsed, seemed no more there.
No whit displeased, she laughed, and laughter
      made
  her eyes so glorious, that my mind compelled
  to quit one object, was distributed
mid many dazzling lights I now beheld
  forming a halo, which encircled us
  with radiance, by their song alone excelled.
The daughter of Latona[9] cinctured thus
  we see at times, when vapour fills the sky
  and makes her girdle's texture luminous.
In the celestial court, where once was I,
  are many jewels so precious, that in vain
  one seeks to pluck them from the Realm on
    high;
and of their number was that heavenly strain:
  who thither soars not on the wings of
    yearning
  may of a dumb man news from thence obtain.
When, chanting thus melodiously, those
    burning
  suns had wheeled thrice about us where we
    stood—
  like stars which round the steady poles keep
    turning,
ladies they seemed, for dancing still in mood,
  who pause in silence at the measure's close,
  listening, till they have caught the strain
    renew'd.
And, from the depth of one, these accents rose:
  'In that the beam of grace, which lights and
    tends
  true love and then, by dint of loving, grows,
multiplied now in thee, so far resplends,
  that it conducts thee upward by that stair,
  which save to re-ascend it none descends,
whoso refused thee, for thy thirst, a share
  of wine from his own vial were no more free
  than water is which doth not seaward fare.
Fain wouldst thou know what blossoms these
    may be,
  engarlanding and with such joy surveying
  the fair dame, who for heaven doth
    strengthen thee.
I was a lamb of the holy flock, obeying
  that Dominic,[10] who hath a pathway shown,
  where is good fattening, if there be no

straying.
My brother and my master, of Cologne:
  neighbours me on my right: Albert[11] his
    name,
  and Thomas, called Aquinas,[12] is my
    own. . . ."

*Saint Thomas tells of the life of Saint
Francis of Assisi.*

PARADISE, CANTO XI, LINES 43-117

'. . . 'Twixt the Tupino and the brook descending
  the blessèd Ubald's chosen hill one sees
  a fruitful slope from a high mount depending,
whence on Perugia's Porta Sol the breeze
  blows hot and cold; rearward her irksome
    sway
  makes Nócera with Gualdo ill at ease.[1]
From this same slope, just where it breaks away
  most gently, to the world was born a Sun,
  as this from Ganges on the timeful day.
Therefore, whene'er the place is named, let none
  call it "Ascesi"[2]—word of meagre sense;
  but "the East" should its title rightly run.
For there he rose, nor far had travelled thence,
  ere he began imparting to mankind
  some comfort from his mighty influence.
Mere boy, and to his father's anger blind,
  he wooed a dame, to whom none opes the
    door
  with pleasure or to death is less inclined,
but he, full fain, his bishop's court before
  et coram patre[3] took her for his own;
  thereafter day by day he loved her more.
Bereaved of her first husband, scorned,
    unknown,
  more than a thousand and an hundred years
  she lived unwooed, till sought by him alone.
In vain the story that she felt no fears,
  but with Amyclas[4] unperturbed had stood,
  when the world-shaker's voice assailed her
    ears;
in vain the loyal, the matchless fortitude
  with which, while even Mary stayed below,
  she wept with Christ upon the very rood.
But lest too little of my meaning show,
  Francis and Poverty henceforward take

at large for this fond pair and call them so.
Their concord and glad looks availed to make
    love, wonderment and contemplation sweet
    cause holy thoughts to blossom in their wake.
The venerable Bernard[5] bared his feet
    first, and ran after peace so great with speed
    he deemed o'erslow, yet was his footing fleet.
Oh unimagined wealth, oh fruitful seed!
    Giles[5] bares his feet, his feet Silvester[5] bares,
    following, for such a bride, the bridegroom's
    lead.
Thenceforth that lord and father onward fares
    with his dear lady and that household, now
    bound with the cord, which each so humbly
    wears.
Nor did a sense of shame weigh down his brow,
    that he was Peter Bernardone's son,
    and was, to look at, passing mean and low;
but he revealed, as might a king have done,
    his stern resolve to Innocent,[6] who granted
    its first seal to his order thus begun.
As multiplied the humble souls that wanted
    to follow one, whose marvelous life were
    theme
    in the empyrean heaven more fitly chanted,
the eternal Spirit made Honorius[7] deem
    the moment wise to crown yet once again
    this archimandrite's consecrated scheme.
Next in the Soldan's haughty presence, fain
    of martyrdom, behold him, dauntless stand,
    preaching of Christ and those, his saintly
    train;[8]
but, loth to waste his labours on a land
    unripe for harvest, he returned to reap
    the Italian crop now ready for his hand,
then took from Christ upon the rocky steep,[9]
    'twixt Arno reared and Tiber, his last seal—
    marks that his limbs were two whole years to
    keep.
When he who chose him for so great a weal
    was pleased at length to raise him to the
    height
    which he had earned by his self-humbling
    zeal,
unto his brethren, as to heirs by right,
    he recommended his own lady dear
    and bade each love her as her faithful knight;

and from her bosom to its kingly sphere
    on high his glorious spirit willed to flee,
    and for his corpse would brook no other
    bier. . . .'[10]

*In the heaven of Mars Dante sees a great
cross in which sparkle myriads of moving
lights; he hears triumphal music and waits,
enraptured, for what is to come.*

PARADISE, CANTO XV

Goodwill that issues as it ever must
    from all true love, even as base desire
    resolves itself into the will unjust,
silence imposed on that melodious lyre,
    and hushed the sacred chords, now loose, now
    taut,
    as heaven's right hand which tunes them may
    require.
How should those glorious spirits hearken not
    to righteous prayers, who, to will me to pray,
    were thus with one accord to silence brought?
Well may he mourn for ever and for aye
    who, for the love of thing which hath nowise
    eternal value, casts that love away.
As through the pure and tranquil evening skies
    there shoots at times a sudden trail of light,
    stirring to movement the late listless eyes,
which well might be a star that takes to flight,
    save that from where it first was kindled none
    is missing, and it quickly fades from sight,
so from the horn which to the right doth run
    darting adown that cross to its foot there
    came
    a star, of those that cluster bright thereon.
Nor parted from its riband was the gem,
    but, like to fire in alabaster, sped
    along the radial shaft its eager flame.
With equal love reached forth Anchises' shade,
    if worthy of credit be our greatest *musa*,
    on seeing his son in the Elysian glade.[1]
'*O sanguis meus, O superinfusa
    gratia Dei, sicut tibi cui
    bis umquam coeli ianua reclusa?*'[2]
The light thus, so on it I fixed mine eye
    then turned, my lady's face to scrutinize,
    and on both sides was awestruck equally;

for such a smile was blazing in her eyes
  methought that mine had touched the deepest
    ground
  both of my grace and of my paradise.
Then, glad alike in aspect and in sound,
  that spirit spake such further things as I
  could understand not, they were too
    profound;
not did it veil its thought deliberately,
  but could no other, for its argument
  soared, for the mark of mortal minds, too
    high.
But when the bow, by warm affection bent,
  was so far slackened that its utterance now
  within our mental range had made descent,
the first I understood was: 'Blest be thou,
  threefold and one,[3] who graciously art
    pleased
  unto my seed such courtesy to show!'
And it pursued: 'My son, thou hast appeased
  in him thou hearest speaking from this light
  a dear, long-cherished thirst, which on me
    seized
when reading in the mighty tome, where white
  and dusky never change—and all by grace
  of her who fledged thee for thy lofty flight.
Thou deemest that to me thy thought doth pass
  from primal thought, as "one," if rightly
    known,
  is of both "five" and "six" the starting-place;[4]
hence askest not my name, nor to be shown
  why in this gladsome concourse of the blest
  the joy of none seems equal to my own.
Thou deemest rightly; for both mightiest
  and humblest here into the mirror gaze
  where thou, ere thinking, hast thy thought
    express'd.
But, that the sacred love which keeps always
  my vision watchful, causing me to pine
  with sweet desire, may yet more brightly
    blaze,
securely, frankly, blithely be it thine
  to voice the will, voice the desire whereto
  my answer stands decreed by will divine!'
I turned to Beatrice, and she foreknew
  my thought ere uttered, and a smile bestowed
  whereby the wings of my volition grew.

Then I began: 'So soon as ye abode
  within the First Equality, your wit
  shone in like measure as your feeling
    glowed;[5]
because the Sun by whom ye are warmed and
    lit,
  with light and warmth so equally doth glow,
  that all similitudes fall short of it.
But in mankind—and well the cause ye know—
  wish and the means to give that wish effect
  have pinions which diversely plumaged grow.
I too by this disparity am check'd,
  as man: hence for thy fatherly accost
  no other thanks than of the heart expect.
I implore thee, living topaz-stone that dost
  ingem this precious jewel, satisfy
  me with thy name: 'tis that I long for most.'
'O leaf of mine, in whom well-pleased was I
  while but awaiting thee, I was thy stem':
  such was the preface to its prompt reply.
Then it said: 'He[6] that gave thy clan its name,
  who after more than five-score years doth yet
  toil round the mount's first cornice[7]—even
    the same
my son was, and thy grandsire did beget:
  well may thy prayers, as it is meet they
    should,
  the long term of his weariness abate.
Florence within her old enclosure stood,
  whence tierce and nones she still hears daily
    tolled,
  and dwelt in peace, sober and chaste and
    good.
No bracelet did she have, no crown of gold,
  no highly-broidered gowns, no girdle in hue
  more striking than its wearer to behold.
No father yet found reason to beshrew
  a daughter's birth; for dower and age to wed
  'scaped not, on either hand, the measure due.[8]
No houses then stood uninhabited;
  no Sardanapálus[9] yet was come to show
  what gallant hearts by chambering are bred.
Nor yet defeat did Montemalo know
  by your Uccellatoi'—to be acquainted,
  swift tho' it rise, with swifter overthrow.[10]
Bellinción Berti[11] saw I pass, contented
  with belt of bone and leather, and his dame

leaving the mirror with her face unpainted;
saw Nerli's[11] lord and Vecchio's,[11] chiefs of
    fame,
    content with plain buff coats, their wives
      withal
    of handling flax and distaff think no shame.
Oh happy they! Each sure of burial
    in her own tomb, none fated yet to lie
    deserted in her bed at Frenchman's call.[12]
One, o'er the cradle, crooned a lullaby,
    using the idiom which in every home
    fathers and mothers first delight to employ;
another to the youngsters bidden come
    and gather round her spinning-wheel would
      tell
    tales of the Trojans, Fiesole and Rome.
Cornelia and Cincinnatus[13] might as well
    be found among you now, as then had been
    such as Cianghella and Lapo Salterel.
Me to a life so lovely, so serene,
    of fellowship with citizens so staid,
    a hostelry so good to sojourn in,
did Mary give, when loudly called to aid;
    and, in your ancient Baptistery, there
    was I both Christ's and Cacciaguida made.
Moronto and Eliséo my brothers were:
    my wife I took me from the vale of Po;
    and thence the surname comes which thou
      dost bear.
Anon with the emperor Conrad[14] did I go
    crusading; and in time he dubbed me knight,
    my gallant deeds of arms had pleased him so.
With him I fought that law's nefarious might
    whose people, by the pastors' fault, the place
    have long usurped which should be yours by
      right.
There was I at the hands of that foul race
    dismantled of the world's deceitful shows,
    the love of which doth many a soul debase;
and came from martyrdom to this repose.'

*Cacciaguida predicts Dante's future and
offers consolation and counsel.*

PARADISE, CANTO XVII, LINES 46-135

'As his stepmother's wiles and cruelty
    from Athens drave Hippolytus,[1] likewise

thyself from Florence driven forth must be.
This would they, this already they devise,
    and soon will do it he[2] that plots it there
    where Christ is daily hawked as merchandise.
The side wronged will, as wont, in rumour bear
    the blame; yet shall the vengeance testify
    unto the truth, whereof 'tis minister.
Thou shalt leave each thing that most tenderly
    thou lov'st; and this, of arrows from the bow
    of exile, is the first that it lets fly.
Thou shalt make proof how salt the taste doth
      grow
    of others' bread, and how it tires the feet
    still up, still down, by others' stairs to go.
And what shall gall thee most, will be to meet
    the company, stupid and evil swine,
    with whom thou shalt be cast into this pit;
who, all mad, all as thankless as malign,
    will turn 'gainst thee; but ere much time hath
      flown,
    theirs shall the crimsoned forehead be, not
      thine.
So shall their brutishness in deeds be shown,
    that 'twill become thee well to have preferred
    to form a party of thyself alone.[8]
First refuge and first inn for thee prepared
    shall be the mighty Lombard's[4] courtesy,
    who on the ladder bears the sacred bird;
who shall have such benign regard for thee,
    that, counter to men's wont, betwixt ye two
    the granting shall before the asking be.
With him shalt thou behold the mortal[5] who,
    at birth, was so impressed by this strong star,
    that wondrous are the deeds which he shall
      do.
Still unobserved of men his merits are,
    by reason of his youth; for this bright coil
    has round him wheeled but nine brief years
      so far:
but ere the Gascon the great Harry foil,[6]
    some sparkles of his temper will he show
    in caring not for money or for toil.
Hereafter shall his deeds be bruited so
    for their magnificence, that they shall let
    no tongue be silent, even of his foe.
Him look to, and upon his favours wait;
    through him shall many be transformed in

kind,
rich men and poor, exchanging their estate.
And thou shalt bear hence, written in thy mind
of him, and tell it not'—and he told things
which those who see them past belief shall
find.
He added: 'Son, these on the happenings
foretold thee are the glosses; lo, concealed
by a few turns o' the year, what ambushings.
Yet to no envy of thy neighbours yield,
in that thy future life shall long outlast
the doom by which their treachery shall be
sealed.'
When, having now from speech to silence
pass'd,
that sainted soul thus showed the web,
whereof
I'd stretched the warp, with woof inwoven
fast,
I spake as one who, doubting, fain would prove
the wisdom of some friend and such doth
seek
as sees and will uprightly and doth love:
'Father, 'tis clear indeed, how time doth prick
tow'rd me, e'en such an arrow to let fly
as woundeth sorest him of eye least quick;
'tis good to be armed with foresight, then, that
I,
if robbed of the place wherein I most delight,
lose not the others through my poetry.
Down in the world of sorrows infinite,
and on the mountain from whose lovely crest
my lady's eyes upbore me by their might,
and, afterwards, through Heaven, as on I
pressed
from light to light, I've learned what, if
retold,
would have for many a harsh pot-herb taste.
And if to truth my friendship turneth cold,
I fear that I may perish among those
who will describe these as "the days of old".'
The light that by its smile I knew to enclose
my late-found treasure flashed with such a
beam
as back to the sun a golden mirror throws,
and then replied: 'To conscience rendered dim
by its own or others' shame (no matter which)

'tis true that sharp will much thou sayest
seem;
but, notwithstanding, see there be no breach
with truth, but publish thou thy vision whole;
which done, e'en let them scratch who feel the
itch.
For though thy voice may cause the palate dole
at the first taste, 'twill later leave behind,
when well digested, that which feeds the soul.
This cry of thine shall do as doth the wind,
which hardest strikes upon the loftiest hills;
and that is no small proof of noble mind.'

*The poet enters the heaven of the fixed
stars through the sign of the Twins, his
natal constellation; he looks down over the
spheres already traversed.*

PARADISE, CANTO XXII, LINES 106-154

So, Reader, may I once again have sight
of that devout triumph, for whose sake my
sin
ofttimes do I bewail and bosom smite,
you had not dipped your finger out and in
the fire so quickly, as I saw the sign
which follows Taurus and was therewithin.
O glorious stars, O radiancy divine
pregnant with mighty power, to which is due
all of whatever genius may be mine,
the father of every mortal life with you
was born, with you was setting, at the time
when first on me the Tuscan breezes blew;
and, after, when within the wheel sublime
that whirls you grace was granted me
thuswise
to enter, yours was my allotted clime.
Yea, and for strength to meet the hard emprise
that draws her to itself, my soul no less
to you now, even now, devoutly sighs.
'Thou art so near the final blessedness'
thus Beatrice began, 'that it is meet
thine eyes the utmost clearness should
possess.
So, ere thou wend yet farther into it,
look down once more, and the vast world
survey,
by me already placed beneath thy feet;

thus shall thy heart, with all the joy it may,
  greet the triumphant throng which, full of
    cheer,
  through this round aether now is on its way.'
In vision I re-travelled, sphere by sphere,
  the seven heavens, and saw this globe of ours
  such, that I smiled, so mean did it appear;
and highest I esteem his mental powers
  who rates it least; and him, whose thoughts
    elsewhere
  are fixed, good sense with truest wisdom
    dowers.
I saw Latona's daughter[1] shining bare
  of all the shadow which some while agone
  had caused me to suppose her dense and rare.
Thine offspring's countenance, Hyperion,[2]
  there I endured and saw how, circling, move
  near him thy child,[3] Dione, and, Maia, thy
    son.[4]
From here I saw the tempering of Jove
  between his sire and son,[5] from here could
    trace
  their true positions and each change thereof.
Likewise did all the seven, how swift their pace,
  how vast their size, unto my vision show,
  and each from each how far removed in
    space.
As for the threshing floor that mads us so,
  I, rolling with the timeless Twins, discerned
  it all, from the hills to where its streams
    outflow.
Then to the beauteous eyes mine eyes returned.

*Dante contemplates a symbolic representa-
tion of Christ in triumph surrounded by
saints; he notes the ever-growing beauty of
Beatrice.*

PARADISE, CANTO XXIII, LINES 25-69

As on a calm and full-mooned summer night
  Trívia[1] smiles mid her immortal train
  of nymphs who spangle heaven from depth to
    height,
outshining myriad lamps beheld I then
  one Sun who kindled each and all, as ours
  kindles the stars that throng his high domain;
and through the rays, poured down in living
    showers,

the radiant substance, blazing on me, tried
  my mortal vision far beyond its powers.
Oh Beatrice, beloved and loving guide!
  She said: 'That power by which thine own is
    quell'd,
  is such as nought created may abide.
There is the might and wisdom which avail'd
  'twixt Heaven and Earth to open every road
  so long from yearning human hearts
    withheld.'
As lightning from a cloud must needs explode
  through room too strait to hold the swelling
    flame,
  which falls to earth against its natural mode,
even so then did my spirit burst its frame,
  grown greater at those banquets through
    excess
  of sweets, and it forgets what it became.
'Open thine eyes to my true loveliness:
  thou hast seen things, from which thou shalt
    derive
  the strength to bear the smile upon my face.'
I was like one who, eager to revive
  some long-forgotten dream, with all his wit
  strives to recall it, yet doth vainly strive,
when I this invitation heard, so meet
  for largest thanks, that it shall aye be found
  traced in the volume where my past is writ.
Should now to aid me all the tongues resound
  which Polyhymnia[2] and her sisterhood
  have with their sweetest milk made most
    abound,
when chanting of her holy smile they would
  not even a thousandth of its charm portray,
  nor how therewith her holy visage glow'd.
So too the sacred poem, which would essay
  to picture Paradise, must leap, like him
  who finds an interruption to his way.
Yet none that ponders on the weighty theme,
  which a mere man sustains, will take amiss
  his staggering under burden so extreme.
No sea-way for a bauble-boat is this
  cut by my daring prow, but one to prove
  the steersman's mettle in extremities.

*Having seen in the primum mobile (the
outermost physical sphere) the angels in*

their perpetual adoration of the divinity,
the poet's thoughts turn towards Beatrice,
whose guidance has made such visions pos-
sible. He rises with her to the Empyrean.

PARADISE, CANTO XXX, LINES 17-132

If all thus far related in her praise
    might now in one stupendous paean close,
    'twould serve me here but as a passing
        phrase.
The beauty I saw, transcending measure, goes
    not only beyond our reach, but I must deem
    only its Maker the full joy of it knows.
Here, I confess, my theme defeats me—theme,
    such as no comic bard, no tragic, e'er
    was baffled by in his sublimest dream;
for, as on feeble eyes the Sun's full glare,
    so to recall her smile's enchanting grace
    lays on my spirit more than it can bear.
From the first day that I beheld her face
    in this life, till this vision, my song with
        power
unfailing hath pursued her loveliness;
but now, as poet, I must needs give o'er
    pursuit that every artist knows is vain,
    when, having done his best, he can no more.
She—such as I bequeath her to the strain
    of loftier trump than mine, now pressing on
    anigh the goal it long hath toiled to gain—
with gesture as of guide whose task is done,
    resumed: 'We have left the world's last
        sphere, and move
now in the heaven composed of light alone:
light of the understanding, full of love;
    love of the true good, full of ecstasy;
    ecstasy sweet all other sweets above.
Here shalt thou look on either soldiery
    of Paradise, and the one host array'd
    as at the final judgment it will be.'
Like to the sudden glare by lightning made,
    which doth the visual spirits so confound
    that from the eye the clearest objects fade,
a living glory compassed me around,
    and left me swathed in such a dazzling sheet
    of its own light, that I saw nought beyond.
'The love that calms this heaven[1] is wont to
        greet

after such fashion all it welcomes here,
    thus for its flame the torch to render meet.'
Scarce had this brief assurance reached my ear,
    when I perceived myself with power endued
    surpassing that of any earthly seer;
and with such ardour was their strength
        renewed,
    that there exists no glory shine it never
    so brightly, which mine eyes had not
    withstood.
And I saw light which flowed, as flows a river,
    blazing between two banks abloom with
        spring
    more marvellous than poet dreamed of ever.
Out of that torrent living sparks took wing,
    and settling on the flowers that by it grew
    glittered like rubies in a golden ring.
Then, as though drunken with the scents they
        drew,
    they re-engulfed themselves in the mystic
        gurge;
    and, as one entered, forth another flew.
'The intense desire that now doth burn thee and
        urge
    for knowledge of what here before thee lies,
    pleases me more the higher its ardours surge.
But, first, drink of this water, for thuswise
    alone canst thou thy raging thirst supply.'
    So spake to me the Day-star of mine eyes.
'The stream, the jewels that thence and thither
        fly,'
    she added, 'and the smiling herbage near
    are but dim proems of their reality.
Not that these things are in themselves unclear;
    rather, with vision still too weak to soar
    at these great heights, 'tis thou that failest
        here.'
No infant ever turned his face with more
    of a rush toward the milk, if wakened late
    from slumbering long past his wonted hour,
than I, to make mine eyes as mirrors yet
    more lucid, bent me to that river's bound,
    which pours its flood to aid us mend our state.
And as the eaves that edge mine eyelids found
    and drunk thereof, so seemed it that instead
    of being long it now was changed to round.
Then as a troop of maskers, if they shed

the semblance not their own, are seen
express'd
in their true likeness, which before was hid,
thus changed, and in more jubilant beauty
dress'd,
the flowers and sparks appeared, so that I saw
both the high courts[2] of Heaven made
manifest.
O splendour of God, by means of which I saw
the truth triumphant reigning without cease,
grant me now strength to utter how I saw!
There's light up yonder, and by means of this
is the Creator to those creatures shown
who only in seeing him possess their peace.
The light I speak of is diffused in one
vast circle, of a rondure so immense,
'twere even for the Sun too loose a zone.
'Tis all one beam, that smites upon the sense
reflected from the summit of the Sphere
First Moved, which draws its power and
motion thence.
And as a slope, rising from some calm mere,
glasses itself therein, as though to espy
its wealth of flowers and grass reflected there,
so mirrored in that light, and round it, I
beheld in countless ranks above it rise
all that of us have made return on high.
If pent within the lowest tier there lies
so mighty a radiance, then how vast the space
that the outmost petals of this rose comprise!
And yet my vision suffered no distress
at breadth or height, but could in full survey
the range and quality of that happiness.
There near and far nor adds nor takes away:
for where, im-medïately,[3] God is king,
the natural law, being void, suspends its
sway.
To the yellow of the Rose which, blossoming
for aye, spreads tieréd petals wafting praise
unto the Sun that makes perpetual spring,
Beatrice drew me, like to one who says
nothing, yet fain would speak, and 'Look',
said she,
'how vast a white-stoled gathering meets they
gaze!
See the vast compass of our city! See
our stalls so crowded, that we need but few

fresh comers to complete our company!'

*Beatrice takes her place in the Celestial
Rose; Saint Bernard appears at Dante's side.*

PARADISE, CANTO XXXI, LINES 42-93

By now my glance had hastily surveyed
the general form of Paradise entire,
and on no portion yet had firmly stayed;
and I turned round with new-inflamed desire
to ask my lady many things that I,
in keen suspense, was eager to enquire.
But other than I purposed came reply:
I saw instead of Beatrice an old man,
like all the rest, apparelled gloriously.
Kindling his glance and o'er his cheeks there
ran
a flush of joy benign, the while on me
he gazed as only a loving father can.
And instantly my cry was 'Where is she?'
'I from my place by Beatrice was stirr'd
to come and end thy longing,' answered he;
'if thou look upward to the circle third
from the highest tier, once more she'll meet
thy gaze
on yonder throne, for her deserts prepared.'
He spake: I answered not by word or phrase,
but looked on high and there beheld her
crown'd,
reflecting from herself the eternal rays.
Not from that heav'n where highest the
thunders sound
is mortal eye so distant, though within
what sea soever it lie deepest drown'd,
as there was mine from Beatrice, I ween;
yet nought it mattered, for her image blest
came down to me unblurred by aught
between.
'O lady in whom my hope is liveliest,
and who for my salvation didst endure
in Hell itself to leave thy footprints traced,
of all the things that I have seen 'tis sure
that from thy power and from thy
bounteousness
alone do they their virtue and grace procure.
Thou hast led me, thou, from slavery to the
place

of freedom, making use, to serve thine aim,
of all the ways and means thou dost possess.
Preserve me in thy great work still the same,
that so my spirit, healed by thy dear might,
may please thee when it quits this mortal
frame.'
Thus I; and from that seeming far-off height
she looked on me and smiled, then turning
bent
her gaze upon the eternal source of light.

*Saint Bernard asks the Virgin to have the
ultimate vision granted to Dante. The poet
gropes for words to describe the indescrib-
able.*

'Maiden and mother, daughter of thy son,
lowly and high above all beings display'd,
chosen of God, ere time had yet begun,
thine was the excellence which so array'd
man's nature that its Maker thought no
shame
to make himself of that himself had made.
Within thy womb rekindled glowed the flame
of love that fed the germ from which this
flower
in timeless peace to such perfection came.
Noon-torch of charity to us in our
world here, thou art a well of hope on earth,
whence mortal men draw draughts of
quickening power.
Lady, so great thou art and such thy worth,
that whoso longs for grace nor calls on thee,
bids the wish fly, yet wingless speeds it forth.
Thy loving heart not only grants the plea
of every suppliant, but ofttimes, ere yet
'tis uttered, answers prayer spontaneously.
Merciful, mighty in deed, compassionate,
all virtues that created being can boast,
in thee, have all in thee, together met.
Behold this man, who from the nethermost
sink of the whole world up to this high place
hath seen the realm of spirits, coast by coast,
and now beseeches thee that of thy grace
strength be vouchsafed unto his eyes yet
higher
to raise him tow'rds the final blessedness.

And I, who for myself was ne'er on fire
more than for him, to see this vision, pray
thee instantly—oh, spurn not my desire—
by means of thy own prayers to chase away
all clouds of his mortality, that so
he see the perfect joy in full display.
Further I pray thee, sovereign, who canst do
whate'er thou wilt, after a sight so fair
keep his affections healthy through and
through.
Control his human springs with watchful care:
behold how many saints with Beatrice
pray thee with claspéd hands to grant my
prayer!'
The eyes which God reveres and loves, at this
gazed on the pleader, and thus proved it right
how dear to her all true devotion is;
then were directed to the eternal light,
into whose essence we must deem no eye
of creature pierces with such keen insight.
And I, who to the end was drawing nigh
of all desires, the yearning deep instilled
within me ended, of necessity.
With nod and smiling visage Bernard willed
that I should upward gaze; but I foreknew
and had already his behest fulfilled;
for more and more my vision, as it grew
purer, was penetrating through the ray
of the deep light which in itself is true.
Thenceforth my seeing surpassed what we can
say
by means of words, which fail at sight so
fair;
and memory to such excess gives way.
As one who sees in dream, remains aware,
when the dream's gone, of all it made him
feel,
while all he saw is lost beyond repair;
even such am I; my vision fades, until
it all but ceases, yet my heart is awed
by its sweet effluence which pervades me still.
Thus melts the imprinted snow by sunshine
thawed;
thus was the wisdom of the Sibyl, writ
on frail leaves, to the breezes cast abroad.[1]
O Light supreme, so far above the wit
of man exalted, let my mind again

with some pale semblance of thy beams be lit,
and make my tongue so eloquent that when
  it chants thy glory, a future age may find
  at least one sparkle of thee inspire the strain;
for, by returning somewhat to my mind
  and sounding faintly in these verses, thou
  wilt make men to thy victory less blind.
Bewildered would mine eyes have been, I trow,
  by the keen living ray, whose utmost brunt
  they suffered, had they turned them from it
    now.
And I remember that on this account
  I endured more boldly, till my look grew one
  with the infinite goodness at its central fount.
Oh abundant grace, whereby thus daring grown
  I fixed my vision through the eternal light
  so far, that sight I wholly spent thereon!
Within its depths I marked how by the might
  of love the leaves, through all creation
    strowed,
  bound in a single volume, there unite;
substance and accidents with each its mode,
  as 'twere conflated, in such wise that what
  I say is a mere gleam of glory untold.
The universal form that ties this knot
  methinks I saw, because, while saying this,
  I feel myself in ampler joy upcaught.
One instant dims my vision more, I wis,
  than dim the emprise, which made old
    Neptune stare
  at Argo's² shadow, five times five centuries.
So gazed my spirit, all suspended there,
  absorbed and steadfast, and the more it tried
  to see, the more its powers enkindled were.
In presence of that light so satisfied
  the mind is, that it never could consent
  to turn therefrom to glance at aught beside;
because the good, on which the will is bent,
  is all there; and, outside it, incomplete
  are things which, in it, find their complement.
Henceforth my tongue, in struggling to repeat
  e'en what remembrance holds, will have less
    power

than hath a babe's which still sucks at the
    teat.
Although there was one aspect, and no more,
  within the living light which met my view—
  for that is always what it was before—
yet as my vision, since it stronger grew
  the more I gazed, kept changing, so it found
  one sole appearance take on changes too.
In the sublime light's deep pellucid ground
  did, visibly to me, three circles show,
  of three hues and in one dimension bound;
the first by the second seemed as bow by bow
  reflected, and the third was like a flame
  which equally from either seemed to flow.
How scant is language, all too weak to frame
  my thoughts! And these are such, that, set
    beside
  my vision, 'faint' is word too weak for them.
O Light that aye sole in thyself dost bide,
  sole understand'st thyself, and being
    self-known,
  self-knowing, lov'st thyself, self-gratified!
That circle which, begotten thus, was shown
  in thee as light reflected, when I turned
  mine eyes and let them somewhile dwell
    thereon,
of the same hue with which it inly burned,
  seemed limned in the similitude of Man;
  which made my sight wholly therewith
    concerned.
As geometrician, trying as best he can
  to square the circle, but without the clue
  he needs to guide him, ends where he began;
so I, before that marvel strange and new,
  strove to discover how the image lay
  within the circle, and how joined thereto—
flight too sublime for my own wings to essay,
  had not a flash of insight countervailed,
  and struck my blindness into sudden day.
The high-raised phantasy here vigour failed;
  but, rolling like a wheel that never jars,
  my will and wish were now by love impelled,
the love that moves the Sun and th' other stars.

Notes

On *VITA NUOVA*

1 heaven of light: the sun. **2** she was called Beatrice, etc.: i.e., even those who did not know her name called her Beatrice, which means "she who makes blessed." **3** starry heavens: the eighth of the physical heavens, supposed to move from west to east one degree in a hundred years. **4** Guido Guinizelli (died 1276), poet admired by Dante. (See *Purgatory* xxvi and note.) **5** close relative: perhaps one of Dante's two younger sisters. **6** sphere that makes the longest round: the *primum mobile,* the outermost physical sphere, which gives motion to all the heavens below it. Beyond the *primum mobile* is the Empyrean, the true heaven beyond space and time.

On *CONVIVIO*

1 philosopher: Aristotle. **2** Beatrice.

On *DE VULGARI ELOQUENTIA*

1 grammar: i.e., Latin. **2** mirror: the mind of God. **3** In fact, however, Adam must have spoken first in the course of naming the animals. (Genesis ii, 20-24).

On *MONARCHIA*

1 possible intellect: while the intellect of angels is always acting to its fullest extent, that of man is not, hence his is a "possible" intellect.

DIVINE COMEDY

On *INFERNO,* CANTO I

1 midway: Dante was thirty-five years old (half of "threescore and ten") in 1300, the year of his poem. **2** planet: the sun, allegorically divine illumination. **3** leopard: allegorically probably lust (or fraud ?). **4** Tradition held that the world was created in springtime. **5** lion: allegorically pride (or violence ?). **6** she-wolf: allegorically avarice (or incontinence ?). **7** *miserere mei:* "have mercy on me." **8** *sub Julio:* "under [the reign of] Julius Caesar." **9** Anchiseades: i.e., son of Anchises: Aeneas. **10** Hound: a deliverer of some kind. It is not sure whom Dante had in mind. **11** Feltro and Feltro: places in Northern Italy. Without capitals the phrase could mean "between coarse cloths," i.e., of humble origin. **12** Turnus, etc.: characters in the *Aeneid.* **13** place: Hell. **14** fire: that of Purgatory. **15** to whom: i.e., amongst the blessed in Heaven. **16** she: Beatrice.

CANTO III

1 Power, Wisdom, and Love are attributes of the Father, Son, and Holy Ghost respectively.

CANTO V

1 Minos: in Greek mythology one of the judges of the underworld. **2** Semiramis: lustful queen of ancient Assyria. **3** queen: Dido, who killed herself when Aeneas deserted her. (*Aeneid* iv) **4** native city: Ravenna. The speaker is Francesca of the Da Polenta family, who married the lord of Rimini. **5** the way 't was done: Francesca was slain *in flagrante,* with no time for repentance.

6 Cain: Caina, lowest region of Hell, reserved for fratricides, among others. **7** in the old romance Gallehault served as an intermediary between Lancelo' and Guinivere.

CANTO VII

1 Each of the heavenly spheres has a guiding angel (or choir of angels) to regulate its light and motion.

CANTO X

1 Farinata degli Uberti was a great Ghibelline leader, victor over the Guelphs at Montaperti (1260). **2** twice: Farinata drove the Guelphs (Dante's party) into exile in 1248 and 1260; they returned in 1251, after the death of Frederick II, and again in 1266, after the defeat of Manfred at Benevento. They were never again dislodged. **3** Guy: Guido Cavalcanti, Dante's friend and fellow poet. He was still alive in the spring of 1300. **4** lady: the moon, in her aspect of Hecate, queen of the lower world. Farinata is saying that before fifty months have passed, Dante will be exiled. **5** rout: a reference to Montaperti on the banks of the Arbia. **6** place: at the Diet of Empoli, which followed the battle of Montaperti; here the victorious enemies of Florence suggested the city should be razed.

CANTO XI

1 Cahors, in southern France, was notorious for its usurers; Sodom is the wicked city of Scripture, associated with unnatural vice. **2** Dis: Satan. **3** those: Dante refers to the souls already seen, the lustful, the avaricious, and the wrathful. **4** *Ethics*: Aristotle's VII, i), where three classes of evil are described, of which incontinence is the least blameworthy (and so not a part of lower Hell). **5** *Physics*: Aristotle's (II, ii). **6** your art: human industry, which imitates nature as nature imitates God. **7** Genesis (iii, 19), where man is told that he must earn his bread in the sweat of his brow.

CANTO XIII

1 Cecina and Corneto: towns marking the limits of the thorny wasteland known as the Maremma. **2** Harpies, etc.: as Virgil sings. (*Aeneid* iii) **3** Virgil (*Aeneid* iii) had told a similar story of a man turned into a tree. **4** Frederick: the Emperor Frederick II. The speaker is Pietro della Vigna, Frederick's secretary and minister. **5** Caesar's household: the imperial court. **6** Augustus: the emperor.

CANTO XV

1 A reference to the dikes of the Low Countries. Wissant, near Boulogne, was an important medieval port. Similar dikes were built by the Paduans as a protection against the floods of the Brenta, swollen in springtime by the melting snows of the mountains of Carinthia. **2** Brunetto Latini (1210?-1294), Florentine statesman and author of the encyclopaedic *Trésor*, written in French. **3** Fiesole: small hilltown above Florence, where, according to tradition, Catiline's army was besieged and compelled to surrender. The new city, Florence, was then founded; its first inhabitants being Fiesolans and a few Roman soldiers.

CANTO XXI

1 Saint Zita: patron of Lucca. **2** Bonturo (Dati): political boss of Lucca; the remark is ironical. **3** Holy Face: an image of Christ revered in Lucca. **4** Serchio: stream near Lucca. **5** Malacoda: lit. "bad tail." **6** Caprona: town on the Arno, surrendered to the Florentines in 1289. Dante was with the Florentine forces. **7** i.e., at the time of the Crucifixion, when Hell was shaken.

CANTO XXV

1 Agnel: perhaps one Agnello Brunelleschi. **2** Lucan in his *Pharsalia* tells of Sabellus, bitten by a snake and melting away like snow, and of Nasidius, swelling and bursting out of his armor as a result of another's serpent's bite. Ovid in his *Metamorphoses* tells the tales of Cadmus and Arethusa. **3** Buoso: possibly of the Donati clan. **4** Puccio: of the Galigai family. **5** the other: Guercio de' Cavalcanti. The folk of the village of Gaville killed him and then suffered under the vengeance taken by his associates.

CANTO XXVI

1 Gaeta: town and cape north of Naples, named, legend says, after Aeneas' nurse, who died there. **2** the Pillars of Hercules: mountains on either side of the Strait of Gibraltar. **3** mountain: the mount of Purgatory.

CANTO XXVII

1 cordelier: a Franciscan. **2** prince: Pope Boniface VIII, at that time waging war against the Colonna family, whose forces had retired to Palestrina, a town not far from Rome (where the Lateran palace stands). Hence the pope's war was not a crusade against the infidel Saracens (who had taken Acre in 1291) nor against Jews and wicked Christians who trafficked with the enemy. **3** Legend says that the Emperor Constantine called on Pope Sylvester, living in a cave near Mt. Soracte (north of Rome), to cure him of leprosy. **4** Celestinus V, who abdicated the papal throne. **5** Saint Francis, founder of the Franciscan Order. (See *Paradise* xi.)

CANTO XXXIII

1 Ugolin: Ugolino della Gherardesca, prominent Pisan Ghibelline, accused of treason because of his alliance with the Guelphs (1275). **2** Roger: Ruggiero Ubaldini, archbishop and leader of the Pisan Ghibellines. In 1288 he captured and imprisoned Ugolino. **3** The mountain of San Giuliano between Pisa and Lucca. **4** Gualandi, etc.: prominent Ghibelline families.

CANTO XXXIV

1 The colors of Satan's three faces symbolize respectively hatred, impotence, and ignorance—a negative trinity. (See canto iii, note 1.)

On *PURGATORY*,

CANTO I

1 Calliope: muse of epic po-

117

etry. **2** Legend tells of the nine daughters of King Pieros who challenged the Muses to a contest of song; defeated and contumacious, they were changed into magpies. **3** Venus. **4** Adam and Eve: Dante puts the Garden of Eden on the top of Purgatory in the southern hemisphere, hence unknown to man since the fall—until the fifteent century explorers. **5** Wain: Ursa Major, the Big Dipper. **6** Cato the Younger, who, defeated at Utica, committed suicide rather than submit to the victorious Caesar.

CANTO II

1 "When Israel went out of Egypt" (Psalm cxiv), a song of emancipation. **2** The constellation of Capricorn fades before the rising sun.

CANTO III

1 The souls notice that Dante casts a shadow. **2** pastor: the archbishop of Cosenza, ordered by the pope to give Manfred's body an unhallowed burial. **3** realm: the Kingdom of Naples. **4** Verde: the Garigliano, boundary between the Realm and the lands of the pope. **5** Constance: Manfred's daughter, wife of Peter III of Aragon and mother (in 1300) of the kings of Sicily and Aragon.

CANTO V

1 The Archiano flows into the Arno at the limit of a region called the Casentino. The "Hermit'ry" was a nearby monastery. **2** Pia: a Sienese lady, married to a nobleman of the

Tuscan Maremma. (See *Inferno* xiii, note 1.) Tradition says he murdered her in order to marry another or because he suspected her infidelity. She is the third soul to speak to Dante in this canto.

CANTO VI

1 Justinian had given Italy an excellent code of laws, but there is no authority to administer it. **2** Albert of Hapsburg, elected emperor, never came to Italy to be crowned. **3** Rudolph, who also neglected Italy. **4** Names of feuding families of Northern Italy. The counts of Santafiora, loyal to the emperor, had lost much of their land to the commune of Siena. **5** Marcellus: an arrogant and loquacious enemy of Caesar. **6** A sardonic allusion to the frequent revisions of the Florentine constitution.

CANTO VII

1 "Hail, Queen," opening words of an evening hymn sung to the Virgin.

CANTO IX

1 she: Aurora (the dawn). **2** A reference to the constellation Scorpio. **3** i.e., almost three hours have passed since nightfall. **4** Dante, Virgil, Sordello, and two penitent souls. **5** Philomela, wronged by her brother-in-law and subsequently turned into a swallow. **6** Ganymede, who while hunting on Mt. Ida was snatched up to Olympus to serve as cupbearer to the gods. **7** It was believed that a sphere of fire surrounded the earth. **8** Achilles'

mother, to save him from going to the Trojan War, carried him, while he slept, from the charge of Chiron, his tutor, to the island of Scyros. **9** Saint Lucy, symbol of illuminating grace. **10** The three steps probably symbolize the three elements of penance: contrition, confession, and satisfaction; or they may be figures of mankind's successive stages: innocence, sin, and atonement. **11** adamant: symbolizing the enduring firmness of ecclesiastical authority. **12** The seven deadly sins. **13** The silver key is that of discernment; the gold one is that of power to judge (or priestly authority), bought by Christ's blood and handed down from Peter (Piers). **14** When the Tribune Metellus abandoned the temple of Saturn under the Tarpeian Rock (where the public treasure was kept), the gates were opened by Caesar's soldiers, whereupon the rock roared. **15** "We praise Thee, God," hymn of praise and thanksgiving.

CANTO XIX

1 geomancers: fortunetellers. One of their figures for divination called *Fortuna major* resembled a combination of stars visible just before sunrise in the spring.

CANTO XXVI

1 An allusion to the wicked cities of Genesis (ix, 1-28); the penitents are accusing themselves of perverted lust. **2** Pasiphaë, legendary queen of Crete; she is said to have had made a wooden cow, which she entered in order to have intercourse with a bull. The penitents of this file were guilty of immoderate sexual indulgence. **3** Riphean mountains: legendarily in the far north; the "sands" are those of Africa, in the south. **4** It is reported that Caesar, during his triumph, was called "queen" by his soldiers, a veiled accusation of sodomy. **5** Guido Guinizelli, poet dear to Dante for the original and idealistic nature of his verse. (See *Vita Nuova*.) **6** The sons of Hypsipyle appeared just in time to save their mother from Lycurgus. (Statius, *Thebaid*, v) **7** bard of Limoges: probably Giraut de Bornelh, Provençal poet of late twelfth and early thirteenth centuries, of whom Dante elsewhere speaks with admiration. **8** Guitton: Guittone d'Arezzo (1225-1294), famous poet of the Tuscan school, whom Dante thought over-rated. **9** he: the speaker is Arnaut Daniel, Provençal poet of the late twelfth century, whom Dante admired and imitated. In Dante's original Arnaut's lines are not in Italian but in Old Provençal; the translator indicates the shift by the use of Middle English. **10** swich: such; curteis: courteous; ple: plea. **11** se: see.

CANTOS XXVII-XXVIII

1 Lèah and Rachel: in the Old Testament (Genesis xxix, 10-35), the fertile and the barren wife of Jacob respectively. **2** lady: Matelda, the presiding genius of the garden, a symbol, probably, of human felicity.

CANTOS XXX-XXXI

1 Psalm xxxi, 1-8. "In Thee, O Lord, do I put my trust. . . . Thou hast set my feet in a large room. . . ." With verse 9 there is a shift in mood. **2** substances: the angels who surround Beatrice. **3** creature: the Griffin, who draws the chariot of the Church, on which Beatrice stands; a symbol, it would seem, of Christ.

On *PARADISE*, CANTO I

1 the heaven: the Empyrean. (See *Vita Nuova*, note 6.) **2** Apollo: god of poetic inspiration. **3** Parnassus: double-peaked mountain on which the Muses dwelt. **4** Defeated by Apollo in a musical contest, the satyr Marsyas was flayed by the god. **5** i.e., so infrequently nowadays is distinction attained either in poetry or service of the state. **6** Peneian frondage: the laurel, symbolic of poetic achievement. **7** Delphi: site of a famous shrine to Apollo. **8** Cirrha: seaport of Delphi. **9** The sun, which rises at a different point on the horizon every day in the year, appears most propitiously at the time of the spring equinox, when the three great arcs—the celestial equator, the ecliptic (the path of the sun through the zodiac), and the equinoctial colure (a circle passing through the celestial poles, and crossing the equator at Aries and Libra)—all intersect on the horizon. **10** there: in the Earthly Paradise. **11** Greek mythology tells how Glaucus the fisherman, having tasted of a special herb, became immortal. **12** what in man, etc.: the

soul, created after the body is complete. **13** the wheel: the circling heavens.

CANTO III

1 Piccarda: of the Donati family, related to Dante's wife. **2** The allusion is to Saint Clare, founder of the order that bears her name.

CANTO X

1 God the Father. **2** the circling heavens. **3** motions: the daily and yearly revolutions of the sun, represented by the celestial equator and ecliptic; they cross at Aries, where the sun is during Dante's journey. **4** the ecliptic. **5** the sun. **6** Aries. **7** i.e., in its springtime "spirals" the sun rises earlier every day. **8** The sun occupies the fourth of the Ptolemaic heavens. **9** daughter of Latona: the moon. **10** Saint Dominic, founder of the Dominican Order. **11** Albertus Magnus (1193-1280), scholar and philosopher. **12** Saint Thomas Aquinas (1226-1274), pupil of Albert; great and authoritative theologian.

CANTO XI

1 lines 43-8: Between two streams of Umbria, the Topino and the Chiascio (where Saint Ubald had had his hermitage), stands Mt. Subasio, facing Perugia; to the east lie the towns of Gualdo and Nocera, dominated by the Apennines. Assisi stands on a spur of the mountain. **2** Ascesi: old form of Assisi, meaning "I have risen." **3** *coram patre:* "in the presence of his father." **4** Amyclas: a poor fisherman, unperturbed by a visit from Caesar, for he had nothing to lose. **5** Early disciples of Saint Francis. **6** Innocent III sanctioned the Franciscan rule (1210). **7** Honorius III confirmed Innocent's action (1223). **8** In 1219 Saint Francis went to Egypt and preached before the sultan. **9** steep: Mt. Alvernia, where in 1224 Saint Francis received the seal, i.e., the *stigmata,* marks of Christ's wounds. **10** Saint Francis died in 1226; he ordered his followers to strip his body and leave it for some time on the bare ground.

CANTO XV

1 Virgil (*Aeneid*) tells of the meeting in the Elysian Fields of Aeneas and the shade of his father, Anchises. **2** "O blood of mine, O lavish grace of God! To whom was Heaven's gate ever twice opened, as to thee!" **3** the Trinity: God. **4** Just as the concept of unity leads to a profound understanding of numbers, so in the "primal thought," God's mind (wherein Cacciaguida can read), many other thoughts, including Dante's, are contained. **5** i.e., the blessed never have a wish that they have not the intelligence to fulfill. **6** He: the first Alighieri. **7** first cornice: that of pride, in Purgatory. **8** In the good old days daughters were not married off too young

nor with excessive dowries. **9** Sardanapalus: luxury-loving king of Assyria. **10** i.e., Rome (symbolized by the hill of Montemario, here called Montemalo) was not yet surpassed by Florence (symbolized by the Uccellatoio, a similar suburban hill), which is destined also to more rapid decline. **11** Names of prominent families in old Florence. **12** at Frenchman's call: perhaps an allusion to the frequent absences of Florentine merchants, whose business called them to Paris. **13** i.e., a Cincinnatus or a Cornelia (characters in Roman history celebrated for their simple virtues) would be as rare in Florence today as a Cianghella (notorious loose woman of Dante's time) or a Lapo Salterello (another bad character) would have been in old Florence. **14** The Emperor Conrad IV, leader of the crusade of 1147.

CANTO XVII

1 The false accusations of his stepmother Phaedra compelled Hippolytus to leave Athens. **2** he: Boniface VIII. **3** Dante, in fact, soon parted company with his fellow exiles. **4** Lombard: the head of the family of La Scala, lords of Verona,

whose arms bore a ladder and an eagle. **5** Can Grande, born in 1290 and hence a child when Dante went into exile. He later became a celebrated soldier and a patron of Dante. **6** Clement V, a Gascon, encouraged Henry VII to come to Italy, but secretly worked against him.

CANTO XXII

1 Latona's daughter: the moon. **2** The "offspring" of Hyperion is the sun. **3** child: Venus. **4** son: Mercury. **5** sire and son: Saturn and Mars.

CANTO XXIII

1 Trivia: Diana, the moon. **2** Polyhymnia: the muse of lyric poetry.

CANTO XXX

1 this heaven: the Empyrean. **2** both the high courts: the angels and the saints. **3** immediately: without any medium; directly.

CANTO XXXIII

1 The prophecies of the Cumaean Sybil, written on fallen leaves, were scattered by the wind. **2** *Argo:* the first ship ever launched, hence a marvel to Neptune.

Characters in the Divine Comedy

Meek and rebellious, feeble and violent, betrayed or betrayers,
Dante's characters span the range of human passions.

Francesca, a Living Woman

Francesca da Rimini is surely among the most famous characters in the *Divine Comedy*. The story of her love is one of the high points in Italian poetry. Indeed, Francesco De Sanctis defines Francesca as the only living woman in Italian poetry.

Historically, Francesca is a shadowy figure. No contemporary document has come down to us about her or about the tragedy at the court in Rimini. Dante is the first to speak of her, and his contemporaries add little to the story. If it had not been for the *Divine Comedy*, perhaps no one would ever have known the tragic events of Francesca's life. She was the daughter of Guido Vecchio da Polenta, lord of Ravenna, and the sister of Lamberto, whom Guido Novello succeeded as governor of the city in 1316. The tragedy must have been fresh in the memory of the Da Polenta family at the time Dante was staying in Ravenna.

In 1275, to guarantee peace between the two families, Francesca's father married her to a son of Malatesta da Rimini. Her husband Gianciotto was a serious and prudent man, destined to succeed his father as lord of Rimini. But he was also ugly, coarse, and deformed. (His name means Gianni the *ciotto*, that is, the "cripple.") Moreover, most unfortunately, his brother Paolo was enchantingly elegant and handsome—"suited more for rest than work," as a contemporary describes him.

The young Francesca could not help adoring the companionship of her brother-in-law, who spoke so persuasively and whose vibrant voice breathed life into the tales of chivalry when he read them aloud. It was inevitable that the two young people should fall in love and that Gianciotto, whether by chance, or guided by his suspicions,

Paolo and Francesca, by Gustave Doré (1833-83)

or because someone had warned him, finally found them out. And having found them out, he killed them, in accordance with the morality of the time.

Giovanni Boccaccio, the great commentator on Dante, gives a more romantic version of the story. He relates that Francesca's father, fearing that she would rebel if she knew she was to marry Gianciotto, let her believe she would marry Paolo—who had come to Ravenna to represent his brother at the wedding. Only the next day in Rimini did the girl discover the trick that had been played on her, and by that time she was already in love with the handsome Paolo. There is no corrobation for Boccaccio's story, which was probably a figment of his splendid imagination.

In Dante's poem Paolo and Francesca are among the damned. Dante the theologist had to place them there; but Dante the man could only be moved by their fate. It is always the human concern that prevails in the poem. In the story of the two lovers, too, it wells up and is expressed in the burning accents of passion.

Farinata, Hero of the Ghibellines

After the battle of Montaperti, the triumphant Ghibellines, maddened with hatred, had only one idea: to destroy Florence. Only one man dared to stand up and defend the city, and so save it from ruin. He was Manente degli Uberti, called Farinata, who headed the Ghibellines until 1239 and was the guiding spirit of all his party's actions in Florence.

The Uberti family had been Ghibelline since 1177, when they had sided with Frederick Barbarossa in his invasion of Italy. The family, which was the most powerful in Florence, had become Ghibelline not only for love of the German emperor, but because they wanted the aid of the imperial forces to help them acquire the government of the city for themselves.

In the next century, when the family's hopes of acquiring power faded, the Ghibelline allegiance of Farinata and his relations was less self-interested. To be a Ghibelline around 1250 meant to be on Manfred's side, and Manfred, although a Swabian by descent, was profoundly Italian in other ways. As a sovereign he was as enlightened as he was powerful. Perhaps Farinata hoped to see a league of all the Italian cities gathered around Manfred—a league that would appease all the internal quarrels and strengthen all its members. Perhaps Farinata, like Dante, confusedly foresaw the existence of an Italian nation. Naturally, we do not know for certain what Farinata thought, but we do know that he was most favorably inclined to the policies of Manfred and that he helped the Swabian in his efforts to find allies among the Italian communes.

But the idea of an Italian confederation did not appeal to Farinata's proud and intolerant fellow citizens. They found his conduct strange, and his admiration for Manfred ambiguous. Then, all of a sudden, the fiery Florentines began to suspect that the Ghibellines were conspiring to hand over the city to the Swabian.

Although it seems the accusation was unfounded, in 1257 the enraged citizens exiled the principal Ghibelline families, with the

Farinata degli Uberti tries to save a friend.

Uberti at their head.

The exiles withdrew to Siena, an old enemy of Florence. But since peace prevailed for the moment between the two towns, Florence asked Siena to expel the Ghibelline refugees. Siena stalled until Florence declared war. Siena, spurred on by the exiles, asked Manfred's help; Farinata himself headed the diplomatic legation. The Swabian king did not want to become too involved, so he prudently pledged only a modest contingent of a few hundred soldiers.

Farinata's companions would have liked to have protested this feeble aid, but Farinata accepted it. He had in mind a shrewd and most ingenious plan that would immediately bring fresh reinforcements. In May, 1260, when the hostilities began and the Florentines beseiged Siena, Farinata led Manfred's Germans in a bold sortie to break the siege. It was a desperate attempt that could not possibly have succeeded, given the smallness of his force. In fact, after an initial success, which they owed to the advantage of surprise, Manfred's soldiers were sur-

rounded and routed. The Florentines captured the Swabian flag, which became an object of jokes and ridicule. This was an affront that Manfred's pride would not bear, and he sent two thousand German soldiers from Sicily to reinforce Siena. In this way Farinata succeeded in getting the help he had wanted in the first place. The Ghibellines won the decisive battle of Montaperti, and the Uberti family and the other exiles returned to Florence.

Pietro della Vigna, Guilty or Innocent?

Pietro della Vigna—the famous suicide changed into a thornbush in *Hell*—was the right-hand man of Frederick II. Of humble birth, he suffered great privations in order to study at the University of Bologna. Then in 1225 he joined the Sicilian court as a notary and scribe. Very soon he earned the esteem and then the trust of Frederick; he came to know all Frederick's secrets and became the irreplaceable friend, confidant, adviser, and secretary

But their good fortune did not last long. Pope Clement IV called on Charles of Anjou to invade Italy and fight the powerful Sicilian prince. Manfred's defeat at Benevento also overthrew the Ghibellines of Florence. In 1267 they were forced to leave again, this time for good. The houses of the Uberti family were razed, and Farinata's brother, who had fallen into the hands of his enemies, was beheaded. But Farinata did not witness the ruin; he had died three years earlier.

to the Swabian emperor. All of a sudden, at the height of his power, the omnipotent minister was discharged, his eyes were put out, and he was imprisoned in the awful dungeons of the fortress of San Miniato.

Why?

There is no truthworthy historical answer that would justify such a lightning-stroke of tragedy. There was talk of jealousy in love, of conspiracy, of an attempted poisoning on the part of Pietro della Vigna, and of betrayal on the part of the sovereign who wished to confiscate the property of this minister who had become more than conspicuous. Some accused the emperor of having betrayed his faithful friend; others accused the minister of having betrayed the faith of his lord. We will never know the truth. Probably a palace conspiracy caused the minister's fall from favor—a conspiracy led by a group of courtiers who accused Pietro before Frederick. And the emperor perhaps reacted too hastily by firing and then condemning his secretary.

But were the accusations well founded? Was the sovereign's conduct determined by his indignation at Pietro's clear guilt or by an impulsive anger aroused only by lies?

Pietro della Vigna killed himself in prison in 1249 by beating his head against the wall. Was his suicide caused by shame at having been found out or was it a gesture of desperate rebellion against an unjust condemnation?

Dante accepts the second hypothesis, and his Pietro della Vigna is a sorrowful, generous figure who still remembers "Frederick's heart" and does not reprove

Dante and the false counselors, by Gustave Doré

him. But above all else, Pietro proclaims his innocence in simple and solemn words—the same words, perhaps, that he used at the terrible moment of his arrest—"But by the strange roots of this tree do I swear that I never with my lord broke faith, whom all so justly held in honor high."

It is one of the most tragic episodes in the *Divine Comedy,* the cry of the just

man who has been condemned and who knows that he will never be able to fully convince anyone of his innocence. The gnarled branches twist and turn, but the innocent man cannot free himself from the lie, just as the suicide cannot shake himself free of his fetters. Dante shudders in anguish and brings the desperate oath back to the world of the living.

125

The Thousand Faces of Ulysses

Ulysses is famous for having invented the enormous wooden horse that brought the Greeks treacherously and cunningly into Troy in 1200 B.C. In the oldest tradition, this Achaean warrior was devilishly astute. But psychologically he was much more complex in the poems of Homer, particularly in the *Odyssey*, where he is definitely the hero. Homer greatly refines and enriches Ulysses' character in the *Odyssey*, observing him from less of a distance than he does in the *Iliad*.

The forest of the suicides, by Gustave Doré

His razor-sharp intelligence becomes the focal point. From it comes the versatile and inexhaustible ingenuity that allows him to extricate himself from difficulties in every dangerous adventure that his avid curiosity to see and to know impells him to undertake—from his dramatic encounter with the giant Polyphemus, who eats men, to his meeting with the beautiful sorceress Circe, who lures men to her in order to change them into pigs.

In later tradition Ulysses' complex character becomes simplified. No longer is he many-sided; each author chooses and magnifies a single aspect of the complex Homeric model. Among the great Greek tragedians, Sophocles sometimes celebrates Ulysses' wisdom, sometimes his guile. Euripides, on the other hand, tends to use the cunning and eloquence of the character in comic schemes—an interpretation that many others took up afterward, until the wily Ulysses figured solely in satiric plots. Then Ulysses was taken up by philosophers, who claimed to judge him from the moral point of view. They made him out to be a subtle intriguer, the typical liar. And in these dreary disguises the hero of Ithaca comes into Latin literature, until the Stoics rediscover his ancient Homeric nobility. Dante relies on the Homeric model of the intelligent hero who hurls himself impetuously against the unknown in a voyage without return—a voyage beyond the fabulous Pillars of Hercules, which were then the impassable limits of the known world, the last boundary before a frozen nothingness.

After Dante, Ulysses comes full circle to his old role of a wise and Machiavellian counselor, as he appears in Shakespeare's *Troilus and Cressida*, only to rise in the warmly romantic nineteenth century to become again the character that Dante visualized—the man born "to pursue virtue and knowledge." It is in this shadowy guise that we find him in Graf and Pascoli, whereas in Tennyson and D'Annunzio he is a daring voyager for whom the sky and the sea are never sufficiently vast. Finally, in that complex and daring modern epic, *Ulysses*, by James Joyce, he becomes the symbol of man in the treacherous sea of the conscious and the unconscious.

The Most Horrible Tragedy

Ugolino della Gherardesca, count of Donoratico, could not be called a model of loyalty. In the intricate fortunes of his country the noble Pisan was often forced to change parties or allegiance.

In the beginning he was a Ghibelline; when Pisa came to an agreement with Charles of Anjou in 1272, he allied himself to the Guelph Visconti. Ugolino

had acquired considerable distinction by a successful invasion of the port of Genoa, but not long afterward, at the battle of Meloria (1284), his behavior gave rise to the suspicion that he was a traitor. This did not stop him the next year from being elected captain of the people for a ten-year term. He was in alliance with his grandson, Nino Visconti. But later he broke with Nino and returned to the Ghibelline faction, siding with Arch-

Count Ugolino, as interpreted by Doré

Another illustration by Doré depicts the tragedy of Ugolino.

bishop Ruggiero Ubaldini and causing the Visconti to be driven out.

At this point it must have seemed to many people that Ugolino had reached the top. But the archbishop, with the help of the powerful Ghibelline families, in his turn betrayed Ugolino. Ruggiero had him arrested (1288) and imprisoned in the fortress of the Gualandi, where he allowed Ugolino to die of starvation along with his sons and grandsons. With justice, Dante puts the traitor in Hell. Imprisoned in the frozen Lake of Cocytus, Ugolino gnaws with bestial hate on the skull of Ruggiero, who is even more guilty than Ugolino because he punished innocent children.

Ugolino does not speak of his deeds. He accuses no one, indulges in no recriminations, and makes no attempt to justify himself. Past actions, betrayals, and deceits no longer have any importance compared with the horrible tragedy in which he was the protagonist—to hear that prison door being nailed shut like the lid of a coffin, to stand by impotently and day after day watch the agony of the innocent boys. "Father, why don't you help me?" says one of them, throwing himself at Ugolino's feet. These simple words sum up the drama of Ugolino better than the other, more notorious ones: "Then fasting was more powerful than grief." (This means that it

was hunger rather than grief that killed him.) Even if we give the ambiguous verse its more macabre meaning—that Ugolino fed on the bodies—it is not that which tormented the father most, rather it is the lacerating memory of seeing the boys drop one by one "between the fifth day and the sixth."

This is the frightful tragedy of Ugolino. He was champion of traitors, champion of those miserable men whom contemporary Christian morality and the chivalric tradition considered unworthy of any pity. At the same time it is the tragedy of Ugolino, always the man of his time, so politically confused and so humanly tragic.

The Glory and Death of Manfred

Not only "golden-haired was he, and handsome, and of noble mien," but brave, refined, cultivated, intelligent. Manfred was the son of Frederick II of Swabia, the splendid emperor, and of Bianca Lancia, a noblewoman from a great family. He had many of his father's qualities. Italian in his tastes and by education, he ruled over the south, his true homeland, supported by his mother's faithful family, which came from Piedmont. He could have become lord of Italy even more easily than his father did, if he had not met the implacable hostility of the papacy. He held his ground for many years, but he was finally overcome.

The popes' struggle against the Swabians was entirely temporal in nature. Rome wished to rule the emperor, and the emperor wished to be free of Rome. For this reason Frederick II was excommunicated and the long war ensued. At the time of Frederick's death, in 1250, his bastard son Manfred was scarcely eighteen; but he showed that he knew how to rule the kingdom as the deputy of his half brother, Conrad III, king of Germany. Then the pope's wrath broke over him, and he was excommunicated in an atmosphere of intrigues and revolts.

The young regent faced the situation skillfully. He fought back with arms and with diplomacy, chivalrously offering the German prince, when he finally came to Italy, a strong and almost entirely pacified kingdom. Fearing the king's popularity, he did not react against the diffidence and humiliations that Conrad inflicted on him. When his mission was over, he returned to the shadows, only to take command shortly afterward on the death of his half brother. At that time the kingdom had in large part fallen into the hands of the papal forces. Region by region, Manfred reconquered southern Italy and Sicily in the name of his nephew, Conradin. Later Manfred was crowned king of Sicily, and he ruled in a most enlightened way, following paternal tradition. Having been left a widower when still young, he remarried in 1259 a most beautiful Byzantine princess, Elena degli Angioli, the seventeen-year-old daughter of Michael Comnensus.

But Pope Urban IV did not lay down his arms, and in order to free himself of the too-powerful Manfred, he offered the crown of Sicily

The excommunication of Manfred

The recovery of Manfred's body

to Charles of Anjou, brother of King Louis IX of France. The fearless Manfred would have been able to conquer the French too, if only he had attacked Charles when the latter was at Rome with only a few troops. But instead, inexplicably, Manfred waited, giving the main part of Charles' army the chance to catch up with their leader. Then, too, Manfred was short of money. Some of his generals willingly accepted papal bribes, and in this betrayal allowed the papal army into the realm. A second betrayal determined the outcome of the decisive battle of Benevento in 1266. Manfred threw himself furiously into the fray and was killed without being recognized. Charles of Anjou later ordered a long search for Manfred's body, and when it was found, he had it buried under a heap of stones by the bridge of Benevento.

According to a legend found in Villani's *Chronicles* and repeated by Dante, the bishop of Cosenza did not wish the body of his excommunicated enemy to be buried there, in ground belonging to the Church. He had him disinterred and taken to the Verde River, a little stream far north of Benevento at the boundary of the kingdom.

The Sad Story of Pia

On the first terrace of Purgatory, among those who died a violent death, Dante meets a spirit who alludes to her story with almost bashful reluctance: "me, who am Pia, may'st thou think of then: 'twas Siena made, Maremma that unmade me: he knows it who with his own jewel, when our mutual troth had first been plighted, wed me." These four verses of gentle sadness trace the sweet figure of an unlucky woman, Pia dei Tolomei.

Pia was a Sienese girl, a member of the powerful Tolomei family. When Nello della Pietra de' Pannocchieschi asked her hand in marriage, her family was delighted to give their consent, because Nello was an important man. He had been mayor of Volterra and Lucca, and he had a brilliant political career before him. Pia believed that all her timid dreams would be realized in marrying Nello. However, reality was quite different.

Nello was on his way to becoming one of the most powerful people in Tuscany by steering a course between the Guelphs and the Ghibellines. But his political plots, his intrigues, and his machinations left him no time to dedicate to his young wife, who passed long days gazing at the hostile landscape of the Ma-

Pia dei Tolomei, by Dante Gabriel Rossetti (1828-82)

remma, which surrounded the castle of Pietra, her husband's manor house.

As if that were not enough, at one point Pannocchieschi found that he urgently needed the support of the Aldobrandeschi, an important Tuscan family that was always at odds with Siena. One of the most notable members of that family was the Countess Margherita, who, widowed by the death of Guido di Monfort, had married Orso degli Orsini, brother of the pope Nicholas III, and later, Loffredo Caetani, the nephew of pope Boniface VIII. In 1297, two years after this last marriage, there was a good deal of scandalous gossip about Margherita;

Boniface VIII intervened, accused the countess of bigamy, and annulled her second marriage.

Nello de' Pannocchieschi had known the countess well for a long time. Indeed, he had had a son by her when she was still married to the count of Monfort and while Monfort was a prisoner in Messina. And now there were political reasons as well for a close alliance with the Aldobrandeschi.

Around 1297 Nello de' Pannocchieschi married the Countess Margherita degli Aldobrandeschi. And what about Pia? The marriage was made possible because several months before Pia died in a fall from a high window of the castle in the Maremma. According to an ancient chronicle, when Nello saw his wife lean out the window, he "sent one of his soldiers to her, who grabbed her by the feet from behind, and threw her out the window into the valley far below."

On top of all that, and perhaps in order to justify himself, Nello spread slanderous lies about Pia. Echoes of these lies have come down to us, so that Nello might be given the benefit of the doubt. Did he kill his wife to free himself for his second marriage or to punish her for a fault? Dante's answer is explicit: Pia is in Purgatory, and from there she will ascend to Heaven.

Sordello, the Mantuan Troubadour

It appears that Sordello is part of the *Divine Comedy* simply to give Dante a pretext for scourging Italy and for proclaiming once again his faith in the empire. It is significant that the poet chose for this task a character who in a number of respects is rather liked him.

The Mantuan troubadour, like Dante, showed his lively passion for politics in his verses. In his poem *On the Death of Ser Blacas*, Sordello brings the weight of his savage satire to bear on the emperor and on the kings of France, England, Castile, and Aragon, without paying any attention to the possibility that this might bring down on his head the wrath of all the great powers.

Sordello's life was full of sensational adventures. Born in 1200 in Goito, he frequented the courts as a jongleur, first for the Este family and then for the powerful San Bonifacio family at Verona.

Count Ricciardo di San Bonifacio was married to Cunizza da Romano, who was the sister of Ezzelino, lord of Padua. The marriage had been arranged by Ezzelino for the usual political reasons. He hoped in this way to gain the friendship of the San Bonifacio family. But this did not happen, and Count Ricciardo remained an intractable enemy of the Da Romano. So Ezzelino conceived the plan of taking back his sister, and Sordello was given the job of abducting her. The jester was most successful, helped by Cunizza herself, either from hatred of her husband or love for Sordello, or from a consuming desire for her homeland—we don't know. After this adventure Sordello thought it prudent to retire to Provence, out of range of the vendettas of Verona. In Provence he enjoyed the friendship and favor of Berengar IV; but even there he managed to stir up jealousy and bad feeling.

Now a famous troubadour, he returned to Italy in 1265 in the suite of Charles of Anjou, who was coming down to fight Manfred. Then he endured other adventures, spent some time in prison, and finally, in 1269, loaded with honors by Charles of Anjou, became lord of certain lands in the Abruzzi.

The impetuous scourge of princes ended his life as a knight.

Sordello meets Ezzelino and Cunizza da Romano at their court.

Light and Shade in the Donati Family

The name "Donati" recurs frequently in fourteenth-century Florentine history and in the *Divine Comedy*. Dante was linked to this family by parental ties and by a tangle of mixed feelings. He puts the Donati in Hell, in Purgatory, and in Paradise.

The head of the family was Corso, a violent, quarrelsome, ambitious man, and a ferocious rival of the Cerchi family. Dante despised him for being the man first responsible for the outburst of civil discord in Florence. Banished in 1300, when the priors impartially decided to exile the chiefs of both the Blacks and the Whites, he was confined in the Massa Trabaria. He returned to Florence in the suite of Charles of Valois, and in 1304 and 1308 tried to make himself lord of Florence. The second attempt cost him his life. He was pierced by two lances while trying to flee the city on horseback. In the poem his brother, Forese, predicts Corso's death to Dante, and it is not difficult to sense the poet's subtle, perfidious pleasure

Forese Donati among the gluttons, by Gustave Doré

in the verses that describe in detail how Corso fell from his horse and how his body was dragged along by the maddened beast and "vilely dismembered."

Forese, on the other hand, was a completely different kind of man: good-natured when his brother was proud; as merry as his brother was stern; vulgar rather than aristocratic.

In Purgatory he is punished for gluttony. He has calmed down and matured, but all the same, something remains of the old self-assurance that carried him into the famous poetic contest with Dante. And pointing out to the poet his companions in expiation, he cannot refrain from making

a few sarcastic remarks in their presence—for example, he notes the surfeit of Bolsena eels, which caused the death of Pope Martin IV. But when he speaks of his wife Nella, Forese finds most tender words, which make a lovely wife of his little widow.

Nella is not the only kind and gentle woman in the Donati family. Forese, answering a question of Dante's, says: "My sister— if more virtuous or more fair she was, I know not— on Olympus high rejoices her triumphal crown to wear." The sister is Piccarda, the mystical girl who fled the world and retired to the convent of Santa Clara to escape the violent behavior of her brothers. But when Corso, for political reasons, needed to marry off his sister, he did not hesitate to take her by force from the cloister and make her the wife of a certain Rossellino della Tosa. There was no escape for Piccarda. Her brother's will was law, and she was forced to make the most painful kind of sacrifice. In Paradise, when Piccarda talks of herself to Dante, she says: "The good Lord knows what my life was like then." This calm state-

Dante meets Piccarda Donati, by C. Laurenti.

ment tells more than any lament could.

After the enemy, the friend, the widow, and the nun, there should be at least a hint in the poem of yet another Donati: Gemma, Dante's wife. But we search in vain for the slightest allusion to her. Dante tells so much about himself —his ancestors, his friends, of the women he loved, of the princes he knew—but he says nothing of his wife. And yet this woman shared his destiny and must have had to bear privations and sacrifices, because, as we know, Dante was not rich and poetry was not a profitable art. She raised four children by herself in a hostile city, while he remained in exile. Perhaps the poet's marriage, arranged by his parents, was a dreary union of two people who had nothing to say to each other.

Certainly, it could not be by chance that Dante never mentions Gemma. Why he never talks of her remains a mystery. This shadowy member of the Donati family was perhaps irritable, perhaps petty, or perhaps (and this seems most likely) unhappy because she felt incapable of rising to her husband's spiritual level.

Cunizza, a Baffling Inhabitant of Paradise

In Paradise, in the sphere of Venus, among the souls of lovers, gleams Cunizza da Romano. To find her in such a place of honor could not fail to have amazed the fourteenth-century readers, who knew her character better than we do. Granted that love "swiftly takes hold of the gentle heart" and that "love to no one loved permits excuse for loving," but Cunizza had gone a little too far. If the poet had wished to see Cunizza's soul saved, he could at least have set her in Purgatory to do penance. But to put her among the blessed a few years after her death does seem truly excessive. The ancient commentators were remarkably direct in referring to the sister of the tyrant Ezzelino. One says that "she spent her life in pleasures," another that she was "a famous whore," and a third, Pietro Alighieri, the poet's son, that "she burned hotly with carnal love." But one of them also said that she was generous and compassionate and that she did her utmost to alleviate the suffering of those whom her brother persecuted.

Perhaps it was this love for her neighbor that redeemed her in Dante's eyes, or perhaps there was another reason, a very personal reason, of the poet's. When Ezzelino da Romano, her powerful and ruthless brother, was deposed by a Guelph coalition in 1259, Cunizza could not escape the fate of the defeated; she, too, had to take the road of exile. Already mature in those years, her wandering led her to the Cavalcanti household in Florence. And there, most probably, the penitent and resigned Cunizza knew the young Dante, leaving a profound impression on him.

So many years later, exiled and overcome with humiliation, the poet, perhaps remembering the meek and frail lady who had suffered the same punishment, may have on an impulse decided to honor her to the best of his ability. It is a rather tenuous hypothesis; but it is pleasant to imagine that in order to console a poor old lady battered by fate, the great Alighieri slipped an incongruous episode into the rigid theological and moral architecture of his poem.

Cunizza allows herself to be abducted by Sordello.

The Illustrators

The following is a survey of the various ways in which artists of every age and every country have interpreted the episodes and mood of the Divine Comedy.

The earliest illustrations of the Divine Comedy *were precious miniatures that embellished fourteenth- and fifteenth-century manuscripts of the poem, interpreting it with naïveté, immediacy, and a rich use of color. Here, for example, Dante and Virgil regard Lucifer, the horrible monster that perpetually gnaws the three worst human traitors (miniature from a manuscript in the Trivulzian Library, Milan).*

Opposite, devils and the damned, by Luca Signorelli (1441-1523), a native of Cortona and the first Italian painter to make such expressive use of the nude (detail from the Brizio Chapel frescoes in Orvieto Cathedral). Below, a conception of Paradise, by Giovanni da Fiesole (1387-1455), a Florentine Dominican monk better known as Fra Angelico (Monastery of San Marco, Florence).

Charon's boat,
by Michelangelo Buonarroti
(1475-1564). The artist
and the poet render the
infernal world with
the same tumultuous
and tragic power.
One of the dominant figures
of the Renaissance,
and certainly its most
dramatic painter,
Michelangelo, like Dante,
was a titan obsessed with
the thought of death
and the world beyond.

Opposite, the
Ascent to the Empyrean,
by Hieronymus Bosch
(c. 1450-1516),
the Flemish painter of
extraordinary allegorical
and imagined scenes
(Ducal Palace, Venice).
Above, Buoso Donati
is attacked by a serpent;
in a colored drawing
from a series done by
William Blake
(1757-1827), the
English mystic
poet and painter
(Tate Gallery, London).
Left, The Burning Tombs,
by Sandro Botticelli
(1444-1510), one of
a series of drawings he made
to illustrate the Comedy
and which are now in Berlin.

143

Right, Count Ugolino, by
Sir Joshua Reynolds(1723-92),
the greatest exponent of
English classicism in the
eighteenth century
(Knole, Sevenoaks).
 Above, Paolo and Francesca,
by Dominique Ingres
(1780-1867) (Musée

des Beaux Arts, Angers).
In the battle
between the classicists
and the romanticists,
Ingres was seen as the
adversary of the romantism
represented by Delacroix;
but Dante fascinated
painters of both schools.

144

Opposite, Dante's Boat
(Hell, canto VIII) by
Eugène Delacroix (1798-1863),
the most illustrious
of the European Romantic
painters (Louvre, Paris).

Below, Dante in the Underworld,
by Anselm Feuerbach
(1829-80),
the German classical painter
and noted man of letters
(Neue Pinakothek, Munich).

Opposite, Rachel and Leah,
by the English poet and
painter Dante Gabriel Rossetti
(1828-82). Of Italian origin,
Rossetti founded the
pre-Raphaelite movement,
which took inspiration
from the primitives,
that is, the painters who
lived before Raphael.
Above, The Misers in Purgatory,
by Gustave Doré (1833-83),
who was perhaps
the most popular
illustrator of Dante.
Right, Paolo and Francesca,
by Amos Cassioli (1832-91).
Francesca and Ugolino
were the characters
in the Comedy most
preferred by the Romantics.

Not only painters but sculptors interpreted Dante.
Below, Count Ugolino, by Auguste Rodin (1840-1917),
one of the foremost sculptors of France.
This composition was part of a grandiose project
for a Gate of Hell (Musée Rodin, Paris).

Opposite, Farinata and Cavalcanti, in the dramatic
interpretation by Amos Nattini (born 1892), a Genoese painter
who has illustrated the entire Divine Comedy in a series of
large canvases. The greatest contemporary artists have tried
their skill illustrating the poem, among them Guttuso,
with his splendid series of paintings of scenes from Hell.

Salvador Dali (born 1904),
the Surrealist painter
of prodigious invention
and great technical ability,
has illustrated
the Divine Comedy in
some seventy compositions
in pen and in watercolor.
Left, his interpretation
of the misers in Purgatory.
Above, the figure of Dante
from an illustration for
the prayer to the Virgin by
Gino Severini (1883-1966).
In the course of his
development
from Futurism to
Abstractionism, Severini
always devoted himself to
a serious study of style.

What the Critics Have Said

Dante has been variously judged in each successive age. Some centuries have praised him; others have ignored him. Sometimes he was labeled a barbarian; sometimes glorified like a god.

What Giosuè Carducci called the shifting fortune of Dante is the complex story of how, through the centuries, Italian civilization approached the poet's works in an effort to understand them, to assimilate them, and at the same time to draw from them a portrait of the author. Compounded of appreciation and condemnation, of painstaking research and polemical refutation, of hate and of love, the critical opinion of Dante at any given time appears to be intimately tied to contemporary philosophical, literary, and political movements.

Because the manuscripts of Dante's works, written in his own hand, and the remains of his library have disappeared, the critical tradition begins in the fourteenth and fifteenth centuries with the diffusion of his works, first in manuscript, then in print. Each of his books became known in a different way, according to the consideration it received at different times. The *Divine Comedy* has always been the poet's most popular work. Even before he died, we find a few verses recorded in the *Memoriali Bolognesi* of 1317. Almost equally early mention of the work appears in the writings of Francesco Barberini and Giovanni del Virgilio. More than six hundred manuscript copies of the poem survive, the earliest dating from 1336, along with an enormous number of printed copies. Numerous too are the manuscripts of Dante's short poems (a few even from the thirteenth century), although the attributions are often untrustworthy and it is difficult to put the poems in chronological order. Incomplete printed editions of the *Poems* appeared in Venice in 1491 and in Florence in 1527 (Giunta edition). The *Vita Nuova* is equally rich in manuscripts—there are forty-two of them—but the book was not printed in its entirety until 1576. Of the *Convivio*, forty-three manuscripts survive, but all are of rather late date and inaccurate. It was a work that spread slowly because Dante had never finished it. The first printed edition appeared in Florence in 1490. The other works were not as well known. The *De Monarchia* has come down to us only in a score of copies—many lacking title and author, for reasons of prudence—in two fifteenth-century Italian-language versions, and in a commentary attributed to Cola di Rienzi. Perhaps its restricted distribution was due to the political and religious opposition in the fourteenth century to the point of view the book expressed. Indeed, *De Monarchia* was burned in Bologna in 1329 by order of Cardinal Bertrando del Poggetto. The first printed version of *De Monarchia* appeared in Basel only in 1559. The *Eclogues* and the incomplete *Letters* were only saved by Boccaccio's efforts. Of the *Letters*, only a few, late manuscript versions survive. Evidently, the fourteenth-century reader cared even less about the *De Vulgari Eloquentia*, given the fact that we have only three contemporary manuscript copies. Copies were made by Bembo and Colocci in the sixteenth century; and the book appeared in printed form in a Paris edition of 1577. Every trace of the manuscript of the *Questio de Aqua et Terra* has vanished. The first version we have is one printed in Venice in 1508.

For the Fourteenth Century, the DIVINE COMEDY is an Encyclopedia of Knowledge

The great and instant success of the *Divine Comedy* little by little overshadowed Dante's other works, such as the *Poems* and the *Vita Nuova*, which were often echoed and imitated by mediocre versifiers and by famous writers like Boccaccio and Petrarch. The *De Monarchia* enjoyed unexpected notoriety in the time of Ludwig of Bavaria and inspired a number of polemical refutations. But Dante's true fame during the fourteenth century, with both cultivated and popular audiences, rests with the *Divine Comedy*. The proof lies in the contemporary "divisions" or "declarations," which were Italian-language summaries presented in tercets, and in the profusion of serious commentaries —sometimes in Latin, sometimes in Italian. The commentaries attest the book's popularity as a learned work—an encyclopedia of doctrine and of theological philosophy that emerged from an examination of its allegorical meaning. This widespread critical point of view also gave rise to the refutations and disputations, like the one Cecco d'Ascoli sustains in the *Acerba* against the allegorical "nonsense" and Dante's greatness. The first two commentaries—an Italian-language one called the *Chiose all'Inferno*, written in 1322 by Jacopo Alighieri, and a Latin language one on *Hell*, written in 1324 by Graziolo Bambagliuoli—are developed according to the allegorical interpretation indicated in Dante's letter to Can Grande. By contrast, Jacopo della Lana in his complete Italian-language commentary of 1324-28 interprets the *Comedy* as a didactic and moralizing encyclopedia, while the so-called *Ottimo Commento*, written between 1333 and 1340 by the Florentine Andrea Lancia, discusses the poem's style with admirable sensitivity. Most important is the *Commentarium*, produced in three versions from 1340 to 1358 by another of Dante's sons, Pietro. It explains the pre-humanistic, classical culture of the poet and brings to light precious firsthand information, like the historical reality of Beatrice and the fact that Dante was the author of the *Questio*. It also contains a polemical treatment of the prophetic interpretation offered by Guido da Pisa in the years from 1343 to 1350. According to this interpretation, the *Comedy* is a biblical vision and Dante is a prophet, not a philosopher. Thus Dante's poem attained fame everywhere because of the commentaries, which demonstrated the value of his work as an encyclopedia of philosophy by explaining the mythological references and the scientific questions. The *Comedy* became officially recognized as a classic when the universities and communes staged public lectures about it. In 1360 a Sienese grammarian offered to read aloud "The Dante," as the *Comedy* had come to be called. But only in August, 1373, did the University of Florence, after a number of citizens had appealed to the priors and the chief justice, decide to set up a chair for Dante studies. Boccaccio, Dante's most illustrious admirer, occupied the chair, and he read the first seventeen cantos of *Hell* from October 23, 1373 to January, 1374. The custom of having a chair in Dante studies spread to Bologna, Verona, Pistoia, Pisa, and Siena, and it continued to be observed in the following century. At the same time commentaries still continued to be published, and more and more they adopted the literal interpretation of the poem and indicated the classical sources that Dante had used. There was the Latin commentary by Benvenuto da Imola (1380), which was more expository than interpretive, and full of pre-humanistic culture in the conception of the poet as theologian and prophet. There was the Italian commentary of Francesco da Buti (1385), which focused on the Christian allegory and grammatical explanations. There were the notes in Italian, written toward the end of the century by an anonymous Florentine, which were interesting for certain linguistic points; and there was the elucidation of the first canto of *Hell*, written in Latin by Filippo Villani around 1403. These last commentaries are more or less faithful to the example of Boccaccio, certainly the most illustrious Dante scholar of his century. In a letter of 1359, Petrarch thanks Boccaccio for a copy of the *Comedy*, which Boccaccio had sent him, and reveals his attitude toward Dante: he admired him, but not without reservations. Still, Petrarch's poetry, particularly in the *Trionfi*, owes a considerable debt to the author of the *Comedy*. Petrarch's praise is fainter than it might be, not because he scorns the vernacular, but because Dante's art is too trenchant and incisive for Petrarch's selective and rather precious taste. It was precisely this vigor that attracted Boccaccio to Dante. He put out three versions of something like a critical edition of Dante, including brief commentaries on each chapter of the *Vita Nuova*, an anthology of the *Poems* and of the *Comedy*. Each of the three large divisions of the *Comedy* is summarized in tercets, and there are precise headings for each canto. As an introduction to each edition, Boccaccio wrote a *Trattatello in Laude di Dante*, an ideal biography of the poet and a eulogy of his poetry. He renews his promise to make of that poetry a monument to Dante, which Florence "ought so magnificently to erect." The real purpose of the book is not so much to give a biography of the poet (which cannot be trusted for its facts) as to celebrate Dante's humanistic learning and

his classical studies. This leads Boccaccio to reprove Dante's political animosity and his amorous passions. Boccaccio concentrates on the *Comedy*, which, he claims, Dante began in Latin, but then continued it in Italian so that it might be accessible to all men. He says

that by writing the work in the vernacular, Dante reawakened the poetry of antiquity from its medieval sleep. With this proposition, the fourteenth-century Latin-vernacular dispute about the *Comedy* comes to an end.

For the Humanists of the Fifteenth Century Dante is a Citizen-Poet and a Poetic Philosopher

The Dante cult continued without interruption into the fifteenth century in the sense that the *Comedy* continued·to be thought of as the only book in the vernacular worthy of being read and publicly interpreted alongside the Latin classics. In Florence there were repeated readings of the poem, but fewer serious commentaries appeared, both because the fourteenth-century ones sufficed and because Italian scholasticism had become almost indifferent to questions of theology and natural philosophy. The commentary by Fra Giovanni da Seravalle was designed to reveal Dante's political and religious message to the foreign prelates attending the Council of Constance (1416-17). It accompanied a Latin version of the *Comedy*, literally translated. Guiniforte Brazizza also did a modest commentary,

limited to *Hell*. However, Dante's prestige stimulated reactions and disputations of various kinds in the learned, literary, humanistic, and refined circles of Florence. In his *De Infelicitate Principum* (1440) Poggio Bracciolini wrote: "If Dante had written his poem in Latin, he would be in no way inferior to the classical poets." This humanistic preference for the ancients is found in various forms in all the contemporary judgments about Dante. Leonardo Bruni later reacted openly against this view in his *Vita di Dante* (1436), the masterpiece of fifteenth-century Dante scholarship. It was written in Latin and then translated into Italian. Bruni proclaims Dante's greatness without reservations and considers it a matter of indifference what language is used. Bruni's book is fundamental to any judgment of the

155

taste of the time, and it is precious not only for the information it contains but also because it leaves us a firm and incisive portrait of a Dante actively involved in the political events of the time. Bruni praises Dante's learning, his studies, his art; but above all, he celebrates the citizen-poet. This work is in contrast to the *Trattatello,* by Boccaccio, which concentrates more on the literature and poetry. Giannozzo Manetti in his *Vita Dantis* recalls Boccaccio's work and abandons the interpretations of the citizen-humanist, to praise instead the contemplative aspect of Dante—that is, his theological and cultural sides—and the artistic qualities of the *Comedy.* The change of perspective was favored by the conditions in Florence (Cosimo de' Medici's elevation to the governing council), and we find the change confirmed in the *Città di Vita,* by Palmieri, written between 1455 and 1464. In it, Dante's work serves as the model for a philosophical poem whose aim is a mystical contemplation of God by a soul that has been freed from earthly life. It is an interpretation in the same neo-Platonic spirit with which Florentine culture was adapting the rediscovered Plato to contemporary life and the Christian tradition. Then, too, there was Lorenzo de' Medici's interest in Dante, which is evident in

many verses of the *Altercazione* and the *Comento.* Lorenzo admired Dante as much for being what Marsilio Ficino called a "poetical philosopher," as for being the writer who made Florentine Italian a worthy literary language. This is the intellectual climate that gave rise to Cristoforo Landino's commentary (1481), the only really important piece of Dante scholarship done in the fifteenth century. It applies to the *Comedy* the same philological and interpretive criteria that were used in commentaries on classical texts. The book also includes a life of the poet, a eulogy, and an introductory letter by Ficino, which claims that Dante is the precursor of contemporary Platonism and the hero of the cultural and political sophistication of Florence under the Medici. In Bruni's wake there was no lack of praise for Dante the citizen-poet or defense of his Florentine origins—a fact that was attacked by publishers in other cities in which the *Comedy* had already appeared. There was also no lack of statements affirming Florence's rights to the glory of its famous son. Indeed, a little earlier Lorenzo de' Medici had tried to bring the poet's body back to Florence. But aside from the critical distortions provoked by the cultural mood of the time, we find in Landino's widely read commentary notable cri-

tiques of the *Comedy.* For example, "The variety of the narration is one of the admirable things about this poet, and he pays great attention to it. He manages to change the form of the narration with great skill and with new inventions, and this variety refreshes the spirit of the reader, and makes the poem far from boring, as a monotonous style would make it." Poliziano is much less generous. He, like Luigi Pulci, finds Dante's vernacular rough and archaic, and when he uses the words and style of the poet in his own writing, he makes sure to give them a more elegant and musical form, thus sapping them of their expressive energy.

In this he is the most prominent precursor of Pietro Bembo and of the taste of the sixteenth century. Girolamo Benivieni's scientific work, *Circa el Sito Forme et Misure dello Inferno di Dante Alighieri Excellentissimo Poeta,* which appeared in 1506, is also written with sixteenth-century critical standards in mind.

Dante Is Almost Forgotten in the Renaissance

In the sixteenth century the cult of Dante suffered a decisive relapse, even though many of his minor works were printed for the first time, and despite the fact that the Manuzio edition of the *Divine Comedy* (Venice, 1502) remained the most correct and reliable of any until the eighteenth century. Pietro Bembo in his *Prose della Volgar Lingua* (1525) excludes Dante from the list of writers worthy of imitation. He calls him a "great and magnificent poet," but also says he is "heavy and without charm." Instead, he favors Petrarch for lyric poetry and Boccaccio for prose. He found them more graceful and charming than Dante. Behind Bembo's attitude is the ideal of measured and harmonious poetry, of a limpid and musical line; this is at the opposite pole from the expressive and complex poetry of the *Comedy*. He compares Dante's poem to "a lovely and spacious wheat field, in which the grain is all mixed up with oats, tares, and sterile and noxious weeds." This opinion was quite widely accepted throughout the century. The rejection of Dante's work as a model of language and style by the sixteenth century was caused by a blunted sense of taste and a lack of willingness to relive the exceptional Dantesque experience. This was shown by the innumerable theoretical discussions in the second half of the century that examined the *Comedy* in the light of Aristotelian principles: whether the poem was a fable or a

comedy, whether it respected the rules of probability, and so forth. These arguments were too abstract to have much to do with Dante's system. In short, precisely because of his greatness, Dante was forgotten almost completely by the Italian Renaissance. Linguistically, he continued to be admired by Tuscan readers, who often defended him simply as a matter of civic and parochial pride. The center of this traditional attachment was first the Florentine Academy (1540) and later the Accademia della Crusca (1582). From the point of view of language, the most passionate defense of Dante came from Niccolò Machiavelli in his *Dialogo sulla Lingua*. Many other writers, in various degrees, also made it their business to rise above the indifference of the century—crystallized by Bembo—and

re-evaluate the particularly Florentine quality of Dante's language. Borghini and Salviati dared to praise Dante's excellence as an epic poet, and they were vehemently refuted by the most famous theorists of the time, such as Giovambattista Giraldi Cinzio, Annibal Caro, and Ludovico Castelvetro, who accused Dante of taking countless and unsuitable liberties. The few commentaries that in their own modest way kept alive the critical tradition of the preceding century were largely written by Tuscans.

In Florence Pier Francesco Giambullari and Galileo Galilei (the latter in *Intorno la Figura, Sito a Grandezza dell'Inferno di Dante*) continued the detailed study of the structure of Dante's underworld which had been begun by Benivieni.

The Seventeenth Century Attacks Dante Bitterly and Pedantically

The linguistic controversy, which had grown during the sixteenth century, was renewed in 1612 by the publication of a dictionary by the Accademia della Crusca. According to the conservative Tuscan traditionalism typical of this academy, the dictionary was based on the works of the fourteenth century, not on more

recent ones. The supporters of Tasso and Marino attacked Dante with bitterness and pedantry. The *Comedy* was printed less and less often, and the vehemence of the controversy that raged around the book tended to hide the century's basic lack of interest in the work. With a few exceptions, the body of Dante criticism seems quite weak because it consists mainly of external, theoretical, and formal considerations, which obscure the real problems of the text. Dante was at the lowest ebb of his popularity; he served almost as a pretext in the dispute between those who fought the privileged position of the Florentine language by scorning the historical, literary, and poetic value of the fourteenth-century classics for a number of unjustified reasons and those who supported the tradition and who were incapable of coming up with really convincing arguments to support their point of view. Indeed, members of the Accademia della Crusca and their opponents, far removed from the spirit and form of Dante's poem, almost always agreed in condemning the language and style of the Comedy as barbaric and archaic. According to the anti-Crusca group, Dante's poetry was inelegant and incapable of expressing great sentiments. Only a few, exceptional readers, like Tommaso Campanella, continued to recognize Dante's greatness.

In this way, through the work of Tassoni and Beni, only the worst was said about the great fourteenth-century poem, which was judged "a jumble or a caprice without rule and form of poetic action."

In the Eighteenth Century Dante is the Father of the Italian Language

The growing number of editions of the Comedy and the interest in the minor works—indeed, an attempt was made to publish Dante's complete works—is indicative of the eighteenth century's increased appreciation of the poet.

New questions were posed about Dante's life, about his relationship to Beatrice, and about textual problems of the Comedy. Historically, it makes no difference that the proposed solutions seem almost totally unacceptable today. What matters is the search for solutions. It proves that during the triumph of "rationalism," when dominant aesthetic theories leaned toward simplicity and clarity, in line with the Arcadian concept of good taste, the cult of Dante revived, though with difficulty after the seventeenth-century lull. From Muratori to Tiraboschi, from Crescimbeni to Cesarotti, the typical Arcadian judgments about Dante—full of obscurity, extravagance, and absurdity—were often repetitious and were finally incorporated in the systematic destructions of Dante by Giuseppe Baretti (in his famous Frustra Letteraria) and Saverio Bettinelli (in his irreverent Lettere Virgiliane). No one could disregard the typically "illuministic" polemics for and against Dante that burst forth following the condemnation of the poet by Voltaire. Many Italian critics rose to defend Dante for reasons of national pride. Even Baretti retracted the improvident condemnation contained in his Frustra. The dispute was rekindled by the savage criticism of the Comedy, undertaken by Bettinelli and based on sixteenth-century rhetorical concepts of genres. At this time Gaspare Gozzi defended Dante with arguments that were scarcely more sound than the criticisms. These debates are of considerable importance, not so much for the value of the arguments of the contenders, but because they started a national cult for Dante. It is also true that the most learned of these readers—Tiraboschi, Quadrio, and above all, Melchiore Cesarotti—recognized the magnitude of Dante's genius and explicitly pointed out the fantastic power and vigor of his imagination, thus intuitively getting at the philosophical and theological profoundness of the *Comedy*. Dante criticism took a new direction with the research and the theories of Antonio Conti, who saw the cultural inspiration for the *Comedy* in the Bible rather than in the writers of antiquity, and with the work of Gian Vincenzo Gravina, who was most attentive to the style and the linguistic richness of the poem. Dante became the father of the Italian language and the father of Italian poetry (as Francesco Algarotti suggests) in Giambattista Vico's revolutionary *Giudizio sopra Dante*. Vico ranks him as the first great poet in Italian civilization, as Homer was in the Greek. He

says that the *Comedy* was the result of a basic and vigorous inspiration that could not be subjected to rational rules. He says that it broke through the restraints of stylistic and rhetorical preciousness because of Dante's fantastic inventiveness and primordial genius. Running counter to the taste of his time, Vico evaluated the art of the *Comedy* according to a new set of concrete and historical rules; this led to future discussions about the relation between the logical and the fantastic in the poem, and about the fascinating process of dramatic transfiguration.

history. In France Chateaubriand noted the beauty of Dante's verse from its fascinating Christian point of view. In Italy opinions were most varied; but at least at first they seemed more purely nationalistic as compared to the European points of view, for Dante was becoming one of the sacred values of the *Risorgimento*.

Dante became the proving ground in the dispute between lay and religious criticism, both of which fought over his thought for patriotic reasons. There was the neo-Guelph interpretation (Troya, Balbo, Capponi, Gioberti, Tommaseo) and the lay, Ghibelline, or revolutionary one (Foscolo, Rossetti, Mazzini, Niccolini, Guerrazzi). Among the first group, Gioberti portrays Dante as the many-sided, universal poet capable of responding to national and universal needs, capable of uniting instinctive poetry with the philosophical ideas of the reformer, and capable, at the beginning of modern civilization, of synthesizing its three elements—the romantic, the barbaric, and the Christian. Better known today is the other critical current, headed by Foscolo. He is undoubtedly the greatest interpreter of Dante, notwithstanding certain inconsistencies in his *Parallelo fra Dante e il Petrarca* (which later appeared in

For the Romantics Dante Was the Genius of the Middle Ages

The rediscovery of the Middle Ages by the Romantic movement, with its deep interest in past civilizations and their origins, intensified and diversified Vico's interpretation of Dante. The poet was seen by various critics as one of the great men of Europe, as a political hero, a revolutionary, a religious reformer, a missionary for a moral revival, or a prophet of Italian virtues. In short, during this period Dante loomed up all over Europe as

a medieval genius. Already in the minds of the first German Romantics—the brothers Friedrich and August Wilhelm von Schlegel—the *Comedy* was considered the center of the medieval Christian epic. Hegel defined the artistic and philosophical components of the work, and Schelling pointed out their decisive importance for all modern poetry. In England Thomas Carlyle celebrated in Dante the triumph of the heroic sense that guides the collection *Saggi sul Petrarca,* 1821), in a series of articles published in the *Edinburgh Review* (1818), and above all in the *Discorso sul Testo della Divina Commedia* (1825). In the *Discorso* the philological interpretation of the text, which the author proposes, becomes a complete historical, philosophical, and religious consideration of the poem. Foscolo interprets the *Comedy* as a sacred vision of the biblical kind, and he suggests that Dante wrote it to reform the Church and contemporary Christianity. The best of Foscolo's critical genius is not to be found so much in this central theme—as bold as it is unacceptable—but rather in his illuminating observations on the poem's style and literary value. In the emotion of his criticism he relives the drama of the exile and the mission of the poet as a prophet. The interpretation by Dante Gabriel Rossetti is developed on a more modest plane and is limited by English Masonic ideology. It is an allegorical and symbolistic interpretation, entirely personal and arbitrary. According to Rossetti, Dante belonged to a contemporary heretical sect, and under the veil of the visionary and amorous language of the time, the poet gives his companions a blueprint for reforming political and religious institutions; it is

the task of the critic to discover these ideas beneath the literal text. Rossetti's capricious identifications, disputed by the positivist critics, bore fruit in the mystic and symbolic interpretation that half a century later Giovanni Pascoli put on the *Comedy,* and which, more recently, Luigi Valli reiterated from a more sharply defined sectarian point of view.

A different orientation in the field of Dante studies developed toward the middle of the century and offered its first fruits on the occasion of the sixth centenary (1865). The new approach was the work of the so-called historical school, with a positivist point of view totally opposed to the earlier philosophical and aesthetic interpretations. It turned with new methods and new documents to the study of Dante's biography (C. Ricci, F. Novati, M. Scherillo); to the study of the historical context in which the *Comedy* was written (D. Comparetti, J. Del Lungo); to the culture the poem reflects (E. Moore, R. Sabbadini); and to the poem's critical fortune (G. Carducci, A. D'Ancona). However, there was still no work that united the useful results of all these critical currents, despite the *Dante* of Nicola Zingarelli, a sensitive monograph that represented a step in that direction, and which is useful even today. During this time the founda-

tions were being laid for a reconstruction of the text of the poem and the cultural interpretation of the *Comedy.* Edward Moore, Karl Witte, Paget Toynbee, and Giovanni Scartazzini prepared better texts of the works of Dante, went back to the classical and Christian sources used by the poet, and provided more precise commentaries for the *Comedy.* The historical school of criticism adopted new standards, rejected the fundamental principle of Vico—which is to say, the Christian-medieval premise—and put Dante's thought into a different historical perspective. They saw him astride the Middle Ages and the Renaissance, in part a synthesis of the past and in part an anticipator of the future.

The great critic Francesco De Sanctis provided a unified critical vision of the world of Dante. He developed and somewhat modified the viewpoint of the lay Romantics, and came to conclusions not so far removed from those of the historical school of criticism. In various essays devoted to the famous characters in *Hell,* and in a long chapter in his *Storia della Letteratura Italiana,* De Sanctis explicitly moves away from the idea of unifying and overcoming the idealistic and abstract definitions of the past and the biased theories of contemporary scholars, to a new, original synthesis of Dante's poetic experience. Temperamentally inclined to systematic investigation, and intellectually faithful to the basic principles posed by Vico, De Sanctis reverses the conclusions of the German Romantics. He explores once again the medieval cultural and ideological framework, and its didactic and moral bone structure, to find the limits of the *Comedy* —the less poetic and in a certain sense the negative part of Dante's masterpiece. This, which he calls Dante's "intentional world," only partly checks the tragedy and the drama, the violence and the contrast of the heroic sentiments and of the piety and suffering that live in the poet's tableau. As the true unifying principle at the center of it all, De Sanctis places Dante's "poetic nature," which made a work of art of the whole spirit of the Middle Ages. But the effective world of Dante's poetry is the here and now, reflected in the tragedy and anguish of *Hell*, not the divine world of the absolute, so cold and distant.

From *Hell* to *Paradise* we are witnessing a progressive ascent from the material to the spiritual, paralleled by a cooling off of the poetry, which little by little gives way to mystical and theological discussions. De Sanctis feels that the key to this ascent is allegory, a logical scheme by means of which, at the summit of *Paradise*, the three-dimensional tragedy of *Hell* and the nostalgic reverberations of *Purgatory* lose themselves in the didactic and abstract tone of the philosophical argument. This general critical vision, inspired by De Sanctis' lay and Romantic ideas, and by his personal sympathy for heroic and titanic poetry, does not detract from the success of the analysis, which with admirable subtlety evaluates even various passages of abstract lyricism in *Paradise*.

Modern Criticism Re-evaluates the "Poetry of Theology"

In the first years of the twentieth century the studies of the historical school dominated the scene, revived, as they were, above all by Michele Barbi and Ernesto Giacomo Parodi. They overshadowed the mystical, allegorical critics inspired by Giovanni Pascoli. Parodi, who succeeded Barbi as director of the Dante Society, published a rich series of linguistic and interpretive notes in the Society's *Bulletin*. He also did the fundamental research on Dante's itinerary in the *Comedy* and published it in *Poesia e Storia della Divina Commedia* (1920). Barbi, founder of the review *Studi Danteschi*, produced an imposing series of works about the biography, thought, and critical success of Dante—impressive testimony to fifty years of passionate activity. A critical and philological school grew up around these two men. For the centennial meeting in 1921 it produced a critical edition of Dante's works (among the contributors: F. Pellegrini, E. Pistelli, P. Rajna, E. Rostagno, G. Vandelli, M. Casella), which remains one of the most valuable and worthy works of the anniversary. In these years there also appeared the monumental work by Karl Vossler, *Die Göttliche Komödie. Entwicklungsgeschichte und Erklärung*. It was first made known in Italy by Giovanni Gentile, and later it appeared in translation with the title (in the second edition) *La Divina Commedia Studiata nella sua Genesi e Interpretata*. The centennial year also signaled the appearance of that fundamental work by Benedetto Croce, *La Poesia di Dante*, revolutionary in its form, its tone, and the substance of its arguments. Croce distinguishes the unpoetic component of the poem—the learning, theology, and allegory—which he calls the "structure," from the true poetry, which is often conditioned by it. In a fragmentary reading of the poetic parts alongside the unpoetic structure, Croce separates Dante the theologian and moralist airing his own thoughts from Dante the pure poet. By affirming the fact that research into the thought and the biographical, moral, and religious aspects of Dante is marginal to an appreciation of the poet's art, Croce eliminated the usefulness of conventional criticism. The discussions of Croce's new theory were lively and fruitful, for the theory itself seriously threatened the unity of the poet's work. To bridge the gap, Luigi Russo, among many others, expanded on the distinction made by Croce and found that there was a simultaneous interaction between the poetry and the structure. In a most sensitive commentary and in various other essays, Attilio Momigliano found an overall principle of unity in the psychological and pictorial atmosphere of the Dantesque landscape. In general, the Dante criticism of the past twenty years (all of it anti-Croce) has tended to focus on the poetry of Paradise —neglected by De Sanctis but not by Croce—and to demonstrate its dramatic sense (Cosmos), the new lyrical harmony imposed on the allegorical chords (Flora), and the religious and metaphysical complexity (Appolonius). And even today, when the anti-Croce polemic has died down, it is to a re-evaluation of the poetry of Paradise that critics turn. Particularly valid in this connection are the conclusions reached by Giovanni Getto in his close reading of Paradise—where the "poetry of theology" makes itself felt thanks to a brilliant and new metaphorical language—and the work of Charles S. Singleton, who traces the allegory and structure of Paradise in the speculative atmosphere of religious culture in the fourteenth century.

Henceforth the aesthetic and philological schools need no longer engage in polemical battle, given the common interests of modern Dante criticism.

Dante Today

Dante lives today, not so much through his ideas, which were necessarily those of his time, but because he knew how to interpret the everlasting grief and joy of the human spirit.

Undeniably, the modern world honors Dante, and modern culture still turns with the liveliest interest to his works. But given these facts, it is a difficult and delicate task to single out the motives. Does Dante's message continue to live in a world like ours, which is politically, socially, and ideologically so different from that of the fourteenth century? Some are quick to say "yes," basing their answer, if the truth be known, on a few weak parallels between the poet's thought and our own.

It is true that Dante anticipated certain modern attitudes —for example, his insistence on the need to think out clearly the limits to be observed in the exercise of political and religious power. In view of changed circumstances, these are only theoretical and wholly relative analogies. There is no doubt that we can call Dante's political sensibility modern. In his time he was a reformer who saw the situation in all its complexity. We must give him credit for thinking things out on a national scale.

In fact, while ruminating on the problems and the ruin of Florence, he continually enlarged his frame of reference to include the political and economic reality in all of the Italian peninsula. For him the troubles of Florence were simply the beginning of a ruination that could not help

Monument to Dante (Piazza Santa Croce, Florence)

but spread to all the other Italian city-states.

For these reasons we cannot and should not try to force the significance of Dante's political views. Rather, we should take note of the deformations and distortions introduced by passionate interpreters of the past—first the reformers, then the patriots and secularists. Dante's political ideas devel-

oped within the confines of religious orthodoxy, even when secular distinctions are made. Dante's conception, marked with a Ghibelline kind of conservative realism, was to check the political disintegration already afflicting the empire; it was a conception conditioned by the events of the time and by his own personal misfortunes. Neither factor exists today, and yet without them, Dante's political outlook would not exist. Moreover, there is a great difference between the craving of our world for peaceful confederations of states and the universalism of those claiming political power—so alive in Dante, owing to his medieval faith in the Holy Roman Empire and in a divine plan. The reasons for the rivalry of empire and papacy are also no longer comprehensible to us. They have the same anachronistic ring as has Cacciaguida's discussion of social problems in *Paradise,* when he talks of the decadence of Florence. However, still relevant today is the poet's invective against corruption and vanity, against factional rivalry and depravity. If, for a moment, we leave to one side the general tenor of the political and economic arguments, and stop to consider the criticisms and reproaches that Dante levels at his fellow Florentines as individuals, his words find a prompt echo in our modern consciousness. The nature of man has not, and perhaps cannot, change. Men's arrogance and ambitions today are very similar to those of Dante's contemporaries. And the fact that Dante transformed that arrogance and dishonesty into verses that speak to us today and still illustrate modern predicaments proves how much Dante lives and is a part of our daily life.

Therefore it would be fruitless to insist on the philosophical foundations of the so-called public problems that Dante would have liked to solve according to the needs of his time, for we, naturally, wish to resolve them according to the exigencies of our time. Trying to find parallels where parallels do not exist will not give a veneer of modernity to Dante's profile. Dante's modernity does not stem from the originality of his philosophy, because, aside from the fact that he was an eclectic rather than an original thinker even in his own time, today his speculations are outmoded.

It will be more useful to point out his exceptional capacity for understanding man in all his bitterness and exaltation, and above all, in the bleakness of his earthly solitude, which can only be seen by looking down from on high. Dante demonstrates that he is not chained to his own time by bringing to life in poetry, in a universal way, the diversity of man. He does not interpret the various aspects of his civilization by dividing them between truth and error, as was the custom in the Middle Ages. He sees them individually, clarifies them, and in a certain sense harmonizes the passionate, the speculative, and the moral aspects of the human soul. In this lies the lasting value of Dante's art and the modernity of his poetic experience.

Petrarch had dominated Italian literary culture for five centuries. But people are increasingly impatient with the Petrarchan model, and today they look with particular admiration at the art of the *Comedy*. The poem runs the gamut of fantasy and expressive techniques; it is the first awakening of the aesthetic consciousness in the modern age.

Today Dante stands as the greatest poet that Italy has given to Europe. In the poem he explained and completely interpreted Europe at the precise moment that the individual nations were beginning to be differentiated politically. The testimony of famous critics, of poets most representative of our generation, even of the avant-garde, confirms a general admiration for a poetic experience carried out on the most diverse levels, all exceptional, all unique—a poetry that passes from the expressionism of verbal violence, in *Hell,* through the delicate vibrations of nostalgia and hope to pure conceptual lyricism in the representation of the divinity. In the Italian tradition it is a unique example, and still an indispensable one, of a synthesis complete in every aspect. Indeed, Dante has touched the extreme limits of human poetry, from the rarified heights of *Paradise* to the dramatic depths of *Hell*.

For this reason he is the poet of our time too.

In the Stanze della Segnatura
in the Vatican, Raphael painted
two vast frescoes celebrating
the triumph of the truths of
the faith and the
glorification of the human intelligence.

They are called the Disputà and
the School of Athens respectively,
and it is significant
that Dante Alighieri
figures in both of them, as is
evident from the two details below.

Picture Credits

The works of art reproduced in this volume are in the following collections:

Angers, Musée des Beaux Arts 144. *Vatican:* Library 14, 16, 143; Sistine Chapel 140, 141; Gallery 23. *Florence:* Riccardian Library 4; Court of Appeals 18; Duomo Museum 52; San Marco Museum 139; Bigallo Orphanage 15; Uffizi 50, 52. *Gradara,* castle 149. *Sevenoaks,* Knole 144, 145. *Liverpool,* Walker Art Gallery 11. *London,* Tate Gallery 10, 143, 148. *Milan:* Arte Library—frontispiece, 22, 23, 45, 47, 121, 126, 127, 128, 149; Trivulzian Library 33, 34, 35, 36, 37, 40, 147; Bertarelli Print Collection 20, 22, 23, 133. *Munich,* Neue Pinakothek 147. *Oxford,* Ashmolean Museum 13. *Paris:* Bibliothèque Nationale 24; Louvre 146; Musée Rodin 150. *Prato,* Galleria Antica e Moderna 22, 123. *Venice,* Ducal Palace 142. Photographic credits: Alinari 10, 22, 23, 61, 123, 163; Böhm 142; Brompton Studio 143-148; Caramelli 151; Costa 2, 3, 4, 5, 22, 23; De Biasi 9, 10, 11, 12, 18, 21, 146, 147; Freeman 144, 145; Giraudon 144; Marzari 139; Preiss & Co. 149; Saporetti 20, 22, 23, 33, 34, 35, 36, 37, 40, 45, 47, 121, 126, 127, 128, 133, 149; Scala 19, 49, 50, 52, 53, 54, 56, 138, 140, 141; Scarnati 150. Others from the Mondadori photographic archives. The Dali and Severini illustrations are reproduced with the kind permission of the Salani and Martello publishing houses respectively; the painting by Nattini with the kind permission of the publishing house A la Chance du Bibliophile and of the Counts Poss of Verbania, owners of the pictures.

Some of the famous drawings made by Botticelli to illustrate the Divine Comedy. They were lost until 1878, when a large number of them turned up in the library of the duke of Hamilton (from where they went to the Museum in Berlin). Subsequently, seven more were discovered in the Vatican Library.

At the end of the Divine Comedy *the reader is left with the celestial vision of Dante and Beatrice ascending toward the light of God. Botticelli captured this moment in a drawing that is itself poetic.*

PRINTED IN ITALY, BY A. MONDADORI - VERONA